# Se

# a Natural Act

## and Other Essays

# Psychology, Gender, and Theory

*Series Editors*
Rachel T. Hare-Mustin and Jeanne Marecek

Focusing on emerging ideas in psychology, gender theory, and the politics of knowledge, this scholarly/trade series examines contemporary developments broadly associated with postmodernism and with feminist critiques of psychology and other social science disciplines. Among the topics explored are gender relations; the social construction of gender, class, race/ethnicity, and other categories of difference/hierarchy; and critical reformulations of therapy theory and practice. We seek manuscripts that propose or exemplify new ways of doing psychology, that reconsider the foundational assumptions of psychology—both in scholarship and practice. Of interest as well are works that examine ways in which the discipline of psychology and its work practices not only reflect arrangements of power and privilege in society but also produce knowledge serving to justify those arrangements.

**Rachel T. Hare-Mustin,** Villanova University, and **Jeanne Marecek,** Swarthmore College, coauthored *Making a Difference: Psychology and the Construction of Gender.*

## BOOKS IN THIS SERIES

*Sex Is Not a Natural Act and Other Essays,* Leonore Tiefer

*Celebrating the Other: A Dialogic Account of Human Nature,* Edward E. Sampson

*Seldom Seen, Rarely Heard: Women's Place in Psychology,* edited by Janis S. Bohan

# SEX
## Is Not a
## Natural Act
### *and Other Essays*

LEONORE TIEFER

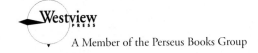

Westview PRESS

A Member of the Perseus Books Group

*Psychology, Gender, and Theory*

Copyright © 1995 by Leonore Tiefer

Published in 1995 in the United States of America by Westview Press, Inc., 5500 Central Avenue, Boulder, Colorado 80301-2877, and in the United Kingdom by Westview Press, 36 Lonsdale Road, Summertown, Oxford OX2 7EW
A Member of the Perseus Books Group

Library of Congress Cataloging-in-Publication Data
Tiefer, Leonore.
   Sex is not a natural act and other essays / Leonore Tiefer.
      p.  cm.—(Psychology, gender, and theory)
   Includes bibliographical references (p.  ) and index.
   ISBN 0-8133-1658-8—ISBN 0-8133-1659-6 (pbk.)
   1. Sex.  2. Sexology.  I. Title.  II. Series.
HQ21.T574  1995
306.7—dc20                                         94-33592
                                                    CIP

Printed and bound in the United States of America

The paper used in this publication meets the requirements of the American National Standard for Permanence of Paper for Printed Library Materials Z39.48-1984.

10    9

PERSEUS
POD
ON DEMAND

# Contents

# Acknowledgments

Although I am the sole author of these papers and speeches, I have neither figured these ideas out all by myself, nor have I lacked for support, encouragement, and help through these past years as an activist and sexologist.

I gratefully dedicate this book to Ann Snitow and the members of the New York Institute for the Humanities Sexuality, Gender and Consumer Culture seminar, which I attended from 1982 (shortly after it formed) until its end in 1993. This group of humanities scholars and progressive intellectuals encouraged me to use the sexological material to which I had professional access to make a contribution to scholarship on the social construction of sexuality. I didn't even know what was meant by *social construction* when I began attending the seminar and wasn't entirely certain for years thereafter. But I eventually got it by osmosis, and I am grateful for all the wonderful discussions we had.

I have been fortunate to have many smart feminist psychologist colleagues to encourage my work. Chief among them is my friend Carol Tavris, who managed to speak so highly of me to people who wanted *her* to lecture that *I* ended up with numerous opportunities around the country to sharpen my ideas. Always willing to suggest a reference or a turn of phrase or to offer encouragement when my motivation faltered, Tavris is inescapably responsible in some measure for this book.

Mary Brown Parlee's analyses of the medicalization of PMS have often pointed the way for me. Charlene Muehlenhard has been a devoted fan of my work and helped me see the value in obtaining a wider audience for these ideas. I am also grateful to all those who have attended conferences sponsored by the Association for Women in Psychology over the years. They have been very supportive since the Pittsburgh meeting in 1979, when, after presenting my first deconstruction of orgasm and the sexual response cycle, I received encouraging thumps on the back from a dozen women who said I had given them a great message that should be shared with others.

My many good and admired friends in sexology are too numerous to name lest I omit and offend, but I cannot neglect mentioning the important work of John Gagnon and William Simon, sociologists wandering in the psychobiological fields of sex research. Their ideas, beginning in 1969, paved the way for this "new" social constructionist trend. My colleague Arthur Zitrin looked at this work from his psychoanalyst's perspective and usually found it wanting, but conversations with him over the years have always stimulated and expanded my thinking. Colleagues and friends in the International Academy of Sex Research, the Society for the Scientific Study of Sex, and the Society for Sex Therapy and Research listened more or less patiently to these talks, and for the opportunities they gave me to work out my analysis I am most grateful. Let me also thank Arnold Melman, chair of the Urology Department at Montefiore-Einstein, for his colleagueship and support over the past decade. Frank Irwin drew the wonderful cartoons for this book.

My brother, Charles, and mother, Rosalind, have supported and encouraged my iconoclasm; likewise, my friends at the Unitarian Universalist Community Church of New York have insisted that being creatively maladjusted is a good thing. They have been my Archimedean point.

*Leonore Tiefer*

# Credits

The chapters in this volume are almost all abridged versions of my speeches and publications concerning sexuality and sexology. Their origins are as follows:

## Part 1. Sex Is Not a Natural Act: Theme and Variations

Chapter 1: "'Am I normal?' The question of sex," in Carol Tavris, ed., *Everywoman's Emotional Well-being* (Garden City, N.Y.: Doubleday, 1986), 54–72. Copyright © 1986 by Nelson Doubleday, Inc. Published by arrangement with Doubleday Book & Music Clubs, Inc.

Chapter 2: "Social constructionism and the study of human sexuality," in P. Shaver and C. Hendrick, eds., *Sex and Gender* (Newbury Park, Calif.: Sage Publications, 1987), 70–94.

Chapter 3: "Sexual biology and the symbolism of the natural." Paper presented at the International Academy of Sex Research, Sigtuna, Sweden, 1990. German translation published in *Zeitschrift für Sexualforschung* 4 (1991): 97–108.

Chapter 4: "Historical, scientific, clinical and feminist criticisms of 'The human sexual response cycle'," *Annual Review of Sex Research* 2 (1991): 1–23.

Chapter 5: "Applications of social constructionism to research on gender and sexuality." Paper presented at the American Psychological Association, New Orleans, August 1989.

## Part 2. Popular Writings on the Theme

Chapter 6: "Six months at the *Daily News*." Selections from weekly "Your sexual self" column, the *New York Daily News,* 1980–1981. Reprinted by permission.

Chapter 7: Text from "The Kiss," by Leonore Tiefer in *Human Nature* Magazine, July 1978, 28–37. Copyright © 1978 by Human Nature, Inc., reprinted by permission of the publisher.

Chapter 8: "Advice to the lovelorn," *Prime Time,* July 1981, 18–20. Publication out of print.

## Part 3. Feminism and Sexuality

Chapter 9: "An activist in sexology." Paper presented at the midcontinent regional meeting of the Society for the Scientific Study of Sex, Cincinnati, May 1993, upon receipt of their 1993 Alfred C. Kinsey Award.

Chapter 10: "Gender and meaning in *DSM-III* sexual dysfunctions."

Paper presented at the American Psychological Association, Boston, August 1990.

Chapter 11: "Deconstructing pre-feminist sexuality research." Paper presented at the American Psychological Association, Boston, August 1990.

Chapter 12: "Feminist revolution and sexuality." Paper presented at New Directions in Sexology conference, Stockholm, August 1990. Portions also presented as the plenary address to the World Congress of Sexology, Amsterdam, 1991, and published in Willeke Bezemer, Peggy Cohen-Kettenis, Koos Slob, and Nel van Son-Schoones, eds., *Sex Matters,* Excerpta Medica International Congress Series (Amsterdam: Elsevier Science B.V., 1992), 3–8. Reprinted by permission.

Chapter 13: "Feminisms and pornographies." Paper presented at New School for Social Research, New York, 1986.

Chapter 14: "Some harms to women of restrictions on sexually related expression." Paper presented at National Coalition Against Censorship conference, New York, May 1993. In press, *New York Law Review Journal,* 1994.

**Part 4. Phallocentrism Redux**

Chapter 15: "Sexism in sex therapy: Whose idea is 'sensate focus'?" Paper presented at the Society for Scientific Study of Sex, New York, 1981.

Chapter 16: "In pursuit of the perfect penis: The medicalization of male sexuality," *American Behavioral Scientist* 29 (1986): 579–599.

Chapter 17: "The medicalization of impotence: Normalizing phallocentrism," *Gender and Society* 8 (1994): 363–377. Copyright © 1994 Sociologists for Women in Society. Reprinted by permission of Sage Publications, Inc.

Chapter 18: "Might premature ejaculation be organic?" *Journal of Sex Education and Therapy* 20 (1994): 7–8.

**Part 5. Conclusion: The Politics of Sexology**

Chapter 19: "Three crises facing sexology." Presidential address given to the International Academy of Sex Research, Pacific Grove, Calif., July 1993. Published in *Archives of Sexual Behavior* 23 (1994): 1–14.

Chapter 20: "New perspectives in sexology: From rigor (mortis) to richness." Plenary address given to the Society for the Scientific Study of Sex, Minneapolis, 1990. Published in *Journal of Sex Research* 28 (1991): 593–602.

Chapter 21: "Women's sexuality: Not a matter of health," in Alice Dan, ed., *Reframing Women's Health: New paradigms for multidisciplinary research and practice* (Newbury Park, Calif.: Sage, 1994), 151–162.

# Introduction:
# An Uphill Battle

$W$e are just at the beginning, I think, of an explosion of fascinating new theory and research about human sexuality, new ideas that will fully take into account the social culture within which each person becomes sexual. My work, preliminary to these insights, has been to analyze and critique the prevailing biomedical and masculinist paradigm dominant in sexology. I believe that this new paradigm, let's call it social constructionism although it goes by various names, is well launched and will provide a more humane and complete successor. But I'm wary of counting the chickens too soon, and so I publish this collection of essays to help hasten the demise of the biomedical approach.

I'm having a strange career—that of a sexologist. It's not the sort of thing you can just study, get a degree in, get hired to do, and do, at least not yet, not in the United States. And it's certainly not the sort of thing you can do without having to deal with other people's projections of what a life spent studying sexuality is all about!

I've learned about human sexuality from my life and my friends' lives, of course, and from reading, writing, and working at various jobs over the past thirty years. Where do you work as a sexologist? I have taught sexuality courses for graduate students and undergraduates as well as medical and nursing students, given many public and professional lectures, evaluated almost 2,000 patients with sexual complaints, provided sex therapy and psychotherapy for many individuals and couples, attended endless research and clinical conferences, conducted laboratory sex research with hamsters and rats, conducted questionnaire and follow-up research with patients, written dozens of articles and one previous book, participated in scientific and humanities sexuality study groups, briefly written columns for magazines and newspapers, and for years and years catalogued newspaper and magazine articles on sexuality in scores of manila folders in a ramshackle collection of filing cabinets in my New York apartment!

Although I earned a Ph.D. in physiological psychology in 1969 from the

1

University of California at Berkeley with a dissertation on hormones and mating behavior in golden hamsters (*Mesocricetus auratus*), my ideas about sexuality underwent a complete transformation over the subsequent decade and I now renounce that dissertation and other early biological work as largely useless in the understanding of human sexuality. In the 1970s, writings from the women's movement convinced me that the primary influences on women's sexuality are the norms of the culture, those internalized by women themselves and those enforced by institutions and enacted by significant others in women's lives. Hamsters had taught me nothing about social norms!

I returned to graduate school and respecialized as a clinical psychologist so I would be able to work with human beings, and I soon began learning about sexuality straight from the humans' mouths. During the 1980s, I was persuaded by the deluge of new historical, feminist, and lesbian and gay writings that sexual behavior and values must be seen in the context of competing ideological and economic interests. Individuals' hormones and individuals' life histories are not enough. No one can resist the influence of the endless debates over sexual identities, the media deluge of sexual images, changes in marriage, work, and parenting, technology and travel, and so on.

As I began to read the new research on sexual history and gender expressions, I could see how the social culture affected the sexual experiences of the thousands of students, individuals, and couples I had talked to as a sexologist. Working within medical center urology departments for more than ten years, I learned firsthand what people do when their familiar sexual routines aren't working and what values and beliefs about sexuality they use as they choose among the options offered to them by contemporary biomedicine.

I have often felt great sadness and frustration as a sexologist to see that for many—perhaps most—people, sexual experience falls far short of what they hoped for and what they believe others may be experiencing. There is so little honest conversation about sex that most people really have no idea what's going on in the lives of others. Even avid readers of self-help books or popular magazines are misguided by the unrepresentative stories presented there. What has irritated me the most about the mystification surrounding sexuality has been the persistent but peculiar idea that "sex is natural"—that is, that sex is a simple and universal biological function that, without any training, all humans should experience, enjoy, and perform in roughly the same way.

This book is a collection of my attacks on this peculiar idea. The concept that "sex is natural" seems to me so illusory and so pernicious that I can work myself into a froth on a moment's notice. It seems such a cruel trick. Notions of "naturalism" position sexuality as important and glorious and yet at the same time help to make it a source of immense anxiety and mystery. As the reader will see from these chapters, I have earnestly tried to overturn this perspective on sexuality by logical argument, by appealing to people's real experiences, by introducing ideas from other cultures and historical periods, and by suggesting metaphors and analogies designed to locate sexuality as just another human potential (like music or spirituality or cuisine). All this so people won't be overcome by giddiness or giggles at the prospect of discussing what kind of a thing sexuality is and how a sensible person can maintain some intelligence while dealing with all the balderdash!

The fact is, however, that although my lectures and individual contacts with people have been positive, and although people have said to me zillions of times, "Gee, I never thought of it that way," encouraging me to believe that I have helped them see something in a new way, I don't really think I've had much impact. Persuading people that sex is not natural really is an uphill sell. The anxiety created by the importance of sex, on the one hand, and the ignorance and insecurity about it, on the other, set people up for confusion and rigid thinking. Their eyes glaze over at the thought of reconsidering the whole enterprise. They falter at the idea of all the regret they will feel over past worries and lost opportunities.

Most of the chapters in this book were initially written for my sexologist colleagues in attempts to shift the thinking in our field. This motivation probably makes for a narrower range than if I hadn't had a particular axe to grind. If only my colleagues had been more receptive, I could have branched out more! However, I have abridged most of the chapters to minimize repetition.

Over the years, just as I have thought that sexology or popular thinking was about to shift away from biological determinism toward a more contextualized perspective, some big media splash about genes or hormones would depress me for a week. The uphill battle of talking about sex as *not* a natural act has required disputing and unraveling both the popular and the sexological establishment perspective over and over and over again. Again, in the mid-1990s, I believe the new wave finally is coming in, and I am excited and optimistic. This collection will be useful, however, in case the pendulum swings back again.

PART ONE

# Sex Is Not a Natural Act: Theme and Variations

$M$y mother is a professional musician, and the metaphor of music has
helped me explain sexuality to numerous audiences. Open a textbook on
human sexuality, and nine times out of ten it will begin with a chapter on
anatomy and physiology. This opening sets the stage for the assumption
that "the biological bedrock," as it is often called, must be understood
before we can look at anything else, such as what people want, what they
experience, how they get their ideas about what sex ought to be, and so
on. Furthermore, the biology presented in these texts always dwells on the
anatomy and physiology of the genital organs, never of the tactile receptors
of the cheek or lips or the physiology of aroma preferences. You'll find the
physiology of arousal but not of pleasure, of performance but not of
fantasy. So, it's not just biology that is being portrayed as fundamental, but
a certain kind of biology.

Open a textbook of music, in contrast, and you will not find chapters on
the bones, nerves, blood vessels, and muscles of the fingers (for playing the
piano), the hands (to play cymbals or cello), or even the mouth or throat
(for flute or singing). And what about the physiology of hearing or of the
sense of rhythm? Why don't music texts start with biology? Isn't biology as
fundamental to music as it is to sexuality?

It is, and it isn't. It depends on what you mean by *fundamental*. If you
mean that music requires human physiology to produce and experience, of
course this is largely true. But if you mean that the physiological aspect is
the most human, the most complex, the most interesting, or the most
important thing about experiencing music, well, then, we are going to
have an argument! By privileging biology within the discourse of sexuality,
and often by reducing sexuality to the biological, I think we've got the cart
before the horse, as the musical analogy suggests. And by privileging
genital physiology over any other aspect of bodily experience, sexology
research and writing make further choices and, I think, further mistakes.
Much of this collection examines these choices and their causes and
implications.

But the rhetoric of sexuality as "natural" is not just about biology; it also
relates to the expanding discussion of sexuality and health. As some of
these writings will show, I worry a lot about the consequences of locating
sexuality within the conceptual model and the material institutions of
health and the health industry. I think the already-accomplished
medicalization of male sexuality shows that sexuality is diminished and
human interests only incompletely served by the medical model, at least at
the present time. Maintaining that "sex is a natural act" identifies as experts
those social actors who know a lot about body mechanics rather than those
who understand learning, culture, and imagination.

Human sexuality is not a biological given and cannot be explained in
terms of reproductive biology or instinct. All human actions need a body,

but only part of human sexuality has to do with actions, and even that part only requires a body in the way that playing the piano does. What is done, when, where, by whom, with whom, with what, and why—these things have almost nothing to do with biology. Giving biology priority in our talking and theorizing about sexuality is called *essentialism* after the mistaken assumption that once you "strip away" all the cultural and historical trappings, the essence of sexuality that is left is biology. This type of thinking used to be called *biological determinism,* a perfectly good term.

So, if sex is not a natural act, a biological given, a human universal, what is it? I would say it's a concept, first of all—a concept with shifting but deeply felt definitions. Conceptualizing sex is a way of corralling and discussing certain human potentials for consciousness, behavior, and expression that are available to be developed by social forces, that is, available to be produced, changed, modified, organized, and defined. Like Jell-O, sexuality has no shape without a container, in this case a sociohistorical container of meaning and regulation. And, like Jell-O, once it is formed it appears quite fixed and difficult to re-form.

A kiss is not a kiss; in this perspective, your orgasm is not the same as George Washington's, premarital sex in Peru is not premarital sex in Peoria, abortion in Rome at the time of Caesar is not abortion in Rome at the time of John Paul II, and rape is neither an act of sex nor an act of violence—all of these actions remain to be defined by individual experience within one's period and place.

In Part 1 I attempt to articulate this antinaturalism perspective further. In these chapters I explain more about the naturalism perspective, where it comes from, how it tyrannizes, what the social constructionist alternative looks like, and how the new approach fits into current theory and research.

# 1

# "Am I Normal?"
# The Question of Sex

*T*hree times in my career I have written regular columns on sexuality for the public—a weekly column for six months for the *New York Daily News* in 1980–1981 and monthly columns for two national magazines, *Playgirl Advisor* and *Playgirl*, for a year and for four months, respectively. In each case I received stacks of letters from readers. The ones below, taken from the newspaper job in 1981, are representative:

> My name is Arlene. I am eighteen years of age. I have a friend [and] we have become very committed to each other in a friendship way, but he thinks that because we have developed this friendly relationship we ought to have a sexual relationship, too. But I am a bit confused [as] to what to do first before I have a sexual relationship with him. I am not sure if I really love him enough. What I am really afraid of is that once I get involved with him, all he will want to do is just have sex, and not be friends anymore.

> I am forty-nine years old and my husband is fifty-five years old. My problem is that we have had sex twice in fourteen months. When I bring the matter up, which I have done twice in this period of time, my husband insists that there is nothing wrong, not in any way, physically or mentally. He says that he is more tired lately, or that our twenty-four-year-old daughter may come in. . . . Two years ago I had a hysterectomy and we both joked about freedom from contraceptives and how we could look forward to "really enjoying it." But, to the contrary, our sex life is almost nil. I miss those intimate moments, preliminary caresses, and the feeling of being desired.

> I am a divorced woman who, in addition to a ten-year marriage, also has had two other sexually satisfying relationships. So I know I don't have a problem. In the past year, however, I have met several seemingly nice men who just don't make love very nicely, and it has created anxieties in me which were never there before. How common are things like this, for example?
>    a. Food, which I believe belongs in the kitchen, not on the body. (This man thought I was unimaginative and unenlightened.)

    b. Such a preference for oral and manual sex that I felt like a masturbating machine, not a lover.

    c. The weirdo who refused to ejaculate inside me, even with rubbers[1] "for the first two or three months until we know each other better." All he could say was, "Look, I've always done it this way. It frustrates me as much as it frustrates you, but I prefer not to just yet."

I know all about "consenting adults," but are these men normal?

God forbids all sex outside marriage—but you encourage it! Which leads to promiscuity and all sorts of trouble. Are you proud of yourself? Someday God will judge you. He will hold you accountable for everything.

There are three things to notice about these letters. First, they don't reveal that the writers themselves have any problems; rather, the partners have problems (2 and 3), the writer has a problem only because of her partner (1), or I, the expert, have a problem (4). This pattern also holds true in questions I've received during radio and TV shows. In part, people are understandably defensive and don't like to admit something is wrong with them. But, also, people who write are not just asking for help; they want to make a statement about how badly they're being dealt with and how they deserve some sympathy.

Second, notice that the question-writers want me to tell them things about their partners—people I've never laid eyes on! These women have been unable to get these men to give them straight answers, have not gotten any answers at all from them, or perhaps have not even been able to ask the men directly about the problem. The average person might not believe how many complex sexual problems are solved "merely" with improved communication, but anyone with any experience in long relationships probably realizes how difficult it is to change the communication patterns a couple has established.

Finally, note that in these letters the emphasis is not on performance (sexual "function") or pleasure so much as on psychological gratifications related to sex. The first woman wants to maintain her self-esteem and does not want to feel betrayed. The second woman misses intimacy, closeness, the feeling of being desired. The third woman wants her expectations met and wants to feel respected. The fourth writer wants me to subscribe to his or her moral vision of sexuality. Far more than is popularly realized, sexual activity is the means to gain or maintain important psychological feelings, and a challenge to one's sexuality is often a personal threat. Self-esteem, closeness, feelings of competence and well-being—these are the feelings sought from sex during modern times.

## What Is Normal?

Why do people write letters like the ones above to media sexuality "experts"? Why are radio phone-in shows on sexuality so immensely popular, night after night, coast to coast? The easy answer is that questions on sexuality have always existed in people's minds, but only recently has there been the opportunity to discuss such matters openly. Dramatic changes in broadcasting and publishing rules about explicit sexual language and imagery, this argument goes, have opened the door to public discussion of issues that have been on people's minds forever.

Another popular hypothesis to explain the explosion of public discussion about sex is that people are less willing nowadays to put up with sexual disappointment and sexual problems and less embarrassed to try and make things better.

Although I agree that as long as there have been human beings there have been questions about sex, I believe that the current deluge reflects less eternal inquisitiveness than a modern epidemic of insecurity and worry generated by a new social construction: the idea that sexual functioning is a central, if not *the* central, aspect of a relationship. Such an emphasis naturally leads to tremendous concern about sex and a greater need for advice, education, support, and a variety of repair services.

The new importance given to sexuality and emotional intimacy in relationships is one result of large social changes in how we view marriage and life:

- The purpose of marriage has shifted from economic necessity to companionship, resulting in dramatic changes in obligations and expectations.
- There has been a shift in how we measure a person's "success" to include physical vitality and life enjoyment along with material achievements.
- Divorce and "serial monogamy" have become increasingly acceptable, making people anxious about maintaining relationships.
- Changes in social attitudes and improvements in contraception have allowed women to view sexuality as separate from reproduction and as an avenue for self-expression and pleasure.
- People are relying on personal relationships to provide a sense of worth they lack in the public sphere due to increased technology, mobility, and bureaucracy.

These social changes provide the backdrop for reconstructing sexuality in modern life. But most people are not prepared for the increased importance of sex for relationships and personal identity. Sex, for the most part, is still a private and secret matter. The majority of people have never seen any genital sex acts but their own.[2] Most people do not talk honestly about sexual activity, and until recently there was no formal education in public schools about sex.

Imagine how you would feel if playing gin rummy, and playing it well, were considered a major component of happiness and a major sign of maturity, but no one told you how to play, you never saw anyone else play, and everything you ever read implied that normal and healthy people just somehow "know" how to play and really enjoy playing the very first time they try! It is a very strange situation.

Norms for sexual activity until recently came from religious authorities primarily concerned about moral boundaries. Sexual activities were governed by a right/wrong mentality, with homosexuality, masturbation, and having many partners among the wrongs and marital coitus, female sexual modesty, and a complete absence of self-disclosure between parents and children among the rights. During the nineteenth and twentieth centuries, religious authority over everyday activities has gradually eroded and the authority of science and science-based medicine to set norms has grown. Various forms of disapproved and deviant behavior (e.g., chronic lying, drinking, disobedience, and sexual "wrongs" of various sorts) came to be seen less as violations of God's law and more as the products of sick minds. The authority for interpreting deviations of behavior shifted almost imperceptibly, category by category, from the domain of sin and evil to that of disorder and abnormality.[3]

## Five Meanings of Normal

Well, what is sexual normalcy? There are at least five ways to answer this question:

1. *Subjective:* According to this definition, I am normal, and so is anyone who is the same as me. Secretly, most of us use this definition a lot, but publicly, few will admit it.
2. *Statistical:* According to this definition, whatever behaviors are most common are normal; less frequent ones are abnormal. If you conduct a survey and ask people how many lies they have told, how often they have drunk alcohol, or what kinds of sexual activities they have engaged in over the past five years and graph the results on a curve, the most frequent responses will be those in the middle, with extreme highs and lows at the ends. The idea of normalcy as something that is not too high and not too low is based on the statistical viewpoint. In the United States today, "too little sex" has joined "too much sex" as cause for worry.
3. *Idealistic:* From this viewpoint, normal means perfect, an ideal to be striven for. Those who model their behavior on Christ or Gandhi, for example, are taking an ideal for their norm, against which they measure all deviations.

4. *Cultural:* Without realizing it, this is probably the standard most of us use most of the time. This measure explains why our notions of normalcy do not always agree with those of people from other countries, regions, cultures, religions, and historical periods. Bare breasts or men kissing in public is normal in one place but abnormal in another. It is common for deviant behavior to be perceived as dangerous and frightening in a culture that rejects it, although the same behavior may be as common and harmless as chicken soup a few tribes or national boundaries away. Mouth-to-mouth kissing is a good example. In much of Oceania, mouth-to-mouth kissing is regarded as dirty and disgusting, and yet in Europe and North America it's a major source of intimacy and arousal.

5. *Clinical:* All the above definitions seem arbitrary, that is, they seem to depend on individual or group opinion rather than on "objective" evidence. The clinical standard, by contrast, uses scientific data about health and illness to make judgments. A particular blood pressure or diet or activity is considered clinically abnormal when research shows that it is related to disease or disability. It shouldn't matter to the clinical definition whether we are talking about the twentieth century or the tenth, about industrial Europe or rural Africa.

Using the clinical standard with regard to psychology is more difficult than using it for physiological matters because it is harder to prove psychological disease, deterioration, or disability. Who's to say, for example, that absence of interest in sex is abnormal according to the clinical definition? What sickness befalls the person who avoids sex? What disability? Clearly, such a person misses a life experience that some people value very highly and most value at least somewhat, but is avoiding sex "unhealthy" in the same way that avoiding protein is? Avoiding sex seems more akin to avoiding travel or avoiding swimming or avoiding investments in anything riskier than savings accounts—it's not trendy, but it's not sick, is it?

Are clinical standards that have been established for sexuality in fact based on valid and demonstrable standards of health and illness, or are they based on cultural and class opinion dressed up in scientific language? Sexual habits and preferences that do not conform to a procreative model for sex are the ones considered abnormal in medicine and clinical psychology. From lack of erection and orgasm to preference for masturbation and oral sex over intercourse to involvement of pain or items of clothing in sexual scripts—everything that is listed in contemporary psychiatric classification texts as abnormal refers to sexual practice that deviates from a preference for heterosexual coitus as the standard fare. Homosexual activities and affections would also still be included, except that political and scientific pressure forced the psychiatric community to "declassify" homosexuality in 1973.

A person's persistent interest in unconventional sexual expression and experience is often seen by clinicians as evidence of that individual's personality immaturity, poor judgment, or extreme needs (e.g., for isolation or for humiliation). Although I agree that such patterns could be evidence of psychological problems, I would want corroborating evidence from other parts of a person's life. And I would want to see that there were negative consequences to the person's well-being other than a sense of shame or guilt from being different. The problem is that the very existence of standards of normality breeds negative psychological consequences for those who deviate— that is known as the "social control" function of norms. And once norms become clinical standards, it's very difficult to identify those psychological problems that might not exist if social conformity weren't so important.

## Why People Care About Being Normal

We don't want abnormal blood pressure because we don't want to feel ill or shorten our lives. But why do people want to be sexually normal if deviance does not have harmful consequences? I think there are three interesting reasons.

- First, centuries of religious injunctions now transferred to medical language have convinced people that "abnormal" sexual desires, actions, or interests are always signs of mental or physical illness—in spite of the limited evidence for this assumption.
- The second reason connects adequate sexuality to relationship success and modern worries about divorce and breakup. Do sexual problems and dissatisfactions lead to divorce? Marriage counselors and therapists say that sexual dissatisfaction is often a *consequence* of marital troubles rather than a cause. An often-quoted study (published in the prestigious *New England Journal of Medicine*) of 100 self-defined "happy" couples found that there was some sort of arousal or orgasm dysfunction in the majority of cases but that the couples considered themselves happy both sexually and nonsexually nonetheless (Frank, Anderson, and Rubinstein, 1978). This is not to suggest that sexual problems or incompatibilities are trivial, but only that they are rarely the linchpin of relationships.
- The third, and I believe most important, reason that people stress the importance of sexual normality has to do with the need for social conformity. The current use of *normal* is code for socially okay, appropriate, customary, "in the ballpark." The average person uses the word in a kind of cultural-statistical way. How people feel about themselves depends to an enormous degree on the comparisons they make between

themselves and others. Leon Festinger, a noted social psychologist, formulated this long-known aspect of human psychology into a formal theory in 1954.

Social comparison is the process by which people evaluate their own satisfactions and adequacy not in terms of some unique internal standard but by looking to see what others get and do. How else to decide "how we're doing"—in work, marriage, tennis, looks, health, church attendance, financial success, or any other social behavior? In the realm of sexuality, however, social comparison becomes difficult because people have no way to know *really* what other people are doing (or how they are doing it, or how they are feeling about it). Maybe that's one reason why exterior "sexiness" has become a stand-in for sexuality—at least people can measure their conformity to a stereotype of sexy looks. To evaluate their adequacy in terms of sexual behavior, people are forced to rely on depictions and discussions provided through books and other media—television, radio, magazines, and movies.

But the agenda of magazines or talk shows is not primarily to educate but rather to attract readers, viewers, and, not the least, advertisers, through providing something new and different. How often have you seen "latest findings" splashed across the cover of a magazine or paperback sex book? I think the public assumes that valid new information is continually emerging and that the media are serving a useful function by presenting it to the public. In fact, guests on "Donahue" and people quoted in magazine articles are usually just promoting their books or expressing their views—which may or may not be backed by valid evidence.

The media have created a class of sex "experts" who write magazine columns, give radio advice, talk on TV, and produce a seemingly endless number of question-and-answer books for the sexually perplexed. Is anyone with an M.D. or Ph.D. after his or her name qualified to speak authoritatively about physiology and medicine, normal and abnormal psychology, couple interactions, child-raising, or sexual abuse and assault? The audience has no idea where the expert's information comes from and only the faintest idea of what might qualify as valid research in this area. Thus it is that contemporary health professionals have replaced religious and moral leaders as sexual authorities in the public's pursuit of sexual "normalcy."

If magazines and nonfiction TV exaggerate the "new" in what they communicate about sexuality, soap operas, nighttime TV dramas, and movies exaggerate the sensational and passionate aspects. If the only knowledge of people's looks came from these media, we would rightly conclude that everyone in the world had perfect skin, hair, and teeth except ourselves. The information about sex from these sources suggests that (1) everyone wants a lot of it; (2) everyone breaks up relationships, families, and lives to get it;

(3) everyone's sexual episodes are full of desperately urgent desire; and (4) the best sex is between strangers, especially strangers forbidden or prevented from consummating their desires. Even though we say that we don't take these images seriously, they shape our ideas of what is true and we end up suspecting that incredibly passionate sex is an immensely important part of many people's lives and perhaps therefore should be just as important in our own lives. A perpetual nagging disquiet is born in many people that shadows their own "ordinary" experiences.

Alfred Kinsey's revelations in 1948 and 1953 about the frequency of various sexual acts in America upset the commonly held belief that in private people were adhering to the official cultural sex norms (no premarital sex, no masturbation, no adultery, especially no adultery by wives, and so on). Prior to publication of those books, most people simply compared themselves to the official moral values and what they knew from rumor about neighbors and relatives. Some people tolerated more discrepancy from the norms than others, but at least they believed they knew where they stood. With the publication of Kinsey's surveys, that comfortable certainty disappeared. Fueled by the increasing emphasis on sexuality as a sign of social adequacy, a new era began in which the public seemed to acquire an insatiable appetite for information to answer the question, "Am I normal?"

# 2

# Social Constructionism
# and the Study of Human Sexuality

*I*n the past ten years, scholarship on human sexuality has been undergoing a radical transformation, but only in some disciplines. Psychology seems not to have noticed that new theories have been proposed that are "potentially explosive in their implications for our future understanding and behavior in regard to sex" (Vicunus, 1982, p. 137). Yet there is an urgent need for new ideas and research in the psychology of sexuality. As feminist anthropologist Gayle Rubin (1984) put it,

> There are historical periods in which sexuality is more sharply contested and more overtly politicized. In such periods, the domain of erotic life is, in effect, renegotiated. . . . Periods such as the 1880s in England and the 1950s in the United States recodify the relations of human sexuality. The struggles that were fought leave a residue in the form of laws, social practices, and ideologies which then affect the way sexuality is experienced long after the immediate conflicts have faded. All signs indicate that the present era is another of those watersheds. (Rubin, 1984, pp. 267, 274)

As I write, places of public sexual activity are closed "for health reasons" because of AIDS and quarantine is being discussed; censorship statutes are being passed to limit production and distribution of explicit sexual images to "protect" women and children; penal codes are specifying in ever greater detail illegal sexual activities between adults and children; and the U.S. Attorney General's Commission on Pornography (the Meese Commission) is blaming explicit sexual materials for sexual violence and abuse in our society.

History may show that the academic community did not, and perhaps could not, take a leadership role in these great sociosexual issues. Perhaps academia speaks with too fragmented a voice or on too slow a time scale. Most recent histories of sexuality (e.g., Weeks, 1981), however, agree that social scientists, physicians, mental health professionals, and other sexuality "experts" are increasingly relied on for advice and authority regarding social sexual policy. For this reason alone psychologists must familiarize themselves with the new scholarship on sex. Unfortunately, psychology has to date

17

been dominated by a limited, medicalized perspective. I want to show how an alternative point of view emerging in other areas of scholarship offers exciting opportunities for psychologists.

# The Social Constructionist Approach

In a recent essay, Kenneth Gergen (1985) defined the social constructionist approach as a form of inquiry indebted to intellectual trends such as symbolic interactionism, symbolic anthropology, ethnomethodology, literary deconstructionism, existentialism, phenomenology, and social psychology. What these disciplines have in common is an emphasis on the person's active role, guided by his or her culture, in structuring the reality that affects his or her own values and behavior. This perspective is to be contrasted with empiricism and positivism, which ignore the active role of the individual in favor of the impact of external forces that can be objectively examined and analyzed.

Gergen identified four assumptions made by social constructionists:

1. The way professionals study the world is determined by available concepts, categories, and methods. Their concepts incline them toward or even dictate certain lines of inquiry while precluding others. For example, the assumption that there really are two and only two genders prevents scholars from designing studies to ask where gender conceptions come from and how they are promulgated or from looking at gender as a dependent rather than an independent variable (Kessler and McKenna [1978] 1985).

2. Many of the concepts and categories people use in scholarship and everyday life vary considerably in their meanings and connotations over time and across cultures. Gergen described considerable variation in concepts such as romantic love, childhood, mother's love, the self, and emotion. Accepting variation in meaning for these abstract notions makes questionnaire research or simple citation of earlier scholarship problematic.

3. The popularity and persistence of particular concepts, categories, or methods often depends more on their political usefulness than on their validity. For example, the positivist-empiricist model of statistics-driven, laboratory-based psychological research has been greatly criticized for its limitations and omissions, yet it persists because of prestige, tradition, and congruence with cultural values (Sherif, 1979; Unger, 1983).

4. Descriptions and explanations of the world are themselves forms of social action and have consequences. Gergen used as his illustration Carol Gilligan's (1982) discussion of the consequences of prominent theories of moral development to show how a system that ignored women's ethical values and ethical development became the academic standard by which moral function was judged.

# Social Constructionism
# and Sexual Scholarship

Many scholars credit Michel Foucault's widely read 1976 essay with popularizing the view that ideas about sexuality arise in particular social-historical contexts. Foucault argued that, contrary to common belief, sexuality was not repressed during the long Victorian era only to gradually reawaken under the warming influence of twentieth-century permissiveness. Instead, he argued that there is no essential human quality or inner drive, sexuality, that is available to be repressed in one era and liberated in another. Rather, there is a human potential for consciousness, behavior, and physical experience that can be developed ("incited") by social forces of definition, regulation organization, and categorization. Sexualities and sexual experiences are produced, changed, and modified within an ever-changing sexual discourse. The modern view of sexuality as a fundamental drive that is very individualized, deeply gendered, central to personality and intimate relationships, separate from reproduction, and lifelong (literally womb-to-tomb) would be quite unrecognizable to people living in different civilizations.

Kenneth Plummer (1982) contrasted the popular drive-based view of human sexuality with the social constructionist dramaturgic metaphor of sexual script (Gagnon and Simon, 1973). Is sexuality better seen as a powerful universal biological drive that can be shaped to some degree by sociocultural forces and individual learning, or is it more akin to a "script" that is enacted in physical performance and created, not just shaped, within the sociocultural moment? The latter position leads to a vision of sexuality (1) as emerging within relationships and situations according to participants' expectations; (2) as needing to be constructed rather than controlled; (3) as available to satisfy needs for affection, protection, and gender-affirmation; and (4) as qualitatively different for children than it is for adults. The idea of a universal, inborn sexual drive is seen as a form of excuse and rationalization rather than legitimate description.

Histories and anthropologies of sexuality are being revolutionized by the new constructionism. Whereas earlier scholarship tabulated cultural and historical variations in acts and attitudes (Ford and Beach, 1951; Lewinsohn, 1958), newer works in history (Weeks, 1981) and anthropology (Ortner and Whitehead, 1981) trace the variation and meanings of the categories and concepts themselves. There's no point in making a cross-cultural table of age at first intercourse, for example, without discussing differences in the meaning of intercourse—and differences in choreography as well. Acts of intercourse, for example, even if they all involve contact between men's and women's genitalia, have no more in common necessarily than haute couture coats and bearskins. And the experience of such acts conducted in wildly different sociocultural settings will have about as much in common as the experience of wearing the Paris coat and the bearskin. As one of the "new" histories put it, "In any approach that takes as predetermined and universal the categories of sexuality, real history disappears" (Padgug, 1979, p. 5).

Most sex researchers, grounded in biology or the decontextualized study of the individual, accept universal categories no matter how much sexual variety they document. As Jeffrey Weeks has pointed out, "Even in the case of writers like Kinsey, whose work radically demystified sexuality, and whose taxonomic efforts undermined the notions of 'normality,' the [naturalistic] concept is still traceable in the emphasis on sexual 'outlet' as opposed to beliefs or identities" (Weeks, 1982, p. 295).

Kinsey, originally a zoologist, uncritically accepted the common idea of an evolutionarily determined drive as the bedrock of sexuality. Only recently has biological determinism been seriously challenged: "Biological sexuality is only a precondition, a set of potentialities, which is never unmediated by human reality, and which becomes transformed in qualitatively new ways in human society" (Padgug, 1979, p. 9).

Patricia Miller and Martha Fowlkes (1980) have suggested that the sociological perspective on sexuality has been limited because the few sociologists who have been interested in sex have focused on deviance and social control and have studied prostitutes, nudists, transvestites, and homosexuals far more than "ordinary" heterosexuals and couples. Now that feminists and gay and lesbian scholars have entered the academy in significant numbers, they can make "dominant" forms of sexuality the object of analysis.

# Aspects of the
# Social Constructionist Approach

## *Analysis and Challenge*
## *of Categories and Concepts*

The most basic, and also most difficult, aspect of studying sexuality is defining the subject matter. What is to be included? How much of the body is relevant? How much of the life span? Is sexuality an individual dimension or a dimension of a relationship? Which behaviors, thoughts, or feelings qualify as sexual—an unreturned glance? any hug? daydreams about celebrities? fearful memories of abuse? When can we use similar language for animals and people, if at all?

As Kinsey, with Wardell Pomeroy and Clyde Martin, plaintively wrote in describing their method,

> In spite of the long list of items included in the present [interview] study [anywhere from 300 to 521 items per interview], and in spite of the fact that each

history has covered five times as much material as in any previous study, numerous students have suggested, and undoubtedly will continue to suggest after the publication of the present volume, that we should have secured more data in the fields of their special interests. Specifically it has been suggested that the following matters should have had more thorough investigation: racial ancestry . . . somatotypes . . . hormonal assays . . . physical examination of the genitalia . . . marital adjustment . . . early childhood and parental relations . . . motivations and attitudes . . . cultural and community backgrounds . . . [and] sperm counts. (Kinsey, Pomeroy, and Martin, 1948, p. 56)

It seems that when sex researchers discuss "terminology," naturalism and essentialism have prevented them from seeing that the discussion of language is not a search for the "real" or "clearest" variables and terms but an exercise in boundary setting. What should we choose, for the purposes of a particular study, to construe as sexual?

Herant Katchadourian's (1979) psychological review of "the many meanings of sex," for example, failed to note that all the terms discussed (gender identity, drive, partner choice, desire, sexual experience, arousability) described individual issues. By contrast, Michel Foucault and Richard Sennett (1982) explicitly problematized the individualized focus of sexuality language. Their examination took them to early Christian theology and nineteenth-century medicine. Theology, preoccupied with sexual purity and personal obedience, and medicine, preoccupied at that time with sexual excess and insanity, construed sexuality as an individual matter within the discourses of personal responsibility and individual disease. Theirs is a discussion of sexual constructionism, showing how concepts are fluid, responsive, and constructed within particular contexts. There is no expectation that "the" definition of sexuality is being sought or found.

Paul Robinson (1976) examined how William Masters and Virginia Johnson's (1966) commitment to equal sexual rights for women led them to force their physiological findings into a procrustean conceptual bed. After selecting a homogeneous sample and testing subjects in an environment where the definition of sexual behavior was physical arousal and orgasm, Masters and Johnson "found" similar patterns between men and women, which they described in terms of a fixed four-stage "human sexual response cycle." The persistence of this arbitrary and ill-fitting model illustrates Gergen's claim about how politics determine many categories in sexology.

## Imagery and Metaphor

What kinds of things is sexuality (or sexualities) like? Sociologists John Gagnon (1973) and William Simon (1973) intended the metaphor of dramatic scripts to draw our attention to learned, planned, external sources. Ethel Person (1980), a psychoanalyst, changed the metaphor to a "sex print . . . in the sense of fingerprint, unchangeable and unique . . . an individualized script that elicits erotic desire" (p. 620). She focused on the learned sources of eroticism, but with Freudian early-life determinism. Ironically, Simon (1973) had intended to exclude psychoanalytic ideas of irreversibility with a metaphor that would underscore "a continuing potential for reorderings of meanings . . . a reordering that has permanent consequences in the sense that later changes are at the very least as significant in informing current behavior as were the original or earlier meanings, and, in many instances, more significant" (p. 70).

Metaphors such as script and fingerprint, like drive and instinct, direct the attention of researchers, scholars, and readers to distinct sexual possibilities. This is what Gergen meant by saying that descriptions of the world are themselves forms of social action and have consequences. The 1973 struggle within the American Psychiatric Association over continuing to classify homosexuality as a mental disorder seemed often to be primarily about imagery in discourse about sexuality, with both proponents and opponents of "declassification" arguing that the presence of homosexuality in the official listing carried a powerful message to young people, parents, legislators, teachers, and homosexuals (Bayer, 1981).

### Historical Dimensions of Sexuality Language

Historical studies are dear to social constructionists because they can point the way to analyses of cultural meanings and changing personal experiences. There's been a great deal of work on historical shifts in the construction of homosexuality, and methods developed in that work should prove extremely useful in studying all aspects of sexual experience, behavior, and identity (Plummer, 1981).

Recently, Mark Elliott (1985) counted the prevalence of the terms *impotence* and *frigidity* in the psychological literature between 1940 and 1983. He found that each term appeared in titles indexed in *Psychological Abstracts* between two and eight times per year until 1970, when titles with *impotence* escalated dramatically. I have written at length about the numerous social forces contributing to this change and about the consequences of the "growth" of "impotence" for sexuality discourse and men's experiences. Historical work is providing the greatest impetus to social constructionism in sexuality, as this work emphatically destabilizes essentialist notions.

### Methods for Studying Sexuality

Gergen (1985) asserted that a constructionist analysis must "eschew the empiricist account of scientific knowledge . . . the traditional Western conception of objective, individualistic, ahistorical knowledge . . . [and embrace criteria such as] the analyst's capacity to invite, compel, stimulate, or delight the audience. . . . Virtually any methodology can be employed so long as it enables the analyst to develop a more compelling case" (pp. 271, 272, 273).

This suggestion is completely in sync with feminist complaints about the limitations and biases in positivist scholarship. To understand sexuality, scholars need to use and respect multiple methods and researcher points of view and to see experimental, correlational, participatory, and clinical methods as complementary, not competing (Carlson, 1971). Individual constructions of sexuality involve an interplay of individual and social processes that cannot be adequately explored with only one method.

Suppose scholars were to start with an idiosyncratic speculation about the psychology of sexuality such as the following:

> It is the recollection rather than the anticipation of the act that assumes a primary importance in homosexual relations. That is why the great homosexual writers of our culture can write so elegantly about the sexual act itself, because the homosexual imagination is for the most part concerned with reminiscing. . . . This is all due to concrete and practical considerations and says nothing about the intrinsic nature of homosexuality. (Foucault, 1982/1983, p. 19)

Following Gergen's lead, scholars who accepted this view would not tend to formulate empirical research to decide whether and under what circumstances it was "true" that homosexuals felt and believed this way. Rather, they would want to explore the now and then, the here and elsewhere, the who, what, when, where, and why of this speculation, without the goal of identifying once-and-for-all-truths about homosexuals. What does clinical work on the nature of fantasy have to teach us? What about theories on the nature of representation? What about cultural variations in myth and the encouragement of individual imagination? How might claims about imagination be affected by mass availability of erotic images?

Unfortunately, both the methodological eclecticism of constructionism and its tendency to place the subject at the center of the method conflict with the quest for "rigor" of many sex researchers. An important conference sponsored by the National Institute of Mental Health underscored sexology's commitment to "unambiguous concepts," "objective measurement," "operationalism," and all possible forms of scientific "control" (Green and Wiener, 1980). Nevertheless, even in that setting, one could find suggestions for more constructionist scholarship, including life histories and analyses of diverse kinds of relationships, and some workers expressed a preference for studying real situations rather than laboratory analogs.

## The Medicalization of Sexuality

The major obstacle to a social constructionist approach to sexuality is the domination of theory and research by the biomedical model. As Catherine

Riessman (1983) defined it, "The term medicalization refers to two inter-related processes. First, certain behaviors or conditions are given medical meaning—that is, defined in terms of health and illness. Second, medical practice becomes a vehicle for eliminating or controlling problematic experiences that are defined as deviant" (p. 4).

The ideological support for medicalization is essentialist, naturalist, biological thinking. The major constructionist project is to define and locate sexuality in personal, relational, and cultural, rather than physical, terms. This is a real uphill battle.

## Analyzing the Privileged Position of Biology in Sexuality

Here's the beginning of a psychoanalytic essay about sexuality:

> The scientific picture of sexual behavior has become so distorted that we must make a serious attempt to rediscover the obvious. In any attempt of this kind, it is always well to begin again at the beginning, in this case with a brief reexamination of the evolutionary differentiation of the sexes, and the physiologic basis of sexual activity. . . . In the most primitive protozoa, the individual propagates by itself. (Rado, 1949, p. 159)

In the beginning we always seem to find the birds and the bees: biology and reproduction, the genes and the genitals. The privileged position of biology in sexual discourse is based on the assumption that the body dictates action, experience, and meaning. Why has biological reductionism retained such a grip on sexology when it has long been dethroned from other aspects of psychology? I think there are two reasons. The contemporary reason, the political one, has to do with legitimacy for sex research. Sex is dirty, or at least risque, but emphasizing the biological bases makes it a more reputable subject of study.

But the more profound answer has to do with Western Judeo-Christian discourse, wherein sex came to be located in the body, separated from the spirit and the mind (Petras, 1973). Foucault and Sennett (1982) argued that the Christian moral agenda of self-purification became linked with an antimasturbation preoccupation in the eighteenth century, which was in turn translated into the medical idea that sexuality exists in the individual prior to any sexual relationship or activity.

Jeffrey Weeks (1985) illuminated the deep faith of early sexologists that in the struggle between sexual ignorance and enlightenment the surest weapon would be biological science. He told how German sexologist Magnus Hirschfeld, founder of sexology journals, research institutes, and international congresses, saw his Berlin Institute seized and its papers burned by the Nazis in 1933 and yet could still write: "I believe in Science, and I am convinced that Science, and above all the natural Sciences, must bring to mankind, not only truth but with truth, Justice, Liberty and Peace" (Hirschfeld, 1935, cited in Weeks, 1985, p. 71). Feminists have also traced the reliance on biological theories to a displaced search for divine guidance. "The laws which Science was uncovering would turn out to be the expression of the will of God—revelations of the divine Plan. Thus, science would provide moral guidelines for living" (Ehrenreich and English, 1978, p. 66).

Sexual biology, at first the study of instincts, later the study of brain centers, germ plasm, hormones, and fetal development, and most recently the study of vaginal blood flow, molecular genetics, nipple enlargement, and clitoral histochemistry, would reveal nature's direction for human sexual conduct. Biological science promised that *what is* would provide direction for *what ought to be*.

Biology's privileged position within contemporary sexuality discourse thus descended from early researchers' hope that "objective science" would replace oppressive orthodoxies of the past. Yet the emphasis on biological variables can create its own oppressive constructions. An example of this is the impact of Masters and Johnson's (1966) research on female sexuality. At the same time that their description and measurement of female orgasm documented some women's physical capacities and changed some old prejudices, their exclusive focus on measurable bodily states mechanized and trivialized sexual experience and mystified social and psychological aspects of sexuality, including those which operated in the laboratory during their research (Segal, 1983).

## Increasing Importance of Sexual "Adequacy"

The social support for sexual medicalization arises in part from the increasing importance of sexuality itself in modern life. Like fitness, sexuality has gained importance as part of society's glorification of youth and health, its "denial of death." German sexologist Gunter Schmidt (1983a) identified three "compensatory" functions that sexuality serves in our time:

> [Sexuality] is supposed to hold marriages and relationships together because they scarcely fulfill material functions any longer; it is supposed to promote self-realization and self-esteem in a society that makes it more and more difficult to feel worth something and needed as an individual; it is supposed to drive out coldness and powerlessness in a world bureaucratized by administration, a world walled-up in concrete landscapes and a world of disrupted relationships at home and in the community. ... All discontent—political, social and personal—is meant to be deflected into the social and relationship sector in order to be compensated. (Schmidt, 1983a, pp. vii–viii)

In a world where gender remains very important while the proofs of gender adequacy become more elusive, sexual knowledge and performance, for both men and women, need to serve the function of proving gender adequacy, too.

## The Media and the Hegemony of Sexual Medicine

As sexual interest and adequacy gain in social importance, weaknesses in one's preparation become more significant. The major source of information for the young has become mass media, both because of parents' silence and because of the dearth of sex education in the current conservative climate (Gagnon, 1985). In the twentieth century, mass media shape popular consciousness by providing language, experts, information, and fictional scripts.

Nonfiction media are dominated by a health model of sexuality, with physicians, psychologists, or other health specialists the authorities. Sex enters the print media either because of a newsworthy event ("new" research or technology, sexual crimes, escapades of celebrities) or in the form of a feature article in which authorities give their opinions of issues of normal "adjustment" ("How to Have Great New Sex with Your Same Old Spouse," Sarrel and Sarrel, 1983) or of deviance ("The Anguish of the Transsexuals," Churcher, 1980). Perhaps because of the history of censorship, the media are more comfortable with the aspects of sexuality that seem least like pornography, that is, closer to medicine and public health.

Even the science articles focus on sensational new developments, typified by "the 'G' spot" flurry of 1981 and 1982.[1] A trade book about the "G" spot (Ladas, Whipple, and Perry, 1982), based on skimpy research that even prior to publication had been contradicted in professional journals and scientific meetings, became a bestseller in 1982. Newslike reports of a scientific "discovery," an area of unusual erotic sensitivity on the anterior wall of the vagina that related to an alleged ability of women to ejaculate fluid at orgasm, appeared in numerous women's magazines, newspapers, and sex-oriented magazines. The authors of the book appeared widely on national television. Seven book clubs purchased the book before publication. The insatiability of the media for the commercial potential of sexual topics results in an endless search for news and advice, whereas disconfirming evidence receives little or no publicity. The combination of scientific (read: biological) "news" and health-expert advice in the nonfiction media reinforces the impression that sex is very important without providing the kind of information ordinary readers or viewers can actually use. People end up with the directive to consult a professional expert—not the most empowering message.

The romantic and passion-filled portrayals of sexuality in the fiction media (e.g., movies, soap operas, television series like "Dynasty") stoke the public's expectations. If sex can provide such power, meaning, and material rewards, if it can make or break relationships, if it is such a large part of people's lives, then the public's dependence on experts and authorities for guidance in this maelstrom increases. A constructionist approach to sexuality can elucidate how individuals, couples, and social groups are affected by the media's various messages.

## Political and Economic Aspects of Professional Expansion

Cultural authority in the area of sexuality is not passively conferred on health authorities; it is actively sought, consolidated, and maintained. Through individual and group efforts, professionals take measures to ensure their autonomy, promote their economic opportunities, and increase their public status (Larson, 1977).

In sexology, professional expansion and control within health fields have been promoted through specialty organizations with restricted memberships, registries of "approved" service providers, advertising by institutional public relations offices, frequent conferences that define professional boundaries, awards, media contacts, and numerous specialized journals and newsletters. The development of "impotence" diagnosis and treatment as a subspecialty within urology illustrates many aspects of professional medicalization, as does having sexual dysfunctions defined as psychiatric disorders by the American Psychiatric Association.

Consider as an example the construction of the condition of "anorgasmia." Based on her wide familiarity with sexual patterns around the world, Margaret Mead (1955) observed, "There seems to be a reasonable basis to assuming that the human female's capacity for orgasm is to be viewed much more as a potentiality that may or may not be developed by a given culture, or in the specific history of an individual, than as an inherent part of her full humanity" (p. 166). Like playing the piano or grinding corn for tortillas, producing an orgasm is probably a universal human potential that depends on opportunity, training, and goals. But, rather than making orgasms an arbitrary matter of talent and predilection, professional interests in medicalization have made them a matter of health and disorder. Social constructionist research can analyze how people internalize the medicalized messages of sexuality professionals and how these messages contribute to their sexual scripts and expectations.

## The Public's Role in the Medicalization of Sexuality

The public is also not merely a passive player reflexively responding to the proselytizing of health experts and the media. Rather, medicalized discourse about sexuality seems to be actively sought to provide both authoritative direction and self-protective attributions. The dearth of sex education plus the high importance attributed to sexuality leave the public eager, even desperate, for information from respected authorities. The morally neutral discourse of "objective medical science" provides ideal cover for sexual claims and desires that might otherwise be questioned. Feminists, for example, embraced Masters and Johnson's (1966) "proof" that women were entitled *by their biology* to sexual activity, pleasure, and orgasm. The gay community cites the American Psychiatric Association's 1973 declassification of homosexuality as evidence of its biological normalcy.

## Sexuality and Psychology

Any research that emphasizes individual and group variations in sexual meaning and experience will undermine the universalistic assumptions central to the medical model. How, from the vast range of physical and mental possibilities, do people come to call certain ones sexual? How do these sexual activities come to be invested with personal meaning? How do these individual constructions change over the lifetime of a person or a relationship? We assume that the contemporary commercialization of sexuality, which has made images so much more available to the public, has changed scripts and expectations, but how? How do people incorporate what is in the culture into their own life course?

Research is needed to examine the psychological experience of words used very often in sexology: *pleasure* and *intimacy*. Pleasure is often rated as the most important element of sexual satisfaction, yet we cannot assume a universal inborn experience and there is no research concerning how people apply a "pleasure" label to aspects of sexual relations. The sex therapy literature is full of claims about the importance of intimacy to clinically healthy sexual performance, although it seems safe to assume that the vast majority of genital unions over the centuries have occurred without the presence of anything remotely like our modern idea of "self-in-intimacy."

Studies of how body image develops and influences sexual experience are also needed—do people compare themselves to cultural ideals of sexiness and, invariably falling short, suffer? Or are ideas of sexiness more dependent on early personal experiences of being praised by doting adults? What factors buffer feelings of inadequacy and which ones add fuel to the fire?

Medicalized discourse, with its smooth, superficial prescriptions for sexual experience, sets up norms and deviations without regard to the range of possible pathways and outcomes for sexual development. If constructionists succeed in reframing sexuality as constructed in interaction as a result of expectations and negotiations, psychology may move to the forefront of sexuality analysis.

John Gagnon, a social constructionist sex researcher for the past thirty years, believes that "people become sexual in the same way they become everything else. Without much reflection, they pick up directions from their social environment. They acquire and assemble meanings, skills and values from the people around them" (Gagnon, 1977, p. 2). Perceiving sexual behavior in this "ordinary" way conflicts with the popular perception of deeply buried instincts and raging hormones. The medicalized discourse has held sway because it offers respectability to sex researchers, entrepreneurs, and customers alike, but it does not offer a route to a rich understanding. It's time to give the social constructionist perspective an opportunity to develop a more compelling case.

# 3

# Sexual Biology and
# the Symbolism of the Natural

## Uses of *Nature* and *Naturalism*
## in Sexology

*I* thought for years that sex was natural, but now I realize that I never stopped to think about exactly what I meant by that statement and what evidence existed for the claim. Let's consider some uses of naturalism language in writings about sexuality.

The whole of sexual experience for both the human male and female is constituted in two . . . separate systems . . . that coexist *naturally*. . . . The biophysically and psychosocially based systems of influence that *naturally* coexist in any woman [can] function in mutual support. . . . Based on the manner in which an individual woman internalizes the prevailing psychosocial influence, her sexual value system may or may not reinforce her *natural* capacity to function sexually. One need only remember that sexual function can be displaced from its *natural* context temporarily or even for a lifetime in order to realize the . . . import [of the sexual value system]. . . . It seems more accurate to consider female orgasmic response as an acceptance of *naturally* occurring stimuli that have been given erotic significance by an individual sexual value system than to depict it as a learned response. (Masters and Johnson, 1970, pp. 219, 297, emphasis added)

Present-day legal determinations of sexual acts which are acceptable, or "*natural*," and those which are "contrary to *nature*," are not based on data obtained from biologists, nor from *nature* herself. (Kinsey, Pomeroy, and Martin, 1948, p. 202, emphasis added)

It is an essential part of our conceptual apparatus that the sexes are a polarity, and a dichotomy in *nature*. (Greer, 1971, p. 15, emphasis added)

The *nature* of the society in which a people live clearly plays a significant part in shaping the patterns of human sexual behavior. . . . Human societies appear

to have seized upon and emphasized a *natural*, physiologically determined in-
clination toward intercourse between males and females, and to have discour-
aged and inhibited many other equally *natural* kinds of behavior. We believe
that under purely hypothetical conditions in which any form of social control
was lacking, coitus between males and females would prove to be the most
frequent type of sexual behavior. (Ford and Beach, 1951, p. 19, emphasis
added)

This *natural* instinct which with all conquering force and might demands fulfillment. (Richard von Krafft-Ebing, *Psychopathia Sexualis*, 1886, quoted in
Weeks, 1985, p. 69, emphasis added)

Raymond Williams (1976), the historian of culture, identified three uses
of the term *nature* and located their origins in seventeenth-century Enlightenment political debates. He began his discussion, by the way, by saying that
*nature* is "perhaps the most complex word in the language" (p. 219).

According to the first use, *nature* refers to the *essential quality* of something. For the author of the fourth quotation above, for example, "the nature of the society in which a people live" means the essential quality of the
society. Nature here is a metaphor for what is bottom, bedrock, fundamental. Once the essence of something is its *nature*, then other uses of *nature*
acquire the connotation of basic, bedrock.

The second use Williams identified is nature as an *inherent force* directing
the world. This meaning can be seen in the second quotation's use of the
phrase "contrary to nature." This legal term, which is still in use, means that
some sexual act is opposed to a higher force directing the world, nature here
as successor or stand-in for God. Don't fool with Mother Nature. Power is
connoted here.

The third use is *nature* as *material world*, particularly as *fixed* material
world. This meaning seems to be the most common one in the sexological
quotes above: The third quote says the sexes are a dichotomy in nature, that
is, they are a fixed dichotomy in the material world; the first quote says female orgasm is natural, that it definitely exists in the material world. Nature
"herself" is referred to in the second quote: "Present-day legal determinations . . . are not based on data obtained . . . from nature herself"; in other
words, the existence of a material world that lies outside of human intervention is assumed. Independence, objectivity, and a contrast with human culture are connoted here.

The term *nature* is often used in sexology for its rhetorical power. By
emphasizing that something is *in nature*, an author gives whatever is being
discussed solidity and validity. That special rhetorical power often seems to
call on nature *by contrast with culture*, as if anything human-made can be the
result of trickery, but something prior to and outside of human culture can
be trusted. The laws of nature, for example, are thought to be above human

politics, while the laws of people are polluted with politics (Schiebinger, 1986). The term confers the authority of something before or underneath culture, something prior to culture. Sexual nature, then, sounds like something solid and valid, not human-made.

But there are two more aspects of the rhetorical power conveyed to orgasm or intercourse or certain sexual acts or instincts by calling them *natural*. The first is *universality*. Part of the rhetorical power comes from generalizing what's natural and therefore presocial into what's natural and therefore *universal*. Because human culture has not yet interfered with something that is natural, the allegedly natural act or instinct is thought to be part of the essence of being human and therefore universal to the human condition.

Finally, the quality of *biological* is implied, since what else is *universal, presocial,* and of the *essence* but *biology?* It is biology that is contrasted with culture when a sexologist uses the term *nature*. *Natural orgasm* is universal and a biological thing; *natural intercourse* is universal and a biological thing; *natural sexuality* is universal and a biological thing.

I submit that the term *natural* is used so frequently in sexologic discourse because of *rhetorical needs for justification and legitimacy*. *Nature* and *natural* are used to persuade, not to describe or to give information. In the quotations above, the rhetorical efforts are most apparent in the language of Masters and Johnson, where presocial, universal, and biological connotations of *nature* help support their theses about the importance and propriety of men's and, especially, women's sexuality.

But sexologists use the rhetoric of naturalism not just to endorse the value of sexuality but to increase their own respectability as scholars of sexuality. Respectability is a chronic problem in this field. Many sex researchers will sympathize with the tone of these words by George Corner, a leading sex endocrinologist of the twentieth century:

> In 1922 the National Research Council was called upon by influential groups . . . to bring together existing knowledge and to promote research upon human sex behavior and reproduction. . . . The Committee for Research in Problems of Sex, with financial support from the Rockefeller Foundation, successfully undertook to encourage research on a wide range of problems of sex physiology and behavior. The younger readers of this book will hardly be able to appreciate the full significance of [this]. . . . It represented a major break from the so-called Victorian attitude which in the English-speaking countries had long impeded scientific and sociologic investigation of sexual matters and placed taboos on open consideration of human mating and childbearing as if these essential activities were intrinsically indecent. To investigate such matters, even in the laboratory with rats and rabbits, required of American scientists . . . a certain degree of moral stamina. A member of the Yerkes Committee once heard himself introduced by a fellow scientist to a new acquaintance as one of the men who had "made sex respectable." (Corner, 1961, p. x)

This quotation highlights an important point about how the language of naturalism, with its implications of biological universality, allows researchers to keep the focus of their work on some phenomenon called "sexuality" even while replacing human subjects with rats and rabbits (Hall, 1974). We sex researchers study "sexual" behaviors in all these species and believe we are studying some uniform and universal phenomenon, albeit manifested in somewhat differing form across species. This paves the way for studies of "homosexuality" and "courtship" in animals and "mating behavior" and "copulation" in humans. It's all sexuality, after all, in one big happy mammalian family.

# Origins of the Use
## of *Nature* and *Naturalism*

I alluded earlier to seventeenth-century European sources that used the language of naturalism (Williams, 1976). Let me say a little more about this period in order to demonstrate that these terms originated in a *particular* time for *particular* purposes and thereby shed some light on the rhetoric involved in contemporary uses of such language.

Philosophers and historians of science remind us that a call for a scientific approach to knowledge—an approach dedicated to studying "the laws of nature" objectively—arose during the Enlightenment to reinforce democratic politics in Britain and Europe (Bloch and Bloch, 1980). Writers of the period called on nature for a source of authority and legitimacy other than mysticism or monarchy; laws of nature were to compete with laws of kings and popes.

Political philosophers of the sixteenth and seventeenth centuries invoked a hypothetical state of nature, subject to the laws of nature, to support political theories based on individuals' free and rational acceptance of the social contract. Such theories were intended to support the right of the people to resist the doctrine of the divine right of kings as well as to resist abuses of power by the church. Recourse to the concept of the state of nature and its laws represented an effort to invoke a presocial design for the world (Williams's second definition) that would trump the mere historical legitimacies of states. Appeals to the reason and dignity of man as given by nature supported claims for individual human rights and aspirations and for equality (Schiebinger, 1986).

At the same time, nature, this time the mere material world, to use Williams's third meaning, was invoked throughout the writings of seventeenth-century scientists such as Francis Bacon and René Descartes as something waiting to be tamed and controlled through man's use of reason (Lloyd, 1984). Emancipated from ignorance and fear, making use of the new economic and technological opportunities of the time, man (often the male of the human species and not the generic *man*) would master nature, rip the veil from nature, and so on. The rhetorical uses of nature as presocial, universal, and biological thus arose as political rhetoric in this intense cauldron of social change and have shaped our language and imagery since.

## Feminist Challenge to the Language of Naturalism

Throughout the current women's movement, the language and implications of naturalism have been a special target of attack (Lowe and Hubbard, 1983). Feminist scholars have attacked the ideology of male supremacy based on assumptions about male and female nature as prime supports for sex-role stereotyping and women's social, economic, and political oppression. Feminists have implicitly recognized the political dangers of the use of naturalism language—on the one hand, *natural* was used in the normative sense to imply good, healthy, and moral, yet at the same time it connoted something biologically based, fixed, and presocial. That is, feminists worried that through the use of naturalism metaphors, what is would be assumed to be what should be. Reflecting these fears, the title of one book was *Woman's Nature: Rationalizations of Inequality* (Lowe and Hubbard, 1983).

The explosive rise of sociobiology in the mid-1970s seemed to be a backlash confirming the feminists' fears. Biological, evolutionary, and animal research was recruited to justify the status quo. Donald Symons' (1979) sociobiology text, for example, argued that "there is a female human nature and a male human nature and these natures are extraordinarily different, though the differences are to some extent masked . . . by moral injunctions" (p. v).

And what are these different sexual natures? Symons compiled field and laboratory studies and made generous generalizations from these studies to support his conclusion that there are "natural" differences in how men and women experience desire, jealousy, sexual pleasure, orgasm, and wishes for partner variety. Perversely, Symons's book seems unusually open-minded in its discussion of language, including issues concerning natural language and the idea of a natural environment, the semantics of ultimate causation, and the relation of human culture to evolution. Symons even concluded his book with this caution: "Tendencies to equate 'natural' and 'good' and to find dignity in biological adaptation can only impede understanding of ultimate causation and distort perceptions of nonhuman animals, preliterate peoples, and history (Symons, 1979, p. 313).

Yet, as reviewers in *Science* (Shapiro, 1980), *The Quarterly Review of Biology* (Hrdy, 1979), and *The New York Review of Books* (Geertz, 1980) all pointed out, Symons's "freewheeling" search for universals through a random pastiche of evidence from academic scholarship to Frank Harris and Shere Hite frequently violated his own cautionary note. He ended up, as might be predicted, even criticizing feminist political demands. Thus is it always, feminists would say, when nature is valorized.

In the 1960s and 1970s, feminist theory and research were directed to patiently correcting ideas about women by identifying the causes of gender differences in the multiple influences of socialization and social structure as contrasted with any "natural" inevitability or biological determinism. This painstaking social science accumulation was and continues to be productive.

But, as Ruth Bleier (1986) finally concluded, research on and claims about sex differences, especially those linked to biology, are, like Banquo's ghost, impossible to kill. If it isn't the size of brains, then it's mathematical ability; if it isn't impulses toward aggression, then it's interhemispheric transfer of information; if it isn't preferences in types of play activities, then it's pleasure in genital sexuality. A modern society built on sex differences requires continual infusions of supportive science, and the media, as Lynda Birke (1986) and others have shown, feeds on conceptual simplicity and polarizations. Thus, studies with positive sex differences are frequently featured in the *New York Times,* and if the evidence can be attributed to biological factors, the study will often make the front page.

In the 1980s a new strategy of feminist scholarship emerged, not to correct false ideas of female nature, not to show the social distortion of natural female capacity by institutionalized oppression, but to challenge the whole notion of naturalism through the idea of social construction. Feminist primatologist Donna Haraway (1986) discussed this shift in an essay entitled "Primatology Is Politics by Other Means."

> The past, the animal, the female, nature: these are the contested zones in the discourse of primatology. . . . [But] rarely will feminist contests for scientific meaning work by replacing one paradigm with another, by proposing . . . alternative accounts and theories. Rather, as a form of narrative practice or storytelling, feminist practice in primatology has worked more by altering a "field" of stories or possible explanatory accounts, by raising the cost of defending some accounts, by destabilizing the plausibility of some strategies of explanation. . . . Feminist science is about changing possibilities. (Haraway, 1986, pp. 115; 81)

While Haraway supports efforts to challenge existing theories of gender difference by showing female primates capable of competition, mobility, aggression, and sexual assertion, she argued that showing that females are "just like and therefore just as good as males" is ultimately a doomed strategy that perpetuates the focus on gender as difference and on male norms.

Narrative analysis, however, along with other forms of postpositivist research (Guba, 1990), conflicts with sexology's continuing needs for legitimacy. Recall George Corner's (1961) comment that studying the sex physiology and behavior of rats and rabbits was the only way early researchers had of getting into otherwise risque and taboo sex research. Writing about psychology, Carolyn Sherif (1979) argued more than a decade ago that reductionism wouldn't disappear until the prestige hierarchy in science changed: "What psychology defined as basic was dictated by slavish devotion to the more prestigious disciplines. Thus, a physiological or biochemical part or element was defined as more basic than a belief that Eve was created from Adam's rib, not because the former can necessarily tell us more about a human individual, but because physiology and biochemistry were more prestigious than religious history or sociology" (p. 100).

Following the lead of scholars examining the particularities of the Enlightenment origins of science, feminists eager to "destabilize the plausibility of these strategies of explanation" have challenged the definition of the experimental "subject," the role of technology, and the role of quantification as they allowed the new field of psychology, particularly in the United States, to differentiate itself from philosophy (e.g., Hornstein, 1989). Psychology strove to gain scientific respectability with displays of technique and language demonstrating alliance and identification with better-established fields. The history of sex research will tell the same tale about the inclusion and exclusion of methods and theories as part of the quest for legitimacy.

Thus, biological sex research is a target for feminist analysis and deconstruction not only because of its ties to notions of male and female nature but because it dominates the scientific prestige hierarchy and prevents alternate forms of knowledge from achieving legitimacy.

## Postmodern Scholarship and "Denaturalization"

Scholars in many disciplines identify postmodernism as a contemporary shift in worldview and the construction of reality. As one leading feminist author has said, "Postmodern discourses are all 'deconstructive' in that they seek to distance us from and make us skeptical about beliefs concerning truth, knowledge, power, the self and language that are often taken for granted within and serve as legitimation for contemporary Western culture" (Flax, 1987, p. 624). *Discourses,* of course, can be scientific or academic treatises or they can be diaries, poems, productions on the analyst's couch, lullabies, or filmscripts. Postmodernism is about challenging absolutes in favor of multiple points of view. It's about honoring the contexts of observations and concepts and contesting objectivity and privileged access to the "way things really are." It's about acknowledging change and the difficulty of definitive pronouncements. It's about permanent instability.

William Simon (1989), discussing postmodernism as it affects sex research, identified the "emergent consensus about the absence of consensus" (p. 18) as the central theme of postmodernism, "a sense of being forced to an unexpected and often discomforting pluralism" (p. 19). Such a skeptical position concerning truth, knowledge, power, the self, and language will inevitably challenge concepts of nature and naturalism. Simon argued that in fact postmodernism *is about* denaturalization: "In effect . . . what is implied is the reading of the sexual 'against the grain,' i.e., reinterpreting the predominant biological explanatory concepts as metaphorical illusions" (p. 24).

This perspective has so far had its strongest impact on the history of sexuality (Duggan, 1990) and the notion of sexual object choice or sexual identity (e.g., Boswell, 1990). The postmodern boom in scholarship, especially in the interpretive disciplines of anthropology and history, offers a powerful opportunity to challenge the "naturalistic" categories, concepts, and metaphors about sexuality.

I view my scholarship in sexology as a version of postmodernism. It is committed to diversity and relativism and regards human physiology as providing a set of physical possibilities unlabeled as to use or meaning. Penile erection, for example, that centerpiece of much contemporary sex research, might or might not have anything to do with pleasure or procreation or display or domination or anxiety or hypochondriasis or ego-satisfaction or intromission into another person. It all depends on the context and how that physical possibility is socially constructed.

## Conclusion

The perspective that biological sex research is more basic than other approaches because it examines something closer to nature, that is, something presocial and thus more generalizable than anything learned or influenced by culture, can be traced to European Enlightenment constructions of nature and the natural world, which served the particularities of Enlightenment politics, and its persistence can be traced to the rhetoric used in scientific and sexological claims to legitimacy. But this construction is coming under challenge from many directions. Historian Ludmilla Jordanova (1989) wrote:

> Over the last 20 years or so historians have become aware of the need to unpack the processes through which "naturalization" takes place, whereby ideas, theories, experiences, languages, and so on, take on the quality of being "natural," permitting the veiling of their customary, conventional and social characteristics. Understanding such naturalization is integral to the project of de-

lineating and explaining the precise nature of scientific and medical power. (Jordanova, 1989, p. 5)

Biological sex research, the language of sex as a "natural act," is popular in large part because it accesses and maintains prevailing scientific authority. But there are other equally persuasive and more inclusive ways to construe sexuality, if we can manage to shake loose of that prestige hierarchy of knowledge. Postmodernism offers feminism a powerful ally for the shaking.

# 4

# Historical, Scientific, Clinical, and Feminist Criticisms of "the Human Sexual Response Cycle" Model

*The sexuality that is measured is taken to be the definition of sexuality itself.*
—Lionel Trilling

## The Human Sexual Response Cycle Metaphor: A Universal Machine Without a Motor

The idea of the the human sexual response cycle (HSRC) by that name was initially introduced by William Masters and Virginia Johnson (1966) to describe the sequence of physiological changes they observed and measured during laboratory-performed sexual activities such as masturbation and coitus. The goal of their research was to answer the question: "What physical reactions develop as the human male and female respond to effective sexual stimulation?" (Masters and Johnson, 1966, p. 4). Although they coined terms for their four stages, it appears that the metaphor of "the" overall sexual "cycle" was assumed from the very outset. They wrote: "A more concise picture of physiologic reaction to sexual stimuli may be presented by dividing *the human male's and female's cycles* of sexual response into four separate phases. . . . This arbitrary four-part division of *the sexual response cycle* provides an effective framework for detailed description of physiological variants in sexual reaction" (p. 4, emphasis added).

The cycle metaphor indicates that Masters and Johnson envisioned sexual response from the start as a built-in, orderly sequence of events that would tend to repeat itself. The idea of a four-stage cycle brings to mind examples such as the four seasons of the annual calendar or the four-stroke internal combustion engine. Whether the cycle is designed by human agency or "nature," once begun it cycles independently of its origins, perhaps with some

41

variability, but without reorganization or added stages, and the same cycle applies to everyone.

The idea of a sexual response cycle has some history, although its precursors focused heavily on an element omitted from the HSRC—the idea of sexual drive. In his intellectual history of modern sexology, Paul Robinson (1976) saw the origin of Masters and Johnson's four-stage HSRC in Havelock Ellis's theme of "tumescence and detumescence."[1]

But the language of tumescence and detumescence was popular even prior to Ellis. In his analysis of Freud's theory of the libido, Frank Sulloway (1979) discussed nineteenth-century German and Austrian sexological ideas in circulation while Freud was writing. Sulloway pointed out that many sexological terms associated with Freud, such as *libido* and *erotogenic zones,* were in widespread use in European medical writings by the turn of the century, and he credited Albert Moll (then "possibly the best-known authority on sexual pathology in all of Europe" though "an obscure figure today") with originating a theory of two sexual drives—one of attraction and the other of detumescence (Sulloway, 1979, p. 302).

It is significant that, despite this long heritage of sexologic theorizing about sexual "energy," Masters and Johnson's model of sexual response did not include initiating components. Their omission of sexual drive, libido, desire, passion, and the like would return to haunt clinical sexology in the 1970s. Actually, in avoiding discussion of sexual drive, Masters and Johnson were following a trend peculiar to sexologists (in contrast to psychiatrists and psychoanalysts) during the twentieth century. Perhaps because of the history of elaborate but vague nineteenth-century writings, perhaps because of the subjective connotations to *desire,* talk of sex drive seemed to cause nothing but confusion for modern sexual scientists interested in operational definitions. Kinsey used the term only in passing, and meant by it "sexual capacity," the capacity to respond to stimulation with physical arousal (e.g., Kinsey, Pomeroy, Martin, and Gebhard, 1953, p. 102). Sexologists could compare individuals and groups in terms of this hypothetical internal mechanism, capacity, by looking at their frequencies of sexual behavior, thresholds for response, and so on with no reference to internal experience.

Frank Beach (1956), writing during the time Masters and Johnson were beginning their physiological observations, argued that talking about sex *drive* is usually circular and unproductive and approvingly noted that even Kinsey "equates sexual drive with frequency of orgasm." Beach suggested that sexual *drive* had nothing to do with "genuine biological or tissue needs" and that the concept should be replaced by sexual *appetite,* which is "a product of experience, . . . [with] little or no relation to biological or physiological needs" (Beach, 1956, p. 4). Although the concept of appetite never caught on in sexology, the recent rediscovery of "desire" indicates that ignoring the issue of initiation of sexual behaviors did not solve the problem.

By omitting the concept of drive from their model, Masters and Johnson eliminated an element of sexuality that is notoriously variable within populations and succeeded in proposing a universal model seemingly without much variability. In what I think is the only reference to sexual drive in their text, Masters and Johnson indicated their belief that the sexual response cycle was actually an inborn drive to orgasm: "The cycle of sexual response, with orgasm as the ultimate point in progression, generally is believed to develop from a drive of biologic origin deeply integrated into the condition of human existence" (Masters and Johnson, 1966, p. 127). The cycle of sexual response, then, reflects the operation of an inborn program, like the workings of a mechanical clock. As long as the "effective sexual stimulation" (i.e., energy source) continues, the cycle proceeds through its set sequence.

## Scientific Criticisms of the HSRC Model

Masters and Johnson proposed a universal model for sexual response. At no point did they talk of "a" human sexual response cycle, but only of "the" human sexual response cycle. The critique of the HSRC model begins with a discussion of the generalizability of Masters and Johnson's research results. Analysis of their work shows that the existence of the HSRC was assumed before the research began and that this assumption guided subject selection and research methods.

### Subject Selection Biases: Orgasm with Coital and Masturbatory Experience

In a passage buried four pages from the end of their text, Masters and Johnson revealed that for their research they had established "a *requirement* that there be a positive history of masturbatory and coital orgasmic experience before any study subject [could be] accepted into the program" (Masters and Johnson, 1966, p. 311, emphasis added). This requirement in and of itself would seem to invalidate any notion that the HSRC is universal. It indicates that Masters and Johnson's research was designed to identify physiological functions of subjects who had experienced *particular,* preselected sexual responses. That is, rather than the HSRC being the best-fit model chosen to accommodate the results of their research, the HSRC actually guided the selection of subjects for the research.

Two popularizations of Masters and Johnson's physiological research commented on this element of subject selection but disregarded its implications for HSRC generalizability:

Men and women unable to respond sexually and to reach orgasm were also weeded out. Since this was to be a study of sexual responses, those unable to respond could contribute little to it. (Brecher and Brecher, 1966, p. 54)

If you are going to find out what happens, obviously you must work with those to whom it happens. (Lehrman, 1970, p. 170)

"Unable to respond"? If you want to study human singing behaviors, do you only select international recording artists? One could just as easily argue that there are many sexually active and sexually responsive men and women who do not regularly experience orgasm during masturbation and/or coitus whose patterns of physiological arousal and subjective pleasure were deliberately excluded from the sample. No research was undertaken to investigate "human" sexual physiology and subjectivity, only to measure the responses of an easily orgasmic sample. The "discovery" of the HSRC was a self-fulfilling prophecy, with the research subjects selected so as to compress diversity. The HSRC cannot be universalized to the general population.

The apparently identical performance requirements for male and female research subjects masked the bias of real-world gender differences in masturbatory experience. Masters and Johnson began their physiological research in 1954. In 1953, the Kinsey group had reported that only "58 percent of the females" in their sample had been "masturbating to orgasm at some time in their lives" (Kinsey, Pomeroy, Martin, and Gebhard, 1953, p. 143). Married women, the predominant subjects in Masters and Johnson's research, had even lower masturbatory frequencies than divorced or single women. This contrasts with the 92 percent incidence of men with masturbatory experience reported by the same researchers (Kinsey, Pomeroy, and Martin, 1948, p. 339). Masters and Johnson had to find men and women with similar sexual patterns despite having been raised in dissimilar sociosexual worlds. Obviously, because of this requirement the women research participants were less representative than the men.

## Subject Selection Biases: Class Differences

Just as Masters and Johnson chose subjects with certain types of sexual experiences, they deliberately chose subjects who did not represent a cross-section of socioeconomic backgrounds. They wrote: "As discussed, the sample was weighted *purposely* toward higher than average intelligence levels and socioeconomic backgrounds. *Further selectivity* was established ... to determine willingness to participate, facility of sexual responsiveness, and ability to communicate finite details of sexual reaction" (Masters and Johnson, 1966, p. 12, emphasis added). Masters and Johnson's popularizers disparaged the possible bias introduced by this selectivity with such comments as, "The higher than average educational level of the women volunteers is hardly likely to affect the acidity of their vaginal fluids" (Brecher and Brecher, 1966, p. 60).

But one cannot simply dismiss possible class differences in physiology with an assertion that there are none. *Could* differences in social location affect the physiology of sexuality? The irony of assuming that physiology is universal and therefore that class differences make no difference is that no one conducts research that asks the question.

In fact, Kinsey and his colleagues had shown wide differences between members (especially males) of different socioeconomic classes with regard to incidence and prevalence of masturbation, premarital sexual activities, petting (including breast stimulation), sex with prostitutes, positions used in intercourse, oral-genital sex, and even nocturnal emissions. For example, "There are 10 to 12 times as frequent nocturnal emissions among males of the upper educational classes as there are among males of the lower classes" (Kinsey, Pomeroy, and Martin, 1948, p. 345). Kinsey noted, "It is particularly interesting to find that there are [great] differences between educational levels in regard to nocturnal emissions—a type of sexual outlet which one might suppose would represent involuntary behavior" (p. 343). Given this finding, doesn't it seem possible, even likely, that numerous physiological details might indeed relate to differences in sexual habits? Kinsey also mentioned class differences in latency to male orgasm (p. 580). The more the variation in physiological details among subjects from different socioeconomic backgrounds, the less the HSRC is appropriate as a universal norm.

### Subject Selection Biases: Sexual Enthusiasm

Masters and Johnson concluded their physiological research text as follows: "Through the years of research exposure, the one factor in sexuality that consistently has been present among members of the study-subject population has been a basic interest in and desire for effectiveness of sexual performance. *This one factor may represent the major area of difference between the research study subjects and the general population*" (Masters and Johnson, 1966, p. 315, emphasis added).

Masters and Johnson do not explain what they mean by their comment that "the general population" might not share the enthusiasm for sexual performance of their research subjects and do not speculate at all on the possible impact of this comment on the generalizability of their results. Whereas at first it may seem reasonable to assume that everyone has "a basic interest in and desire for effectiveness of sexual performance," on closer examination the phrase "*effectiveness* of sexual *performance*" seems not so much to characterize everyone as to identify devotees of a particular sexual style.

We get some small idea of Masters and Johnson's research subjects from the four profiles given in Chapter 19 of *Human Sexual Response* (1966). These profiled subjects were selected by the authors from the 382 women and 312 men who participated in their study. The two women described had masturbated regularly (beginning at ages ten and fifteen, respectively), had begun having intercourse in adolescence (at ages fifteen and seventeen), and were almost always orgasmic and occasionally multiorgasmic in the laboratory. For the first woman, twenty-six and currently unmarried, it was explicitly stated that "sexual activity [was] a major factor in [her] life" (Masters and Johnson, 1966, p. 304) and that she became a research subject because of "financial demand and sexual tension" (p. 305). No comparable information was given about the second woman, who was thirty-one and married, but she and her husband had "stated categorically" that they had "found [research participation] of significant importance in their marriage" (p. 307).

The unmarried male subject, age twenty-seven, was described as having had adolescent onset of masturbation, petting, and heterosexual intercourse as well as four reported homosexual experiences at different points in his life. The married man, age thirty-four, had had little sexual experience until age twenty-five. He and his wife of six years had joined the research program "hoping to acquire knowledge to enhance the sexual component of their marriage" (Masters and Johnson, 1966, p. 311). The researchers noted, "[His] wife has stated repeatedly that subsequent to [research project] participation her husband has been infinitely more effective both in stimulating and satisfying her sexual tensions. He in turn finds her sexually responsive without reservation. Her freedom and security of response are particularly pleasing to him" (p. 311).

Every discussion of sex research methodology emphasizes the effects of volunteer bias and bemoans the reliance on samples of convenience that characterizes its research literature (e.g., Green and Wiener, 1980). Masters and Johnson make no attempt to compare their research subjects with any other research sample, saying, "There are no established norms for male and female sexuality in our society . . . [and] there is no scale with which to measure or evaluate the sexuality of the male and female study-subject population" (Masters and Johnson, 1966, p. 302). Although there may not be "norms," there are other sex research surveys of attitudes and behavior. For example, volunteers for sex research are usually shown to be more liberal in their attitudes than socioeconomically comparable nonvolunteer groups (Hoch, Safir, Peres, and Shepher, 1981; Clement, 1990).

How might the sample's interest in "effective sexual performance" have affected Masters and Johnson's research and their description of the HSRC? The answer relates both to the consequences of ego-investment in sexual performance and to the impact of specialization in a sexual style focused on orgasm, and we don't know what such consequences might be. I cannot specify the effect of this sexually skewed sample any more than I could guess what might be the consequences for research on singing of only studying stars of the Metropolitan Opera. The point is that the subject group was exceptional, and only by *assuming* HSRC universality can we generalize its results to others.

## Experimenter Bias in the Sexuality Laboratory

Masters and Johnson made no secret of the fact that subjects volunteering for their research underwent a period of adjustment, or a "controlled orientation program," as they called it (Masters and Johnson, 1966, p. 22). This "period of training" helped the subjects "gain confidence in their ability to respond successfully while subjected to a variety of recording devices" (p. 23). Such a training period provided an opportunity for numerous kinds of "experimenter biases," as they are known in social psychology research, wherein the expectations of the experimenters are communicated to the subjects and have an effect on their behavior (Rosenthal, 1966). The fact that Masters and Johnson repeatedly referred to episodes of sexual activity with orgasm as "successes" and those without orgasm or without rigid erection or rapid ejaculation as "failures" (e.g., Masters and Johnson, 1966, p. 313) makes it seem highly likely that their performance standards were communicated to their subjects. Moreover, they were candid about their role as sex therapists for their subjects: "When female orgasmic or male ejaculatory failures develop in the laboratory, the *situation is discussed* immediately. Once the individual has been *reassured, suggestions* are made for improvement of future performance" (p. 314, emphasis added).

Another example of the tutelage provided is given in the quotation from the thirty-four-year-old man described in Chapter 19 of their book. He and his wife had entered the program hoping to obtain sexual instruction and seemed to have received all they expected and more. Masters and Johnson appeared to be unaware of any incompatibility between the roles of research subject and student or patient. Again, this reveals their preexisting standards for sexual response and their interest in measuring in the laboratory only sexual patterning consisting of erections, orgasms, ejaculations, whole-body physical arousal, and so on, that is, that which they already defined as sexual response.

In addition to overt instruction and feedback, social psychology alerts us to the role of covert cues. Research has shown that volunteer subjects often are more sensitive to experimenters' covert cues than are nonvolunteers (Rosenthal and Rosnow, 1969). One could speculate that sex research volunteers characterized by a "desire for effective sexual performance" may well be especially attentive to covert as well as overt indications that they are performing as expected in the eyes of the white-coated researchers.

## The Bias of "Effective" Sexual Stimulation

As mentioned near the beginning of this chapter, Masters and Johnson set out to answer the question, "What physical reactions develop as the human male and female respond to effective sexual stimulation?" (Masters and Johnson, 1966, p. 4). What is "effective" sexual stimulation? In fact, I think this is a key question in deconstructing the HSRC. Masters and Johnson stated, "It constantly should be borne in mind that the primary research interest has been concentrated quite literally upon what men and women do in response to effective sexual stimulation" (p. 20).

The *intended* emphasis in this sentence, I believe, is that the authors' "primary" interest was not in euphemism, and not in vague generality, but in the "literal" physical reactions people experience during sexual activity. I think the *actual* emphasis of the sentence, however, is that the authors were interested in only one type of sexual response, that which people experience in reaction to a particular type of stimulation. Such a perspective would be akin to vision researchers only being interested in optic system responses to lights of certain wavelengths, say, red and yellow, or movement physiologists only being interested in physical function during certain activities, such as running.

In each of the book's chapters devoted to the physical reactions of a particular organ or group of organs (e.g., clitoris, penis, uterus, respiratory system), Masters and Johnson began by stating their intention to look at the responses to "effective sexual stimulation." But where is that specific type of stimulation described? Although the phrase appears dozens of times in the text, it is not in the glossary or the index, and no definition or description can be found. The reader must discover that *"effective sexual stimulation" is that stimulation which facilitates a response that conforms to the HSRC.* This conclusion is inferred from observations such as the following, taken from the section on labia minora responses in the chapter on "female external genitalia": "Many women have progressed well into plateau-phase levels of sexual response, had the effective stimulative techniques withdrawn, and been unable to achieve orgasmic-phase tension release. . . . When an obviously effective means of sexual stimulation is withdrawn and orgasmic-phase release is not achieved, the minor-labial coloration will fade rapidly" (Masters and Johnson, 1966, p. 41).

Effective stimulation is that stimulation which facilitates "progress" from one stage of the HSRC to the next, particularly that which facilitates orgasm. Any stimulation resulting in responses other than greater physiological excitation and orgasm is defined by exclusion as "ineffective" and is not of interest to these authors.

This emphasis on "effective stimulation" sets up a tautology comparable to that resulting from biased subject selection. The HSRC cannot be a scientific *discovery* if the acknowledged "primary research interest" was to study stimulation defined as that which facilitates the HSRC. Again, the HSRC, "with orgasm as the ultimate point in progression" (Masters and Johnson, 1966, p. 127), preordained the results.

## Clinical Criticisms of the HSRC Model

The HSRC model has had a profound impact on clinical sexology through its role as the centerpiece of contemporary diagnostic nomenclature. In this section, I will first discuss how contemporary nomenclature came to rely on the HSRC model and then describe what I see as several deleterious consequences.

### HSRC and the DSM Classification of Sexual Disorders

I have elsewhere detailed the development of sexual dysfunction nosology in the four sequential editions of the American Psychiatric Association's *Diagnostic and Statistical Manual of Mental Disorders* (*DSM*) (Tiefer, 1992b). Over a period of thirty-five years, the nosology evolved from not listing sexual dysfunctions at all (APA, 1952, or *DSM-I*) to listing them as symptoms of psychosomatic disorders (APA, 1968, or *DSM-II*), as a subcategory of psychosexual disorders (APA, 1980, or *DSM-III*), and as a subcategory of sexual disorders (APA, 1987, or *DSM-III-R*).

The relation of this nosology to the HSRC language can be seen in the introduction to the section on sexual dysfunctions (identical in both *DSM-III* and *DSM-III-R*):[2]

> The *essential feature* is inhibition in the appetitive or psychophysiological changes that characterize *the complete sexual response cycle*. The complete sexual response cycle can be divided into the following phases: 1. Appetitive. This consists of fantasies about sexual activity and a desire to have sexual activity. 2. Excitement. This consists of a subjective sense of sexual pleasure and accompanying physiological changes. . . . 3. Orgasm. This consists of a peaking of sexual pleasure, with release of sexual tension and rhythmic contraction of the perineal muscles and pelvic reproductive organs. . . . 4. Resolution. This consists of a sense of general relaxation, well-being, and muscular relaxation. (APA, 1987, pp. 290–291, emphasis added)

In fact, this cycle is not identical to Masters and Johnson's HSRC (although it, too, uses the universalizing language of "the" sexual response cycle). The first, or appetitive, phase was added when sexologists confronted clinical problems having to do with sexual disinterest. In their second book (1970), Masters and Johnson loosely used their HSRC physiological research to generate a list of sexual dysfunctions: premature ejaculation, ejaculatory incompetence, orgasmic dysfunction (women's), vaginismus, and dyspareunia (men's and women's). These were put forth as deviations from the HSRC that research had revealed as the norm. By the late 1970s, however, clinicians were describing a syndrome of sexual disinterest that did not fit into the accepted response cycle. Helen Singer Kaplan argued that a "separate phase [sexual desire] which had previously been neglected, must be added for conceptual completeness and clinical effectiveness" (Kaplan, 1979, p. xviii). *DSM-III* and *DSM-III-R* then merged the original HSRC with the norm of sexual desire to generate "the complete response cycle" presented above.

Clearly, the idea and much of the language of the nosology derived from Masters and Johnson's work, and in fact they are cited in the *DSM* footnotes as the primary source. Is it appropriate to use the HSRC to generate a clinical standard of normality? Is it appropriate to enshrine the HSRC as the standard of human sexuality such that deviations from it become the essential feature of abnormality?

Let us briefly examine how sexual problems are linked to mental disorders in the *DSM* and how the HSRC was used in the sexuality section. The definition of mental disorder offered in *DSM-III* specifies:

> In *DSM-III* each of the mental disorders is conceptualized as a clinically significant behavioral or psychological syndrome or pattern that occurs in an individual and that is typically associated with either a painful symptom (distress) or impairment in one or more areas of function (disability). In addition, there is an inference that there is a behavioral, psychological or biological dysfunction. (APA, 1980, p. 6)

In an article introducing the new classification scheme to the psychiatric profession, the APA task force explained their decisions. With regard to sexual dysfunctions, the task force members had concluded that "inability to experience *the normative sexual response cycle* [emphasis added] represented a *disability* in *the important area* of sexual functioning, whether or not the individual was distressed by the symptom" (Spitzer, Williams, and Skodol, 1980, pp. 153–154). That is, deviation from the now-normative sexual response cycle was to be considered a disorder even if the person had no complaints.

The diagnostic classification system clearly assumed that the HSRC was a universal bedrock of sexuality. Yet I have shown that it was a self-fulfilling result of Masters and Johnson's methodological decisions rather than a scientific discovery. It was the result of a priori assumptions rather than empirical research. Arguably, a clinical standard requires a greater demonstration of health impact and universal applicability than that offered by Masters and Johnson's research.

In fact, it is likely the case that the *DSM* authors adopted the HSRC model because it was useful and convenient. Professional and political factors that probably facilitated the adoption include professional needs within psychiatry to move away from a neurosis disorder model to a more concrete and empirical model, legitimacy needs within the new specialty of sex therapy, and the interests of feminists in progressive sexual standards for women (Tiefer, 1992b). Thus, the enshrinement of the HSRC and its upgraded versions as the centerpiece of sexual dysfunction nomenclature in *DSM-III* and *DSM-III-R* is not scientifically reliable and represents a triumph of politics and professionalism.

## Sexuality as the Performances of Fragmented Body Parts

One deleterious clinical consequence of the utilization of the HSRC model as the sexual norm has been increased focus on segmented psychophysiological functioning. Just for example, consider the following disorder descriptions, which appear in *DSM-III-R*:

1. "partial or complete failure to attain or maintain the lubrication-swelling response of sexual excitement [Female Arousal Disorder]"
2. "involuntary spasm of the musculature of the outer third of the vagina that interferes with coitus [Vaginismus]"
3. "inability to reach orgasm in the vagina [Inhibited Male Orgasm]"

In the current nosology, the body as a whole is never mentioned but instead has become a fragmented collection of parts that pop in and out at different points in the performance sequence. This compartmentalization lends itself to mechanical imagery, to framing sexuality as the smooth operation and integration of complex machines, and to seeing problems of sexuality as "machines in disrepair" that need to be evaluated by high-technology part-healers (Soble, 1987). If there is a sexual problem, check each component systematically to detect the component out of commission. Overall satisfaction (which is mentioned nowhere in the nosology) is assumed to be a result of perfect parts-functioning. Recall that subjective distress is not even required for diagnosis, just objective indication of deviation from the HSRC.

This model promotes the idea that sexual disorder can be defined as deviation from "normal" as indicated by medical test results. A bit of thought, however, will show that identifying proper norms for these types of measurements is a tricky matter. How rigid is rigid? How quick is premature? How delayed is delayed? The answers to these questions are more a product of expectations, cultural standards, and particular partner than they are of objective measurement. And yet a series of complex and often invasive genital measurements are already being routinely used in evaluations of erectile dysfunction (Krane, Goldstein, and DeTejada, 1989). Norms for many of the tests are more often provided by medical technology manufacturers than by scientific research, and measurements on nonpatient samples are often lacking. Despite calls for caution in use and interpretation, the use of sexuality measurement technology continues to escalate (Burris, Banks, and Sherins, 1989; Kirkeby, Andersen, and Poulson, 1989; Schiavi, 1988; Sharlip, 1989).

This example illustrates a general medical trend: While reliance on tests and technology for objective information is increasing, reliance on patients' individualized standards and subjective reports of illness is decreasing (Osherson and AmaraSingham, 1981). The end result may be, as Lionel Trilling (1950) worried in a review of the first Kinsey report, that "the sexuality that is measured is taken to be the definition of sexuality itself" (p. 223). Although it seems only common sense and good clinical practice to want to "rule out" medical causes prior to initiating a course of psychotherapeutic or couple treatment for sexual complaints, such "ruling out" has become a growth industry rather than an adjunct to psychological and couple-oriented history-taking. Moreover, there is a growing risk of iatrogenic disorders being induced during the extensive "ruling out" procedures.

The HSRC has contributed significantly to the idea of sexuality as proper parts-functioning. Masters and Johnson's original research can hardly be faulted for studying individual physiological components to answer the question, "What physical reactions develop as the human male and female respond to effective sexual stimulation?" But once the physiological aspects became solidified into a universal, normative sequence known as "the" HSRC, the stage was set for clinical preoccupation with parts-functioning. Despite Masters and Johnson's avowed interest in sexuality as communication, intimacy, self-expression, and mutual pleasuring, their clinical ideas were ultimately mechanical (Masters and Johnson, 1975).

## *Exclusive Genital (i.e., Reproductive) Focus for Sexuality*

"Hypoactive sexual desire" is the only sexual dysfunction in the *DSM-III-R* defined without regard to the genital organs. "Sexual aversion," for example, is specifically identified as aversion *to the genitals*. The other sexual dysfunctions are defined in terms of *genital* pain, spasm, dryness, deflation, uncontrolled responses, delayed responses, too-brief responses, or absent responses. The *DSM* locates the boundary between normal and abnormal (or between healthy and unhealthy) sexual function exclusively on genital performances.

"Genitals" are those organs involved in acts of generation, or biological reproduction. Although the *DSM* does not explicitly endorse reproduction as the primary purpose of sexual activity, the genital focus of the sexual dysfunction nosology implies such a priority. The only sexual acts mentioned are coitus, [vaginal] penetration, sexual intercourse, and noncoital clitoral stimulation. Only one is not a heterosexual coital act. Masturbation is only mentioned as a "form of stimulation." Full *genital performance during heterosexual intercourse is the essence of sexual functioning,* which excludes and demotes nongenital possibilities for pleasure and expression. Involvement or noninvolvement of the nongenital body becomes incidental, of interest only as it impacts on genital responses identified in the nosology.

Actually, the HSRC is a whole-body response, and Masters and Johnson were as interested in the physiology of "extragenital" responses as genital ones. Yet the stages of the HSRC as reflected in heart rate or breast changes did not make it into the *DSMs*. As Masters and Johnson transformed their physiological cycle into a clinical cycle, they privileged a reproductive purpose for sexuality by focusing on the genitals. It would seem that once they turned their interest to sexual problems rather than sexual process, their focus shifted to *sexuality as outcome.*

There is no section on diagnosis in Masters and Johnson's second, clinical, book (1970), no definition of normal sexuality, and no hint of how the particular list of erectile, orgasmic, and other genitally focused disorders was derived. The authors merely described their treatments of "the specific varieties of sexual dysfunction that serve as presenting complaints of patients referred" (Masters and Johnson, 1970, p. 91). But surely this explanation cannot be the whole story. Why did they exclude problems like "inability to relax, . . . attraction to partner other than mate, . . . partner chooses inconvenient time, . . . too little tenderness" or others of the sort later labeled "sexual difficulties" (Frank, Anderson, and Rubinstein, 1978)? Why did they exclude problems like "partner is only interested in orgasm, . . . partner can't kiss, . . . partner is too hasty, . . . partner has no sense of romance," or others of the sort identified in surveys of women (Hite, 1976)?

In fact, the list of disorders proposed by Masters and Johnson seems like a list devised by Freudians who, based on their developmental stage theory of sexuality, define genital sexuality as the sine qua non of sexual maturity. Despite the whole-body focus of the HSRC physiology research, the clinical interest of its authors in proper genital performance as the essence of normal sexuality indicates their adherence to an earlier tradition. The vast spectrum of sexual possibility is narrowed to genital, that is, to reproductive performance.

### Symptom Reversal as the Measure
### of Sex Therapy Success

A final undesirable clinical consequence of the HSRC and its evolution in the *DSM* is the limitation it imposes on the evaluation of therapy success.

Once sexual disturbances are defined as specific malperformances within "the" sexual response cycle, evaluation of treatment effectiveness narrows to symptom reversal.

But the use of symptom reversal as the major or only measure of success contrasts with sex therapy as actually taught and practiced (Hawton, 1985). Typical practice focuses on individual and relationship satisfaction and includes elements such as education, permission-giving, attitude change, anxiety reduction, improved communication, and intervention in destructive sex roles and life-styles (LoPiccolo, 1977). A recent extensive survey of 289 sex therapy providers in private practice reinforced the statement that "much of sex therapy actually was nonsexual in nature" and confirmed that therapy focuses on communication skills, individual issues, and the "nonsexual relationship" (Kilmann et al., 1986).

Follow-up studies measuring satisfaction with therapy and changes in sexual, psychological, and interpersonal issues show varying patterns of improvement, perhaps because therapists tend to heedlessly lump together cases with the "same" symptom. It is erroneous to assume that couples and their experience of sex therapy are at all homogeneous, despite their assignment to specific and discrete diagnostic categories based on the HSRC. Citing his own "painful experience" (Bancroft, 1989, p. 489) with unreplicable results of studies comparing different forms of treatment, John Bancroft suggested that there is significant prognostic variability among individuals and couples even within diagnostic categories. He concluded, "It may be that there is no alternative to defining various aspects of the sexual relationship, e.g., sexual response, communication, enjoyment, etc. and assessing each separately" (p. 497).

It might be thought that using symptom reversal as the measure of success is easier than evaluating multiple issues of relationship satisfaction, but this is not true, since *any* measure of human satisfaction needs to be subtle. That is, it is indeed easy to measure "success" with objective technologies that evaluate whether a prosthesis successfully inflates or an injection successfully produces erectile rigidity of a certain degree. When evaluating the human success of physical treatments, however, researchers invariably introduce complex subjective elements. The questions they select, the way they ask the questions, and their interpretations of the answers are all subjective (Tiefer, Pedersen, and Melman, 1988). In evaluating patients' satisfaction with penile implant treatment, asking the patients whether they would have prosthesis surgery again produces different results from evaluating postoperative satisfaction with sexual frequency, the internal feeling of the prosthesis during sex, anxieties about the indwelling prosthesis, changes in relationship quality, and so on.

The present diagnostic nomenclature, based on the genitally focused HSRC, results in evaluation of treatment success exclusively in terms of symptom reversal and ignores the complex sociopsychological context of sexual performance and experience. The neat four-stage model, the seemingly clean clinical typology, all result in neat and clean evaluation research—which turns out to relate only partially to real people's experiences.

## Feminist Criticisms of the HSRC Model

Paul Robinson (1976) and Janice Irvine (1990) have discussed at length how Masters and Johnson deliberately made choices throughout *Human Sexual Response* and *Human Sexual Inadequacy* to emphasize male-female sexual similarities. The most fundamental similarity, of course, was that men and women had identical HSRCs. The diagnostic nomenclature continues this emphasis by basing the whole idea of sexual dysfunction on the gender-neutral HSRC and by scrupulously assigning equal numbers and parallel dysfunctions to men and women. (Desire disorders are not specified as to gender; other dysfunctions include one arousal disorder for each gender, one inhibited orgasm disorder for each gender, premature ejaculation for men and vaginismus for women, and dyspareunia, which is defined as "recurrent or persistent genital pain in either a male or a female.")

Yet, is the HSRC really gender-neutral? Along with other feminists, I have argued that the HSRC model of sexuality, and its elaboration and application in clinical work, favors men's sexual interests over those of women (e.g., Tiefer, 1988a). Some have argued that sex role socialization introduces fundamental gender differences and inequalities into adult sexual experience that cannot be set aside by a model that simply proclaims male and female sexuality as fundamentally the same (Stock, 1984). I have argued that the HSRC, with its alleged gender equity, disguises and trivializes *social* reality, that is, gender inequality (Tiefer, 1990a) and thus makes it all the harder for women to become sexually equal in fact.

Let's look briefly at some of these gender differences in the real world. First, to oversimplify many cultural variations on this theme, men and women are raised with different sets of sexual values—men toward varied experience and physical gratification, women toward intimacy and emotional communion (Gagnon, 1977; Gagnon, 1979; Gagnon and Simon, 1969; Simon and Gagnon, 1986). By focusing on the physical aspects of sexuality and ignoring the rest, the HSRC favors men's value training over women's. Second, men's greater experience with masturbation encourages them toward a genital focus in sexuality, whereas women learn to avoid acting on genital urges because of the threat of lost social respect. With its genital focus, the HSRC favors men's training over women's. As has been mentioned earlier, by requiring experience and comfort with masturbation to orgasm as a criterion for all participants, the selection of research subjects for *Human Sexual Response* looked gender-neutral but in fact led to an unrepresentative sampling of women participants.

Third, the whole issue of "effective sexual stimulation" needs to be addressed from a feminist perspective. As we have seen, the HSRC model was based on a particular kind of sexual activity, that with "effective sexual stimulation." Socioeconomic subordination, threats of pregnancy, fear of male violence, and society's double standard reduce women's power in heterosexual relationships and militate against women's sexual knowledge, sexual assertiveness, and sexual candor (Snitow, Stansell, and Thompson, 1983; Vance, 1984). Under such circumstances, it seems likely that "effective sexual stimulation" in the laboratory or at home favors what men prefer.

The HSRC assumes that men and women have and want the same kind of sexuality since physiological research suggests that in some ways, and under selected test conditions, we are built the same. Yet social realities dictate that we are not all the same sexually—not in our socially shaped wishes, in our sexual self-development, or in our interpersonal sexual meanings. Many different studies—from questionnaires distributed by feminist organizations to interviews of self-defined happily married couples, from popular magazine surveys to social psychologists' meta-analyses of relationship research—show that women rate affection and emotional communication as more important than orgasm in a sexual relationship (Hite, 1987; Frank, Anderson, and Rubinstein, 1978; Tavris and Sadd, 1977; Peplau and Gordon, 1985). Given this evidence, it denies women's voices entirely to continue to insist that sexuality is best represented by the universal "cycle of sexual response, with orgasm as the ultimate point in progression" (Masters and Johnson, 1966, p. 127).

Masters and Johnson's comparisons of the sexual techniques used by heterosexual and homosexual couples can be seen to support the claim that "effective sexual stimulation" simply means what men prefer. Here are examples of the contrasts:

> The sexual behavior of the married couples was far more performance-oriented. ... Preoccupation with orgasmic attainment was expressed time and again by heterosexual men and women during interrogation after each testing session. ... [By contrast] the committed homosexual couples *took their time* in sexual interaction in the laboratory. ... In committed heterosexual couples' interaction, the male's sexual approach to the female, ... rarely more than 30 seconds to a minute, were spent holding close or caressing the total body area before the breasts and/or genitals were directly stimulated. This was considerably shorter than the corresponding time interval observed in homosexual couples. (Masters and Johnson, 1979, pp. 64–65, 66)

After describing various techniques of breast stimulation, the authors reported that heterosexual women enjoyed it much less than lesbians but that "all the [heterosexual] women thought that breast play was very important in their husband's arousal" (p. 67). The authors repeatedly emphasized that the differences between lesbian and heterosexual techniques were greater than between heterosexual and male homosexual techniques.[3]

The enshrinement of the HSRC in the *DSM* diagnostic nomenclature represented the ultimate in context-stripping, as far as women's sexuality is concerned. To speak merely of desire, arousal, and orgasm as constitutive of sexuality and ignore relationships and women's psychosocial development is to ignore women's experiences of exploitation, harassment, and abuse and to deny women's social limitations. To reduce sexuality to the biological specifically disadvantages women, feminists argue, because women as a class are disadvantaged by *social* sexual reality (Laws, 1990; Hubbard, 1990; Birke, 1986).

Finally, the biological reductionism of the HSRC and the *DSM* is subtly conveyed by their persistent use of the terms *males* and *females* rather than *men* and *women*. There are no men and no women in the latest edition of the diagnostic nomenclature, only males and females and vaginas and so forth. In *Human Sexual Response,* men and women appear in the text from time to time, but only males and females make it to the chapter headings, and a rough count of a few pages here and there in the text reveals a 7:1 use of the general animal kingdom terms over the specifically human ones. A feminist deconstruction of the HSRC and of contemporary perspectives on sexuality could do worse than begin by noticing and interpreting how the choice of vocabulary signals the intention to ignore culture.

## Conclusion

I have argued in this chapter that the human sexual response cycle (HSRC) model of sexuality is flawed from scientific, clinical, and feminist points of view. Popularized primarily because clinicians and researchers needed norms that were both objective and universal, the model is actually neither objective nor universal. It imposes a false biological uniformity on sexuality that does not support the human uses and meanings of sexual potential. The most exciting work in sex therapy evolves toward systems analyses and interventions that combine psychophysiological sophistication with respect for individual and couple diversity (e.g., Verhulst and Heiman, 1988). Subjective dissatisfactions are seen more as relative dyssynchronies between individuals or between elements of culturally based sexual scripts than as malfunctions of some universal sexual essence.

Defining the essence of sexuality as a specific sequence of physiological changes promotes biological reductionism. Biological reductionism not only separates genital sexual performance from personalities, relationships, conduct, context, and values but also overvalues the former at the expense of the latter. As Abraham Maslow (1966) emphasized, studying parts may be easier than studying people, but what do you understand when you're through? Deconstructing and desacralizing the HSRC should help sex research unhook itself from the albatross of biological reductionism.

# 5

# Applications of Social Constructionism to Research on Gender and Sexuality

*I* want to suggest that doing the work of social constructionism involves four tasks and that one can work on those tasks utilizing various methods drawn from various disciplinary perspectives. The unity is not in the specific method used, although I will discuss why interpretive, qualitative methods predominate. The unity of the work is rather in the goals and the guiding philosophy.

## Deconstructing Existing Texts

*Deconstructing a text produces many meanings and opens up possibilities of conflicting meanings by bringing into the foreground what is marginalized, minimized or silenced in the text.*

—Daphne Read

Deconstructing texts takes the form of *critical analyses* of existing *concepts, categories, and metaphors.* From the point of view of social constructionist theory, this type of exercise serves to reveal a multiplicity of potential conceptual perspectives. Deconstructing texts serves to destabilize existing frameworks by taking an emperor's-new-clothes approach: "Look! This is what everybody says is going on here, but let's take a closer look. What rhetoric is being used? What's left out as well as what's included?" By challenging dominant and conventional thinking, by destabilizing existing explanations, the work is basically defiant and subversive. The approach has become popular with women's and gay and lesbian studies specialists, who have embraced it to examine canonical texts from which they have been excluded.

The first volume of Michel Foucault's *The History of Sexuality* ([1976] 1978) is the best known contemporary *sexual* deconstruction project. It has certainly destabilized prevailing explanations. Foucault argued at the large, conceptual level that, contrary to conventional claim, the past two centuries of Western history have *not* exemplified sexual repression but rather, just the opposite, have displayed *production* of ever-expanding sexual discourses. Foucault analyzed Catholic confession rituals and medical and psychoanalytic texts to show how they served to shape sexual experience. This text has made a major contribution to social constructionist thinking in sexology.

Another favorite work of sexual deconstruction is Paul Robinson's (1976) *Modernization of Sex*. He examined the works of modern sexologists Havelock Ellis, Alfred Kinsey, and William Masters and Virginia Johnson:

> In the three intellectual portraits that follow, I have examined their writings very much as one might those of a major philosopher or political theorist. That is, I have been concerned to identify the assumptions, the biases, the tensions and the modes of reasoning that characterize their work. . . . [This] is an unusual . . . approach. . . . But I have risked it in order to emphasize the role of my protagonists as theoreticians . . . as men and women who have fashioned distinctive ways of thinking about the human sexual experience. (Robinson, 1976, p. viii)

That is, Robinson showed his readers how these sexologists *constructed models* of sexuality. He examined their underlying philosophies and their rhetoric and showed how they selected and sometimes distorted facts to conform to their philosophies about grand issues like human sexual nature or gender difference or similarity.

Any text can be deconstructed. And a *text* can be, for psychologists, not just a scientific work but an article in a professional newsletter, an experimental design, a figure or table in a publication, a family photograph, a case report, a test, a transcript, a field report, a course outline, or a meeting agenda.

The remaining three tasks of deconstruction involve demonstration projects. The message of social constructionism is that persons actively construct the meanings that frame and organize their perceptions and experience (Gergen, 1985). To understand people's experience, the deconstructionist must try to get inside their perspectives. The three tasks described below suggest ways of showing this process in the flesh, as it were, rather than in the text.

# Describing the Experiential
# and Behavioral Range of Constructions

Carol MacCormack and Alizon Draper (1987) conducted field studies in Jamaica between 1983 and 1985 to obtain information about sexuality, health, and various other topics from structured interviews, informal observations and discussions, and government demographic surveys. In prenatal clinics and fruit and vegetable markets, women were interviewed and asked to *draw* the female reproductive system on a female outline. Jamaican women's drawings featured a large and elaborated uterus with little attention to the vagina as contrasted with the drawings of British and U.S. women. These findings were corroborated by interviews with the Jamaican women, who expressed the view that female sexuality has its primary meaning in conjunction with having children to achieve adult status and self-esteem.

Celia Kitzinger (1987) used a combination of structured interviews, a forced-choice card-sorting task ("q-sort"), and factor analysis to learn how British lesbians construct their identities and to investigate their politics and their attitudes toward lesbianism. She wrote: "My aim is not to reveal the 'real' histories, motives and life events of the participants, but to understand how people construct, negotiate and interpret their experience" (p. 71).

We learn from Kitzinger's method about lesbian heterogeneity, that is, that meanings of lesbianism differ widely. What it means to be a lesbian varies from a highly personal psychologized perspective ("lesbianism is a route through which happiness, personal growth and fulfillment can be obtained") to a romantic perspective ("It all depends on who you fall in love with"), to a focus on lesbianism as a fixed, private, innately determined orientation, to lesbianism as a strategy of feminism and women's liberation. There is no assumption that there is a *real* lesbianism and that these are alternate forms; there is no assumption that these variations represent a hierarchy of differential lesbian enlightenment; and there is no assumption that some of these women are deluded and others are being honest—there is just the assumption that single concepts do not reflect unitary experience.

Margaret Nelson (1983) gave 127 working-class women and 124 middle-class women a questionnaire to complete during their ninth month of pregnancy, another one several days after their babies were born, and a third one about six weeks later. She was able to show important group differences in attitudes toward childbirth during the pregnancy, different experiences during childbirth, and different postpartum experiences. What makes this study an example of social constructionism is that Nelson did not discuss these differences hierarchically or normatively. That is, she did not assume or point out that the model of a less informed, less prepared, more doctor-dependent, less "natural" childbirth, which influenced working-class women's attitudes, was inferior to the middle-class model of greater autonomy, family-centeredness, and special-experience-ness. Rather, she argued, "Each of the two models of childbirth makes sense within the context of the lives its adopters lead. Each model confers benefits on the women who adhere to it. . . . A single model of childbirth has too often been held up for all women. . . . We have to learn more about what women at different locations in the social structure want for themselves" (p. 296).

Theo Sandfort (1983) used what he called the "self-confrontation" method to study the relationships of twenty-five Dutch boys, all ten to sixteen years old (fifteen of whom were from the lower classes) with men twenty-six to sixty-six years old. He held repeated interviews, asking the boys about positive and negative aspects of their lives, including their sexual relationships. He concluded,

> Instead of speaking in terms of 'victims,' 'offender,' and sexual assaults, which is still the usual way in scientific writing to refer to pedophilia, this research approaches pedophile relationships as simply another form of relationship children can have. In putting aside our own value judgements and letting the children describe their own experiences, we saw that both partners in pedophile relationships can, probably in a different manner, feel attracted towards each other. . . . The relationships emerge as positively valued aspects within the boys' worlds. (Sandfort, 1983, p. 180)

Social constructionist work focusing on the *range* of constructions allows people to describe their activities, attitudes, and feelings in their own words, pictures, and metaphors. Constructionist theory has thus opened up a broad range of ways of construing experience that can be related to diverse historical, physical, and social locations. A social constructionist perspective may seem more congenial to nonjudgmental anthropology than to psychology, but these studies all seemed quite psychologically minded to me, and all seemed to open up new ways to understand sexuality.

## Describing Individual and Social Change in Constructions

Showing the processes by which concepts and categories become constructed in interaction and socialization is especially important to combatting essentialist thinking. If fundamental conceptions of sexuality and gender can change, then such conceptions are not part of human hardwiring.

An unusual project had a group of twelve West German Marxist feminists study the socialization of female sexuality through "group memory-work" (Haug, 1987). Going a step beyond the individual and nonjudgmental storytelling of consciousness-raising groups toward something more akin to leaderless group therapy, these women divided into task forces to study how their sexuality had developed. One woman would write out a specific event-memory related to the theme at hand, and others would critique, expand, and free-associate to her story. Revised and expanded versions were rediscussed. In this way, extended analyses emerged of forces influencing girls' values and ways of sexual behaving and feeling. Much of the group's work focused on the ways that women participate in the reinforcement of their subordinate status, an aspect of their work they called "the slavegirl project." They repeatedly emphasized how important it was that they not defer to familiar theories and concepts but merely stick to the data of memories and associations and try to figure out what sexuality was coming to mean, year by year, body-part by body-part. This is the only collectivist method of social construction work I have come across.

In a classic piece of research, Suzanne Kessler and Wendy McKenna ([1978] 1985) were able to show how gender is constructed during children's development. Using a variety of figure-drawing and verbal tasks, they showed how children move from vague gender categories to two definite ones and from using a variety of attributions to relying exclusively on the presence or absence of a penis for deciding gender.

The data, of course, are hardly new. Many developmental psychologists over the years have invented creative nonverbal tasks involving dolls and drawings to find out when young children developed two categories of person and what cues they used at different ages (e.g., Katcher, 1955). Such studies were usually presented, however, in terms of developmental "mastery" of the biologically "correct" two-category system. Kessler and McKenna embedded their findings in anthropological data showing that the cues and categories for gender in other cultures were different and thus that the children they studied had acquired a construction of gender appropriate to modern Western culture. Once one steps back from assumptions about the inevitability of conventional categories and concepts, one can watch what people do and how they grow to do it from a different perspective.

## Manipulating Social Constructions (Creating Change)

The final task for social constructionists is not merely to observe changes in constructions but to proactively create such changes. Psychotherapists do this all the time in the form of "cognitive reframing." Any situation involving change—education, job training, self-help group socialization—could provide a longitudinal fieldwork opportunity to see changes in action. A lot of AIDS research is addressing sexuality in this framework, showing how individuals who perceive themselves to be at risk are working to reconceptualize sexual activities, feelings, and fantasies.

## Conclusion

Many but not all of the research methods mentioned above take a qualitative approach or combine qualitative with quantitative methods. Looking for diversity rather than for laws of behavior, trying to understand how others see the world rather than slotting people into preconceived categories—these goals are better suited to open-ended, interpretive types of approaches. Anyone attracted to this work must go beyond experimental methods of psychology to aspects of phenomenology, participant observation, experiential research, and different forms of groupwork and interviews.

Finally, as I said at the outset, social constructionist work has been attractive to socially marginalized groups seeking to destabilize accepted theories. I was drawn to it as a feminist looking for new ways to think about sexuality and gender and new ways to criticize the old ways. Along with furthering our political goals and seeing familiar topics with fresh eyes, feminists and others who undertake this work will inevitably deepen their understanding of the human experience.

PART TWO

# Popular Writings
# on the Theme

*T*he chapters in this section are efforts at deconstruction, although I had never heard of the term or the movement when I wrote them. In retrospect, I can see that my theme in these popular writings was to challenge conventional meanings and relocate authority away from experts. I kept trying to take the familiar and make it unfamiliar, the classic approach in deconstruction. And this was not only in the essays included here but in articles that I wrote for *Ms., Redbook, Playgirl Advisor, Glamour,* and other popular magazines. I gave it a royal try!

I don't write for the mass media anymore. My experiences were so negative that I eventually realized I was part of the problem and not part of the solution. In fact, I do not even usually take the time to answer journalists' queries on the telephone anymore. The journalists seem wildly ignorant of the subjects they are researching and usually begin with something like "Could you tell me what's new about transsexuals?" I used to answer with, "Well, how much do you know already?" only to hear, "Well, not much, I heard you were an expert and I was hoping you could tell me." They would always be "on deadline" and needed my time immediately! If I did take time to explain some of the complexities, I would invariably find little of my perspective in the final article. Some throwaway line I'd tossed out would be quoted, but not the careful analysis, and certainly not the complexities and limiting qualifications. The journalist, despite my urgings to do otherwise, would adhere to the most conventional, most simpleminded, most sensationalized level of discourse. I won't even bother describing what it was like to try to talk seriously about sexual subjects on TV or radio. I felt validated in my disappointment, anger, and ultimate hopelessness after I read a history of journalism that stressed the widespread incompetence and gradual takeover by commercial values in the science and health media (Burnham, 1987).

What was consistently distressing was the "naive realism" of the media on sexual subjects. The notion that media are major players in the process of social construction, that they create and define categories of analysis as well as helping to set values, seemed completely unfamiliar and unacceptable to them. As I look back over the essays I wrote for the popular media, I see that I was straining constantly to persuade readers toward skepticism and away from gullibility, toward complexity and overdetermined motives, and toward cultural variables but that this message often got lost in the editing and was never acceptable as a central theme.

I used to try to imagine who was the audience for these writings. I could actually see people reading the *Daily News,* for example, on the New York subway. They were ordinary, middle-aged (more or less) women and men, black and white, blue collar and white collar. They were not glamorous or trendy-looking. They rarely had manicures or perfect teeth. Sitting alone in a room with a typewriter (my mass-media period was before the PC came along), I would try to recall the masses who read these magazines and newspapers and speak to their experience.

It was when I decided I was inescapably part of the problem that I finally gave up. I had heard once too often that "our readers aren't interested in those topics" when I brought up painful realities of poverty, coercion, or ignorance. I felt there was no way to avoid assumptions that seemed to me complacent and middle class. Readers were never supposed to be homeless or in prison, realistically depressed about life prospects, in dead-end jobs, uneducated, in violent relationships, disgusted with their bodies, more interested in history than in sex, or nonconsumers. They were all assumed to have privacy for their sexual lives, to take restful vacations, to be able to buy aromatic candles or bath oils to enhance sensuality. Some of the views I wanted to advocate, and that seemed fundamental to me—like the concept that intravaginal intercourse should be considered only one of many equally pleasurable heterosexual acts—were considered too "radical." Of course, this was all pre-AIDS. Now, what was once radical is pushed as "healthy." But the media still tout a message of conformity with prevailing norms.

I finally realized that the only part of the sexologist's message that was welcomed was actually the conservative part, not the part that promoted social analysis and social change. The issues I was interested in were too complicated, and I could agree to 5,000 interviews and never see those ideas in print. When I finally realized that selectivity and bias among journalists, editors, and publishers were undermining the larger message I wanted to deliver about sexuality, I quit playing the game.

# 6

# Six Months
## at the *Daily News*

*In 1980 I was invited to write a weekly 200-word column for the* New York
Daily News, *which advertises itself as the largest-circulation daily in the country. I knew they wanted something popular and a little titillating, not academic or political, but I thought I would see if I could find some way to present
the ideas I was interested in anyway. The* News *called the column "Your Sexual
Self," exactly the sort of privatized perspective I planned to preach against! I
had to repeatedly resist the editors' request that I answer readers' questions in
the column. I got lots of mail, but none of it ever commented on the columns; it
all wanted advice. The* News *called it quits after six months; I have selected a
few of those columns to include here.*

## The Myth of Spontaneity

Nowadays we are expected to be sexually spontaneous. Scheming and playing games are out. But good sex doesn't strike like lightning. Only in romantic novels do lovers swoon from a single glance or pant from a passing
touch. Getting turned on in real life is more like warming up an engine than
flicking on a light switch.

Such is the power of our ignorance on this subject that many people suspect organic or hormonal weakness if they are not aroused at a moment's
notice. Even those informed about the importance of mental preparation
may wrongly label themselves psychologically undersexed. Not to mention
the names they hurl at their partners.

In fact, seasoned lovers often deliberately put themselves in the mood.
Thinking about sex usually tops their list of preliminaries. Like John Tra-
volta, leisurely and lovingly combing his hair before going out to disco in
*Saturday Night Fever,* anyone can tune into sensual, sexual feelings by imag-
ining good times ahead. Relaxing, mentally and physically, is important. A
shower works for some, a quiet time alone for others.

Some people complain that all this groundwork is too mechanical and time-consuming. Working at sex, they say, defeats the whole purpose. Ironically, these same people don't grouse over warming up for tennis or deny themselves an appetizer before dinner. One of the real reasons people are shy about making preparations for sex is that it seems sinful. Planning for sex runs counter to much of our early learning. Willfully conjuring up a lusty fantasy is wicked. Even sex within marriage can be tainted for some by too voluptuous an attitude.

People may also avoid planning because whenever you plan you risk disappointment. What if you dab on a little perfume and he isn't interested? What if you shave just before bed and she laughs at your obviousness? The risks feel greatest when you are insecure about yourself or your partner. This can make any negative thing feel like a catastrophe. In fact, I believe the risks in warming yourself up for sex (not every time—let's not get compulsive about this) are trivial compared to the possible benefits. Being embarrassed isn't shattering.

In our rush to celebrate spontaneous sex, we may have forgotten a childhood phenomenon—that waiting for Christmas was a big part of the fun. Can we abandon the trickery of seduction without losing the delicious excitement of the tease? Can we remember that a few solitary moments in the bullpen can make all the difference when we finally get into the game?

## Bring Back the Kid Stuff

Poor little petting. Lost in the great big world of grownup sex. Somewhere along the line, kissing and tickling, rubbing and hugging became mere preliminaries to the main event.

A lot more is being lost than you might at first realize. Deprived of touch, many of us get a kind of itchy skin hunger. Sexual petting has been one of the primary ways adults can obtain the comforts of touch. While petting, many lovers murmur of their admiration and affection, talk baby-talk, or whisper and giggle—in a way that's not possible during intercourse. Exchanging endearments creates a special emotional bond. You may smile at the memory of a lover's nickname long after you've forgotten the physical details of sex together. Before we can value such indulgence, however, petting would have to lose the stigma of being kid stuff. As most of us grew up, intercourse was rated X: For Adults Only. It acquired the lure of the forbidden and the status of the big leagues.

At a time when lovers complain about insufficient variety, petting should become more popular. The skin is the largest sex organ, yet many of us have learned to regard as sexual only a tiny percentage of the available acreage.

On the Polynesian island of Pnape, partners spend hours petting and nuzzling before they begin to think about intercourse.

Couples who seek out sex therapists because of sexual disinterest or difficulty in sexual function are often thunderstruck to hear that the first homework assignment of the treatment is to pet with each other. They can't imagine how avoiding intercourse and just playing around will help. They want help with "real" sex. Therapists explain that petting will lead their clients to discover (or rediscover) a wide variety of erotic sensations while positive emotions generated by the mutual stroking will strengthen the couple's attachment.

But, as clients soon realize, it may be easier to have intercourse than to hug and kiss! The task is better defined: a clear goal, a standard method, easy-to-locate equipment, and a socially defined endpoint. It can be accomplished with a minimum of communication. With petting, the script is more vague. Over what path do the hands and mouth wander? What words are said? How do you know when you're through?

You can have successful intercourse with a stranger, but you have to like someone to enjoy petting. Because the physical sensations are less intense, much of the reward must come from the closeness. It's joyless and burdensome to cuddle and embrace with someone you neither know well nor want to know better. The petting assignment is very revealing for many couples.

Calling kissing and hugging "foreplay" reveals their status as means to an end. Anything that is sometimes an appetizer and sometimes the main dish is worthy of a name other than foreplay. Let's save that one for something more appropriate—like golf.

## Shedding Light on Sex in the Dark

Sex is the only game we play in the dark. Are we ashamed to watch what we're doing, or is darkness necessary to liberate our intimate passions?

In the darkness, lovers are safe from the prying eyes of children, parents, neighbors—and each other. To the extent that you want to deny others knowledge of you as a sexual person, you will welcome the protection of the dark.

Under cover of darkness, we are all beautiful. Flab, sag, spots, and wrinkles are mercifully hidden. With the contortions and grimaces of sexual exertion out of focus, we seem graceful as gazelles. To the extent that you find earthy images of skin and sweat distracting, you seek the camouflage of darkness.

In the permissive darkness, sin is softened. Taboos occur without witness. To the extent that your upbringing stressed the prohibitions surrounding sex, you may require the tolerance afforded by darkness.

Concealed by darkness, cracks in the ceiling—or your life—lose their immediacy. It's just the two of you, close together, with the colored lights flashing in your heads. The details of existence fade away.

Blinded by darkness, we are forced to use our other senses. We rediscover touch, aroma, sound. Covered with clothes, we are chronically deprived of the variety of pleasures and comforts available through touch. To the extent that vision distracts you from concentrating on other sensations, you will prefer darkness.

Screened by darkness, we become bold. Our words and our rhythms reveal a lusty eagerness we might deny by day. Shyness can be slain by the dark. In the privacy of darkness, we can exaggerate and improve our actual experience through imagination. Our wishes fulfilled, we feel deeper love and greater passion. Through illusion, we become more involved in reality. To the extent that imagination enriches the moment, darkness is a friend.

The trouble with darkness is that you can't see what you're doing. You can't see how your partner is reacting. You can't gaze into each other's eyes. Travelers ignorant of the territory tend to stick to familiar and well-marked routes. Sex in the dark often becomes routine. Many people protest that seeing themselves and their partners is immodest. But we're talking here about moonlight and 40-watt bulbs, not airport runway approach beacons.

Yet many of us have the greatest difficulty believing that anyone would enjoy seeing our genitals. We've been told they're cursed, or dirty. Many women are so paralyzed by shame they even avoid medical examination "down there." Modesty is often shame in disguise.

Perhaps because of the taboos on showing and looking, such acts can be the final revelation of trust between lovers. Like all proofs of acceptance, they must be mutual—forced, they become empty gestures of intimacy.

## Sex Is an Unnatural Act

I have a T-shirt that reads, "Sex is a natural act." I used to think it was at least amusing, at best profound. If people would only relax and let their natural reactions flow, I thought, sex would be more of a pleasure and less of a Pandora's box.

I'm wiser now. I think the sentiment of the T-shirt distorts the truth. The urge to merge may be natural for birds and bees, but the biological takes a back seat in our own species. We humans are the only ones with a sex drive that isn't solely related to procreation.

Originally, the message that sex is natural was meant to relieve guilt feelings—you can't be blamed for doing what is healthy and normal. Such permission was extremely useful for a time. It enabled many people to break free from choking inhibitions.

But the message was taken too literally. I now meet people who believe hormones control their sex life. They feel no pride when sex is good and have no idea what to do when it is not. Letting Mother Nature do the driving sounds like the lazy person's dream; actually it makes you feel powerless and ignorant.

Belief that sexuality comes naturally relieves our responsibility to acquire knowledge and make choices. You don't have to teach your kids anything special—when the time comes, they'll know what to do. You don't have to talk with your partner about your love life—it'll all just happen automatically.

What happens automatically is often brief, routine, and more in the category of scratching an itch than indulging a beautiful expression. Such a sexual style may satisfy a person for whom sex has a low priority. It is unreasonable to expect mutual pleasure, variety, or emotional intimacy without some information and a lot of practice. If all you need for fulfilling sex comes already built in, then any difficulties must be due to physical breakdown. Many couples seek medical help when what they need is a course on communication. Sexual enrichment workshops mixing film, lecture, discussion, and time for private practice present an approach to sex that emphasizes the relationship.

You can't ignore the way worry and anger affect desire. You need to learn how to give suggestions and feedback without putting each other down. There's no way but trial and error to identify forms of effective stimulation. Most important, the attitude that sex is a natural act implies that great sex occurs early in a relationship and stays constant throughout. A dynamic vision of continuing change and adjustment is more realistic—it's not failing memory that leads some older couples to report that sex keeps getting better.

Unfortunately, most sex education has not caught up with what people need in the 1980s. High school and college classes dwell at length on statistics, plumbing, and contraception. Students rarely read about connections between sexuality and feelings. Nor do they discuss what influences sexual attraction or how psychological needs are met through sex. Often students enter a course and leave it still thinking that love will guide the way to sexual happiness.

Limiting instruction to issues like birth control and venereal disease prevention may promote public health goals, but it does little to enrich the quality of sexual experience. Techniques of pregnancy prevention don't work to prevent sexual disappointment.

Natural sex, like a natural brassiere, is a contradiction in terms. The human sex act is a product of individual personalities, skills, and the scripts of our times. Like a brassiere, it shapes nature to something designed by human purposes and reflecting current fashion.

# Sex as Communication?
# Save Your Breath!

It seems that every new sex book proclaims, "Sex is the ultimate form of communication." What does this mean? How can I figure out if it's true if I can't figure out what it means?

I go to my local guru. He tells me it means that people are most honest, most open, most truly themselves during sex. I ask why. You never really know a person until you've had sex together, he says. I say, I thought you never really knew a person until you got drunk together, or until one of you got cancer. Same thing, he says. Extreme situations cause people to reveal themselves. I'm dubious. Sex may be an extreme situation, but it makes as many people clam up as open up.

I go to another guru. This one tells me that sex is the ultimate form of communication because sex allows a person to express the broadest range of intimate feelings. People fumble for words, she says. They get tongue-tied and choked by emotion. Ah, but in bed they can let themselves go. Love, fear, tenderness, trust, generosity, sensitivity, respect, even anger. But what about those people whose sexual vocabulary is a one-note song? What about those who can emit volumes over breakfast, but only paragraphs in bed? Is sex the ultimate form of communication for them, too?

Another guru, another explanation. This one tells me sex offers the best hope for communication because words can lie, but bodies tell the truth. But I know bodies can lie. Or, rather, that reading body language can lead as often to misunderstanding as revelation. People mistake fatigue for rejection or disinterest. Physical arousal doesn't necessarily reflect desire for the partner in one's arms. Behavior isn't that easy to interpret; smiles and caresses can be as deceptive as words.

Maybe the best approach is to abandon the jargon. What does one person tell another by means of sex? Is the message unique to sex? Can it be delivered better for some people in words, other gestures of tenderness or intimacy or devotion?

The truth seems to be that people express themselves during lovemaking just as they do by all their activities. There tends to be a lot of consistency to the messages, as couples in sex therapy frequently discover. If one partner dominates sex so the other can't get a move in edgewise, it's a safe bet the same thing occurs during a discussion of how to discipline little Billy.

The gurus' basic error is overgeneralization. To claim sex is the ultimate form of communication sounds as if something fundamental about sex were being revealed that was true for all people. In fact, some people express their feelings better with caresses than words, but others don't. Some people reveal more of their inner feelings in sex than over coffee; others don't. Some people are closer to their lovers than to other companions, but many are not.

Like all generalizations, this one bulldozes individual differences. And like all hype about sex, it makes most of us wonder what we're missing. The word "ultimate" is the tipoff. No one human activity could possibly be the ultimate everything to anyone. We're just not that much alike.

## Free Love and Free Enterprise

Every war has its profiteers, and the sexual revolution is no exception. Did you notice the moment when the movement to decrease sexual guilt and ignorance suddenly became big business? The question now is whether the run for the bucks will completely obliterate the original liberatory impulse.

Imagine a sex show at the New York Coliseum. Products and services once available only to decadent aristocrats are now accessible to everyone. Let's tour around and assess the impact of this commercial boom.

The first booth salutes the information explosion. Textbooks and visuals for schools and professional training line one wall; popular books, magazines, and TV presentations on sex cover the other. Soon every citizen will have been interviewed and observed and will have written a book about the experience. Yet, though many of the materials repeat the same points over and over, the public's appetite for such materials seems inexhaustible. Will we ever overcome our ignorance?

The second booth advertises help for the sexually troubled. Lists of disorders reach from floor to ceiling. Different schools of treatment challenge each other's success statistics and argue about causes and cures. Their standards for adequacy make most people feel inadequate, generating perpetual business. Fortunately, for a price, they're all available to treat your "problem." It's a little confusing, though, when you see ads for treatment in newspapers or telephone directories and have no idea about the qualifications of the providers. Can you be helped by a sexual surrogate? Don't look to science for an answer.

The next booth moves us into the world of stuff. Under the banner, "Bare-handed sex is boring," we find equipment to enhance the senses and the imagination. Massage oils and flavored lotions lie next to vibrators and dildos. Alarming displays of bondage equipment are shown along with phony organ enlargers. There are life-size "sex partners" in different colors of plastic. Underwear comes in sequined, leather, very skimpy, and edible versions. There are records and tapes of love sounds (orgasmic sighs and ocean waves), satin sheets, aromatic candles, incense, mirrored beds with built-in bars, fluffy rabbit-fur mitts. Parents worry where they'll put their toys so the kids don't find them.

A fourth booth displays aphrodisiacs—substances that allegedly arouse desire or intensify experience. Few have been scientifically tested, and those few have proven ineffective. Nevertheless, the supply of potions and pills expands as people chase their rising expectations. Next door is the hygiene and fitness booth. Leotards, instruction books, and gym business cards promise that if you change your body, you'll build up your chances for sexual success.

The sixth booth is for the vast world of visual erotica. Some educational, some offensive, some conventional, some unusual—but who can draw the lines? The flood of sexually explicit material for the home market looms on the horizon. Since the major use of pornography has always been for masturbation, sex experts and commercial interests seem in collusion as they sing the praises of solo sex.

Another booth is plastered with brochures that promise the zing of sex away from home. Bring your honey to a hot-tub motel (with waterbed, whirlpool, and X-rated TV movies), or make it with a stranger in a local orgy room. There's something about the unfamiliar that makes us pay attention and feel more intensely. Bring your checkbook and check it out.

The final booth contains the business cards of people who want to have sex with you—for a price. "Dates" are available for out-of-town visitors to fill a lonely evening. Bars with runways have dancers who strip or parade to inflame your fantasies. Models will pose, and participate. Massages can be had without sex—or with. And prostitutes of every age and talent are available, as they have always been.

Commercial interests exist to make a profit. Contributions to human well-being are incidental. Sexual commercialism surely exploits and preys upon insecurity, but it also stimulates and expands the imagination. It's difficult to find the line between moralistic or embarrassed kneejerk rejection ("What do they need *that* for?") and simplistic and indiscriminate acceptance ("Everybody should do their own thing"), but we owe it to ourselves to try.

# 7

# The Kiss

Nothing seems more natural than a kiss. Consider the French kiss, also known as the soul kiss, deep kiss, or tongue kiss (to the French it was the Italian kiss). Western societies regard this passionate exploration of mouths and tongues as an instinctive way to express love and to arouse desire. To a European who associates deep kisses with erotic response, the idea of one without the other feels like summer without sun.

Yet soul kissing is completely absent in many cultures of the world, where sexual arousal may be evoked by affectionate bites or stinging slaps. Anthropology and history amply demonstrate that, depending on time and place, the kiss may or may not be regarded as a sexual act, a sign of friendship, a gesture of respect, a health threat, a ceremonial celebration, or a disgusting behavior that deserves condemnation.

Considering the diversity of kissing customs, it astonishes me that so few social scientists have given the kiss any attention. Kissing is usually relegated to an occasional footnote, if authors bother to mention it at all. My computer search of kissing references in *Psychological Abstracts* and the *Index Medicus* turned up some papers on mononucleosis ("the kissing disease"), one article on a fish known as the "kissing gourami," and unrelated work by people with names like Kissing and Kissler. Even sex researchers are uninterested. *Sex* now refers to intercourse, not kissing or petting. In textbooks on human sexuality, kissing rarely appears in the index.

## Anthropology and Kissing

I became fascinated by the remarkable cultural and historical variations in styles and purposes of kissing, given how "natural" it seems to pursue whatever customs each of us has grown accustomed to. Clellan Ford and Frank Beach (1951) compared the sexual customs of the many tribal societies that were recorded in the Human Relations Area Files at Yale. Few field studies mentioned kissing customs at all. Of the twenty-one that did, some sort of kissing accompanied intercourse in thirteen tribes—the Chiricahua, Cree,

Crow, Gros Ventre, Hopi, Huichol, Kwakiutl, and Tarahumara of North America; the Alorese, Keraki, Trobrianders, and Trukese of Oceania; and the Lapps in Eurasia. There were some interesting variations: the Kwakiutl, Trobrianders, Alorese, and Trukese kiss by sucking the lips and tongue of their partners; the Lapps like to kiss the mouth and nose at the same time.

But sexual kissing is unknown in many societies, including the Balinese, Chamorro, Manus, and Tinguian of Oceania; the Chewa and Thonga of Africa; the Siriono of South America; and the Lepcha of Eurasia. In such cultures, the mouth-to-mouth kiss is considered dangerous, unhealthy, or disgusting, the way Westerners might regard a custom of sticking one's tongue into a lover's nose. Ford and Beach reported that when the Thonga first saw Europeans kissing, they laughed, remarking, "Look at them—they eat each other's saliva and dirt."

Deep kissing apparently has nothing to do with degree of sexual inhibition or repression in a culture. On certain Polynesian islands, women are orgasmic and sexually active, yet kissing was unknown until Westerners and their popular films arrived. Research in parts of Ireland, by contrast, where sex was considered dirty and sinful, and, for women, a duty, shows that the Irish also were oblivious to tongue kissing until recent decades.

Many tribes across Africa and elsewhere believe that the soul enters and leaves through the mouth and that a person's bodily products can be collected and saved by an enemy for harmful purposes. In these societies, the possible loss of saliva would cause a kiss to be regarded as a dangerous gesture. There, the "soul kiss" is taken literally. (It was taken figuratively in Western societies; recall Christopher Marlowe's "Sweet Helen, make me immortal with a kiss! Her lips suck forth my soul.")

Although the deep kiss is relatively rare around the world as a part of sexual intimacy, other forms of mouth or nose contact are common—particularly the "oceanic kiss," named for its prevalence among cultures in Oceania but not limited to them. The Tinguians place their lips near the partner's face and suddenly inhale. Balinese lovers bring their faces close enough to catch each other's perfume and to feel the warmth of the skin, making contact as they move their heads slightly. Another kiss, as practiced by Chinese Yakuts and Mongolians at the turn of the century, has one person's nose pressed to the other's cheek, followed by a nasal inhalation and finally a smacking of lips.

The oceanic kiss may be varied by the placement of the nose and cheek, the vigor of the inhalation, the nature of the accompanying sounds, the action of the arms, and so on; it is used for affectionate greeting as well as for sexual play. Some observers think that the so-called Eskimo or Malay kiss of rubbing noses is actually a mislabeled oceanic kiss; the kisser is simply moving his or her nose rapidly from one cheek to the other of the partner, bumping noses en route.

Small tribes and obscure Irish islanders are not the only groups to eschew tongue kissing. The advanced civilizations of China and Japan, which regarded sexual proficiency as high art, apparently cared little about it. In their voluminous display of erotica—graphic depictions of every possible sexual position, angle of intercourse, and variation of partner and setting—mouth-to-mouth kissing is conspicuous by its absence. Japanese poets have rhapsodized for centuries about the allure of the nape of the neck, but they have been silent on the mouth; indeed, kissing is acceptable only between mother and child. (The Japanese have no word for kissing—though they recently borrowed from English to create *kissu.*) In Japan, intercourse is "natural"; a kiss, pornographic. When Rodin's famous sculpture *The Kiss* came to Tokyo in the 1920s as part of a show of European art, it was concealed from public view behind a bamboo curtain.

Among cultures of the West, the number of nonsexual uses of the kiss is staggering: greeting and farewell, affection, religious or ceremonial symbolism, deference to a person of high status. (People also kiss icons, dice, and other objects, of course, in prayer, for luck, or as part of a ritual.) Kisses make the hurt go away, bless the sacred vestments, seal a bargain. In story and legend a kiss has started wars and ended them, awakened Sleeping Beauty and put Brunnhilde to sleep.

## Classifying Kisses

Efforts to sort all of these kisses into neat categories apparently began centuries ago. According to Christopher Nyrop (1901), a Danish linguist who wrote a history of the kiss, the ancient rabbis recognized three kinds: greeting, farewell, and respect. The Romans also distinguished three kinds of kisses: *oscula* (friendly kisses), *basia* (love kisses), and *suavia* (passionate kisses). The most imaginative system was proposed in 1791 by an Austrian writer, W. von Kempelen, who divided kisses according to their sound: the *freundschaftlicher hellklatschender Kerzenskuss* (the affectionate clear-ringing kiss coming from the heart), the acoustically weaker discreet kiss, and the *ekeljafter Schmatz* (a loathsome smack). Von Kempelen's categories did not gain widespread use.

When Nyrop wrote his book, he reported no fewer than thirty different German words to indicate types of kisses, from *Abschiedskuss* (farewell kiss) to *Zuckerkuss* (sweet, or "candy" kiss). The structure of the language permits composite nouns, but even so, German shows a remarkable linguistic richness in its variety of kisses. Today, *abkussen* means to give many little kisses all over; *erkussen* is (slang) for getting a gift or favor by kissing ("sucking up"?); *fortkussen* is to kiss away tears; and *wiederkussen* is to return a kiss you have been given.

The Germans are not the only ones to classify their kisses. Allan Edwardes, in *The Jewel in the Lotus* (1959), described the Hindu science of kissing: There is *sootaree-sumpoodeh* (the probing, tongue-sucking kiss), to be distinguished from *jeebh-juddh* (tongue-tilting), *jeebhee* (tongue scraping), and *hondh-chubbow* (lip biting). Of course, the question sexologists cannot yet answer—because research to date has been more descriptive than subjective—is to what extent Germans and Hindus actually have more diverse experiences than the French, who struggle along monolinguistically with *embrasser*, the Spanish, who have only *besar*, or the Russians, with *tselovat*.

## Ceremonial Kisses

Classifications are entertaining but not especially illuminating. Types of kisses overlap and change over time. For example, St. Paul may not have known what would come of his simple advice to Christians to "salute one another with an holy kiss," a brief admonition in *Romans* 16:16 that is repeated in *Corinthians* I and II. Over the centuries, the "holy kiss" was interpreted and reinterpreted; it found expression in baptism, marriage, confession, and ordination. The *osculum pacis*, or kiss of peace, supposed to represent God's kiss of life and Christ's kiss of eternal blessing, was exchanged in some locations between priest and congregant, in others between clergy only. It passed out of common practice after the Reformation but is enjoying a renaissance in modern Catholic, Anglican, and Episcopalian congregations.

The famous kiss between bride and groom that concludes a wedding ceremony was actually part of ancient pagan rites and signified that legal bonds were being assumed. I've always thought the clergy's injunction to the groom "I now pronounce you husband [or 'man'] and wife, you may kiss the bride" represented the clergyman's quasi-parental permission to the new couple to be sexual (though it can't be an accident that the permission has typically been extended to the new husband!).

There are many more stories about holy and profane kisses, social and ceremonial kisses, changing customs (e.g., how European customs of kissing changed to bowing and hat lifting during the time of the plague), but by now I have made my point that an act like kissing cannot only be choreographed in very different ways but can serve many functions and carry many different meanings, all depending on the customs of a particular era. And, amazingly, each social group, each generation, feels its kisses are the normal, the natural ones.

# Importance of Kissing

Why is kissing so popular, and why does it adapt to so many meanings? There have been some theories. Desmond Morris, following Freud, noted that a baby experiences its earliest joys, gratifications, and frustrations through its mouth, which becomes a site of emotional associations. In many cultures infants are lavishly touched, cuddled, and kissed all over their bodies, not only by their mothers but also by other relatives and friends. The infant learns that touching something soft with the mouth is a calming and pleasurable sensation. Adult kisses recall some of this infant gratification. Kissing symbols for luck, Morris argued, is emotionally reassuring—it's not just a random gesture to appease the gods or fate.

It certainly is true that the lips, mouth, and tongue are among the most exquisitely sensitive parts of the body. The tongue itself is sensitive to pressure, temperature, taste, smell, and movement. Lips, tongue, and mouth detect and transmit to the brain a range of incoming sensations; and the brain, in turn, devotes a disproportionate amount of its resources to processing their messages and linking them up to behavioral reactions and psychological functions. The space devoted to messages from and to the lips alone is far greater than that devoted to sensory or motor function for the entire torso.

Opportunities for kissing to develop multiple social meanings also arise because of variations in elements such as posture and facial expression—an especially important factor in communicating emotion. Through processes of social learning, trial and error, imitation, and reward and punishment, kisses acquire their multiple meanings and intense associations. Rules for social and sexual kisses vary not only across cultures but even among social classes and subcultures in the United States, making research into the social scripting of kissing a fertile area for those interested in how sexual choreography develops and what the various components mean to participants. The "naturalness" of kissing, as with so many other aspects of social life, turns out to be a biological potential shaped and cultivated by the real human nature—culture.

# 8

# Advice to the Lovelorn

*I* have a recurring nightmare. I am sitting at my desk when a big canvas mailbag is delivered. Envelopes of every size spill over the desk as the bag is emptied. With an odd foreboding, I reach for a small, white, neatly penciled envelope lying on top. It snaps up toward me, taking a vicious bite out of my finger. Cringing, my heart racing, I bind up the injured finger as, oh horror, another mailbag is carried in.

The dream isn't far from my waking feelings while writing weekly columns on sexuality for the *New York Daily News*, a job I held recently. Although each column specifically stated that I would neither print nor answer individual letters, nonetheless a couple hundred threaded their way through to the mailroom and found me.

True, no letter ever even nibbled my cuticle, but many mangled my heart, and I came to dread opening the envelopes. The more people unburdened themselves to me, the more I felt burdened. There I was trying to write trenchant little essays exploring the complexities of modern sexuality, and my correspondents persisted in treating me like a Mother Confessor. The letters that begged me for help each week began to plague my thoughts and gray my mood. Who knew this was on the agenda when I blithely took this job?

## Columnists and Column Readers

Nathanael West, for one. His brilliant 1933 novel, *Miss Lonelyhearts,* details the decline and fall of a newspaperman assigned to write an "advice to the lovelorn" column. The columnist becomes obsessed with the misery of people and his own Christ-like fantasies. I read that book three times during the *Daily News* era, hoping that, like a voodoo doll, *Miss Lonelyhearts* would absorb my gloom and leave me cool inside a cocoon of professional objectivity. Unfortunately, suggestible creature that I am, each reading only magnified my sense of responsibility and impotence. I ended up thinking a lot about newspaper advice columnists and the peculiar doctor/minister/teacher/neighborhood gossip/sharp-tongued big-sister role they perform.

Take a close look at those columns sometime. The way people describe their problems seems so stereotyped, as if they had learned to identify and define their own suffering by reading earlier columns. There's never enough detail about the authors' circumstances to give readers a solid understanding of their plight. This is not just a function of editing, by the way, since the letters I received were more often than not the same kind of telegrammatic complaints you see published: "I am a man of fifty, [and] I have recently become impotent. Can you tell me of any new treatments? I don't have much money."

If people really do see themselves as such stick figures and imagine that any usable advice can be given in response to such sketchy information, then maybe the multipurpose commonsense answers they usually get are appropriate, "Read factual books. Consult reputable professionals. Think about why this problem started and why it continues."

The trouble is, though, that generalized advice is not especially usable in real people's real lives, maybe because demoralization and anxiety cloud the brain and snarl up good judgment. The platitudes seem to make sense ("Communicate more with your partner. Try to look on the bright side."), but they can't be put into practice ("What should we communicate about? What if I can't look on the bright side?"). Readers end up blaming themselves or thinking that counseling is a crock.

## The Community of Readers

Advice columns, of course, are not meant only for the letter-writers. Neither the columnists nor the circulation managers would be at all happy with that! Every correspondent is but the spokesperson for a large, silent iceberg of those with more or less similar worries. This subsurface community of readers is occasionally roused to a passionate wave of cheers or hoots in response to some controversial problem or reply, but it soon subsides back into mute anonymity. Heed for this larger audience leads the columnist to weigh the advantages of precision in answering a particular letter against the desire to say something general that might reach more of the eavesdroppers.

Those tensions have been part of newspaper advice columns since their beginnings in 1691 (Kent, 1979). In that year, shortly after the beginnings of modern-style newspapers, *The Athenian Gazette* (later *The Athenian Mercury*) began to publish letters from readers together with answers from the paper's founder (a young English printer named John Dunton) and a few friends who were disguised as a scholarly team called "The Athenian Society." The letters, which focused on moral, scientific, literary, and, of course, sexual topics, inspired other readers to send in their comments, thereby helping to fill the newspaper's space (a tactic still in use today).

Why are advice columns so popular? Are they a force for good? The success of advice columns rests on an odd mixture of entertainment and education. The columnist deficient in either sphere is unlikely to make the big time.

As entertainment, the column is full of titillation, shock, and wit. The columnist joins readers in playing that ever-popular American contest game "Stump the Expert." Safe in their anonymity, readers compare their responses to those of the authorities and take ecstatic delight in finding omissions or inaccuracies. The columnists' frequent put-downs ("Dump the slob. He's had plenty of time to see the light.") allow readers to feel superior and to vicariously vent their spleens against the bumblers and meanies of society. These one-liners are useful for grabbing readers' attention as they ride the deteriorating subways, but the question must be raised whether they help unscramble the maze of real life.

As educator, the advice columnist wears the mantle of mental or medical health authority, either by virtue of personal training or by relying on an invisible advisory panel. The mantle is respected because it means the adviser's recommendations come from scientific research, not personal feelings or religious tenets.

But readers rarely ask for scientific facts, like how many sperm swim in the average ejaculate or what are the effects of anger on sexual arousal. They pose more complex questions: "How can you tell love from lust?" "Can a sexless marriage be psychologically healthy?" These seem to be factual questions, but they're not. No amount of survey or laboratory research can ever define love or lust or generate advice on making the distinction. These are moral questions, questions about the right and wrong way to live a sexual life.

To answer such questions, columnists are forced to go beyond documented knowledge. They fall back on the very kinds of responses the questioner thinks are being avoided by a professional consultation: religious doctrine, personal experience, hearsay, cliche, speculation. Moreover, because advice columnists rarely disclose (and I bet would be hard pressed even to articulate) their own personal values, neither the source of their authority nor the legitimacy of their wisdom is clear. Those columnists who truly educate raise more questions than they answer. They recommend study, introspection, patience, and discussion with friends and family about these ambiguous, insoluble life dilemmas.

Unfortunately, newspaper editors have a powerful preference for peppy and pithy prose, for simple and action-oriented solutions, for an upbeat attitude. The columnist is continually told that no one wants to read complex, tedious, turgid, convoluted analyses of the psychological, social, economic, historical, blah, blah, blah of human misery.

In *Miss Lonelyhearts*, the columnist resolved these pressures by stepping out of the pages of his newspaper into the real-life sexual trauma of one of his correspondents. Predictably, he died in the process. Somehow that seems not quite the right approach. Too grandstandy; too short-term! And yet, dispensing snappy Chinese fortune cookie slogans and teary homilies on the power of love seems to fall far short of what is needed, too.

As I brooded over the "desperate for advice" sixteen-year-olds, or the "too embarrassed to ask my doctor" sixty-year-olds, I kept asking, "Why do you all write this stuff to me, a total stranger? Isn't there anyone in your real life you can count on for advice or instruction or consolation?" It dawned on me that the real misery in some people's lives lay not in their official "problems" but in the fact that they had no one close by whom they trusted or respected enough to ask for help.

Maybe advice columns could address this unspoken dilemma. For a change they could sing the praises of kitchen conversations and downplay authoritative deliverances. Maybe they could even reach out and help to create neighborhood networks among their readers.

It's not that I want to eliminate the advice column business, not at all. It's just that dialogue is needed to help the people at their wits' end who send in these handwringing letters, and dialogue is what the columns can't provide. When correspondents see columns merely as one of several sources of ideas, they and their letters will be less desperate. We in the business will be able to write our trenchant little essays that entertain and inform as they encourage people to think for themselves. And I, for one, will sleep a lot better.

PART THREE

# Feminism and Sexuality

*I* can't imagine what I would have been thinking about for the past
twenty-five years if there had not been a women's liberation movement.
Would I have just plugged along, using my training in physiological
psychology to continue studying hormones and rat copulatory behavior
as I had done in graduate school? Many people do begin and continue
academic careers in just such a way, but such was not my fate. As the essays
in this section demonstrate, I became a critic within sexology rather than
simply a placid practitioner. I had no sooner gotten a lab of my own than I
began to question the very purpose of lab research within sexology, and
soon afterward I turned my back on that kind of work for good. Once I
realized that sexuality was a social construction, I was a changed person.

It was feminism that more and more showed me the incompleteness of
the sexology paradigm. With the hindsight of these twenty-five years, I can
now see that by even having an academic career in sexology I was taking
part in the same large political shifts that produced intellectual feminism.
The same irreversible processes of gender change that created intellectual
feminism—which so affected the content of my professional work—gave
me the independence to go to graduate school (and, though divorced, to
finish!) and to pursue a career in teaching and research. Everything is
connected.

Feminist theory has come a long way in twenty-five years, and I continue
to read the new literature avidly. Intellectual feminism is all of a piece, and
I have had exciting insights about sexology while attending conferences
such as the triennial Berkshire conference on the history of women or
while reading books like Jeffords's (1989) feminist analysis of the Vietnam
war. It's more and more evident that we are a gender-schematic society
(Bem, 1993, 1981) that is overprepared to use gender to explain behavior.
This predilection is exceptionally evident in sexology, and I have worked
hard these years to reveal the consequences: obscured situational and
structural factors, overemphasized biological causes with implied
unchangeability, and overemphasized genital components of sexuality. I
have often tried to suggest that gender could be a dependent variable in
our research, not just an independent variable, but I've yet to see this idea
catch on.

The articles in this section were all originally written as speeches, in the
heat of some moment and the midst of some argument. Seeing my work as
part of a struggle with ideological opponents has characterized my
professional outlook. In addition to the usual professional attitude—the
belief that I have certain insights and knowledge to share by virtue of
my training and professional experiences—I have often felt an activist's
call to challenge some of the shibboleths prevailing in my fields of
expertise.

This zeal, of course, has come from being a feminist first and a psychologist/sexologist second. There are real injustices and oppressions in the world, and I've never been absolutely certain that being a "professional" is compatible with trying to end these oppressions. So much of professional life seems to be involved with income, status, and hierarchy. But from the moment in 1972 when I first began reading feminist literature, I have known with certainty that being a feminist has meant to promote human betterment, and whatever I have been able to do to advance feminism has seemed to me worthwhile.

I have tried to apply the insights of feminism within sexology and have been greatly supported in this work by colleagues in the Association for Women in Psychology (AWP), a feminist group founded in 1969 (and that I found in 1977). I have often presented one or another of the papers in this section to a sexologist audience and gotten a wary and dubious response. "Gee, some of those ideas are really interesting, Leonore, but is it necessary to be so ideological/strident/militant/repetitious/angry?" But when I would present the same ideas at an AWP meeting, or to other feminists, I got affirmation and encouragement. I learned to see how academics preserve the political status quo by resisting any really challenging intellectual analysis. The first chapter in this section tells the story of the very first time I met that resistance, back in 1976. That experience set the tone for the years to follow.

# 9

# An Activist in Sexology

This award recognizes not only me, but my ideas, a notion that terrifies me a little, since my ideas are fundamentally iconoclastic.[1] What does it mean when a critic, an outsider, gets recognition?

I've received considerable criticism over the years for being *political and ideological* about sexuality when I should have been *professional,* for somehow confusing what should be separate life departments, and I would like to take the opportunity of receiving this Kinsey award to ruminate a little about these issues.

## Becoming an Activist

I have discovered that I have the soul of an activist, a person committed to social change and the amelioration of social problems. The eldest child of leftist Jewish New Yorkers, it should have been obvious that I would grow up expecting to be involved in the struggle against injustice and oppression. The locale of struggle, the particular issues, these would depend on the social and personal vicissitudes of my life and times, but my background inescapably oriented me toward involvement in progressive issues.

I was on the University of California campus at Berkeley from 1963 to 1969 throughout the Free Speech Movement and the various antiwar campaigns, and I must tell you that *then* I didn't lift a finger. I felt agitated a lot; I went to rallies; I watched. I wanted to get involved. But I was frightened and alienated by mass events, no one I knew was involved, and I really didn't understand the politics. Despite my background, political reality really only began for me when the women's movement came along in the 1970s. I became an activist in Fort Collins, Colorado, where I had gone to teach psychology at Colorado State University after getting my Ph.D. from Berkeley in 1969.

As I look back, I realize that these were the questions that concerned me in the early 1970s: How do you maintain your commitment when it becomes clear that the struggle will not soon be over? How do you deal with disappointment and victory? How do you choose which issues to engage? How do you balance the mixed feelings that come with coalitions? How do you deal with the social marginalization of activism? Especially marginalizing was the fact that it seemed that very few people in my profession were active in political change movements and my colleagues often criticized my activities.

For years my feminist activism was separate from my "career" as a sexology researcher and teacher. Although I spent endless hours working for equal access to sports facilities for women students, founding town and campus feminist organizations, advocating gender equity in faculty salaries and promotions, developing a course in the psychology of women, and writing letters to newspapers protesting sexism in news stories and advertisements, I was at the same time publishing my research on prenatal hormones and mating behavior in the golden hamster and the rat and going to conferences listening to other papers on prenatal hormones and mating behavior in the golden hamster and the rat. And in the 1970s, although I noticed the sexist behavior of colleagues at these conferences, and I noticed the paucity of women scientists, I did not see the sexism in the paradigm or in the methods. And I did not see the racism at all.

Beginning with a publication in 1978 (just forget everything before then—for example, my first publication, in 1969, entitled "Mating Behavior of Male *Rattus norvegicus* in a Multiple-Female Exhaustion Test"!), I gradually became aware of how sex research is shaped by social and political values. The single most helpful factor in raising my consciousness about my profession was reading the growing literature in women's, ethnic, and gay and lesbian studies.

In 1982 I joined a biweekly seminar at the New York Institute for the Humanities called "Sex, Gender and Consumer Culture." It was full of politically active New York journalists and humanities professors trained to look at meaning and to disdain universals. The seminar had no other psychologists or health-domain types at all. Here were people who relished the links they made between intellectual theories and political context, the complete opposite of the "neutral, objective" stance I had been taught in my profession. Although I admit I was often over my head in that seminar, and for years I couldn't figure out how understanding Picasso in Barcelona or turn-of-the-century French postcards could help me understand sexuality in people's lives today, I gradually underwent a sea change in my perception of how sexual lives are shaped by sociohistorical context.

I began to blend politics with my profession when I volunteered to give a talk on "Changing Conceptions of Sex Roles: Impact on Sex Research" for my graduate school mentor Frank Beach's sixty-fifth birthday celebration in 1976. The theme of the celebration was "Sex Research: Where Are We Now, Where Are We Going?" I volunteered for two reasons. First, I was under the spell of the women's movement, which said, "Speak out!" Since I had been giving countless speeches in Fort Collins about equal pay and equal athletics and equal graduate admissions, I guess I thought I could somehow easily segue into a speech on equal sexology.

Second, I was having a sabbatical year at Bellevue Hospital in New York to learn about human sexuality. At Colorado State I had been assigned the task of teaching human sexuality because I knew a lot about the sexuality of hamsters and rats, and I had learned pretty fast that a background in comparative psychology was not an adequate preparation for teaching human sexuality. New York has more bookstores than Fort Collins, and I was doing a lot of reading that year. I was terrifically excited by one book I read—the first-ever collection of essays on feminist social science. The editorial introduction began:

> Everyone knows the story about the Emperor and his fine clothes. Although the townspeople persuaded themselves that the Emperor was elegantly costumed, a child, possessing an unspoiled vision, showed the citizenry that the Emperor was really naked. The story instructs us about one of our basic sociological premises: that reality is subject to social definition. The story also reminds us that collective delusions *can be undone* by introducing fresh perspectives. Movements of social liberation are like the story in this respect: *they make it possible for people to see the world in an enlarged perspective.* . . . In the last decade no social movement has had a more startling or consequential impact on the way people see and act in the world than the women's movement. (Millman and Kanter, 1975, p. vii, emphasis added)

In retrospect, I realize now that part of my motivation at Beach's sixty-fifth birthday party in giving a very provocative paper about feminism and sex research was anger—I wanted to show that the emperor birthday boy and all his buddies were naked, that is, intellectually. In this way, I now realize, I intended to get intellectual revenge for the sexist prejudice I had suffered during my years of graduate training. In addition, as any good clinician will point out, at the very same time I was attempting to win, through some sort of tour de force presentation, the intellectual recognition and approval denied to me by those sexist practices.

The paper criticized biological determinism and genital preoccupations in sex research, exposed the stereotyped assumptions about males and females that limited research designs, and called for more qualitative and subjective elements in sex research. Although my ability to make those arguments was pretty thin in 1976, it surprises me how well the general points have stood the test of time.

The paper was received with quite a lot of anger. People felt it was inappropriate to a birthday celebration to criticize the assumptions guiding the past fifty years of work of the guest of honor, and, of course, now I can see that they were right. Personal motives frequently incite social justice actions, and it neither justifies nor dismisses those actions to acknowledge the motives. People often look for motives of maladjustment in the work of social activists, and indeed, activists *are* maladjusted, "creatively maladjusted," as Martin Luther King, Jr., said. Indeed, if activists weren't maladjusted, they would be adjusted—adjusted to the status quo—and that is the whole point. But there is a time and a place for everything, even social justice, although it's hard sometimes in the heat of the struggle to understand that.

After the party and ceremonies, as I was preparing the chapter based on my talk for publication in the celebration volume, I received several letters from male colleagues suggesting I tone down the feminism. One colleague wrote: "Do you think you can modify your chapter to meet these criticisms? You obviously had something on your mind and you got it said. . . . But, I'm not sure that putting all your thoughts and speculations in the 'permanent record' is a good idea for you [or] for the point of view you champion" (Tiefer, 1992c). I opted not to change much of the speech for the published version (Tiefer, 1978), and in 1979 I received a Distinguished Publication Award from the Association for Women in Psychology for my chapter.

These two extremes have characterized reactions to my work ever since, up to 1993. Until now, my sexologist colleagues have persistently told me that although I had some interesting observations, basically I was too strident, too political, too angry, and too repetitious. In contrast, feminist audiences persistently embraced me, encouraged me, and thanked me for bringing a message about sexuality that they found illuminating and liberating. In all honesty, it's hard to say which reaction has been the greater source of motivation. After all, I am the daughter of a Communist whose passion in life was playing the stock market. I'm used to having my feet in very different camps, to having a fragmented identity, to reading disparate literatures always looking for syntheses. I have kept going to sexological meetings, and I have kept going to feminist meetings.

## A Midlife Crisis?

In 1991, I published a record seven papers, most of which were based on speeches I had been invited to give. Two things seemed to have happened. First, I found that I suddenly had a lot to say, and second, to my astonishment, I found that people in my field wanted to hear me. Why?

I had a lot to say partly because ethnic, gay and lesbian, and women's studies had provided fascinating material that I thought could be relevant to sexology and the study of human sexuality. I was particularly taken with the efforts of feminist writers to show how science constructs nature, rather than discovering it, and in particular how animal research is used to construct images of "human nature" that may not be in women's best interests (e.g., Haraway, 1991). The new *Journal of the History of Sexuality* (volume 1, 1990), dominated by gay, lesbian, and feminist scholars, has been making available dozens of fascinating examples of the varying construction of sexualities in the past. And ethnic minority intellectuals have been exposing the limitations of many academic concepts and categories that are blind to factors of race and class (e.g., hooks, 1984, 1989).

I also had a lot to say because I could tell a narrative of social construction, the story of the medicalization of male sexuality, from the inside (Tiefer, 1986a). This narrative gave my years of criticism of sexology's biological reductionism, phallocentrism, stereotyped gender assumptions, and context-stripped research a credibility that overcame, for the moment, the stigma of being an ideologue.

Also, sexologists have wanted to hear my kind of ideas recently because it's become so obvious that sex research is inexorably political. AIDS, abortion, pornography, homosexual rights, and child sexual abuse claims and counterclaims have put sex and sex research continually on the front page. Time has caught up with me in a funny way.

It seems quite possible, however, that my time in the sun may be brief. A recent analysis argues that the radical critique of science, as found over the past twenty-five years in *Science for the People,* has given birth and given way to professionalized sociological treatments of scientific knowledge in a newly reputable subspecialty in sociology (Martin, 1993). Even if many of my suggestions for transformation and reform are heeded, a similar fate may befall sexology if it continues to privilege its own survival rather than the improvement of people's sexual understanding and sexual lives. The transformation of sexology into a tool to fight oppression and injustice is still only a dim possibility far out on the horizon.

But, popular or not, I expect to continue to look for opportunities to move the struggle forward. Let me conclude by describing two I have recently taken. This past year I was able to participate in the National Institutes of Health (NIH) Consensus Development Conference on Impotence. This conference marked the first time the NIH chose a topic in sexuality (Tiefer, 1992a). *Impotence,* I believe, is a term essential to maintaining phallocentrism in sexology and therefore a term I agitate against wherever I can. Discussion of impotence converts problems of the penis into problems of the man, converts problems with sexual performance into weakness and lack of masculine control. Thus, a field devoted to the diagnosis and treatment of impotence supports the quest for phallic perfection—a quest that ignores women and women's sexual interests—recruiting enormous economic resources for this purpose.

I was invited to speak at the NIH conference about ethnic and cultural influences on impotence, an important topic, but one about which there is no research. Instead, I insisted on discussing nomenclature and partner issues, topics that weren't even on the schedule. I was determined to bring women into this "all boys' toys" situation. And I did make a difference, albeit a small one, in the final report of the NIH consensus panel. Activism extends not only to such participation but also to telling the story of the consensus conference, as I have at several meetings this year, to show how the social constructions of sexuality and gender actually proceed daily in minute ways.

## Conclusion

What can I abstract from this odyssey of an activist who happens to be a sexologist? It's important to view whatever subject you are interested in from many perspectives by reading, joining interdisciplinary seminars, and participating in out-of-venue activities. It's important to understand political reality and to see how the subject you are interested in fits into politics. Professions exist to perpetuate themselves, and any good they do must be effortfully worked into their mission. You need another place to stand in addition to just being a competent professional. If you are committed to social betterment, you must take action; analysis alone is insufficient. Unfortunately, it's never clear that a particular moment is the right one or that a particular action will make a difference, so you will have to take action without certain knowledge of its impact. Since challenging the status quo is likely to make you unpopular, make sure you have a political base of some sort to provide moral support when the going gets rough.

I said I would mention two opportunities I've recently taken to move the struggle forward. The second one is to put these ideas into speeches such as these. Is this again the manifestation of maladjusted motives? I feel that any venue is the right one to say that feminism is a struggle to eradicate the ideology of domination—the cultural basis of group oppression—(hooks, 1984, p. 25) and to remind anyone within the sound of my voice to extend their feminist thinking to contend with racism as well as sexism.

We live in a time of intensely competing sexual discourses, and sexuality is one of the arenas for struggle against oppression and injustice. There is really no way to be apolitical as a sexologist—every action supports some interests and opposes others. My message as I thank you for honoring me with this award is a call for you to choose your work with intentionality and to incorporate race and class analyses into your research and clinical efforts.

# 10

# Gender and Meaning
# in the Nomenclature
# of Sexual Dysfunctions

$M$ichel Foucault ([1976] 1978) argued that sexuality has been constructed over the past 150 years as "a domain susceptible to pathological processes and hence calling for therapeutic or normalizing interventions" (p. 68). How best can we understand today's constructions? One clue comes from Foucault, who suggested, "The history of sexuality must first be written from the viewpoint of *a history of discourses*" (p. 69, emphasis added). A fundamental task for feminists interested in sexuality is to read texts so as to *reveal and decode* their *gender meanings* and significances.

## APA's Diagnostic Manual
## as a Text of Gender Politics

The first edition of the *Diagnostic and Statistical Manual of Mental Disorders* was published by the American Psychiatric Association in 1952 (*DSM-I*); the second in 1968 (*DSM-II*); the third in 1980 (*DSM-III*), and the revised third (*DSM-III-R*) in 1987 (the fourth edition was just released in 1994). Remember "The Great Misdiagnosis Debate of 1985–1986" wherein feminists successfully agitated to keep new psychiatric inventions such as "self-defeating personality disorder" and "premenstrual phase dysphoria" out of the *DSM-III-R*? Why did we care so much? Simply because the *DSM* is the standard naming text of mental health and mental disorders used throughout the world. It has been translated into dozens of languages and is used everywhere as the authoritative reference to current psychiatric conceptualizations. As the *New York Times* said in covering the misdiagnosis debate, "The *Diagnostic and Statistical Manual of Mental Disorders* is the official standard by which psychiatric diagnoses are made. Diagnoses listed in the manual are generally recognized in the courts in making legal decisions, by hospitals and psychotherapists in keeping records and by insurance companies in reimbursing for treatment" (New psychiatric syndromes spur protest, 1985).

Add to that list researchers who want a standard language for classifying subjects and behaviors, and teachers, who often teach classification language uncritically as a straightforward description of reality, and you have extraordinary opportunities for social influence. Classification of behavior offers fertile terrain for social control at both the material and imaginative levels (Schneider and Gould, 1987). Classification is about *creating differences,* which seem inexorably, in our culture, to entail inequality and hierarchy (Rhode, 1990). Thus, classification sets into motion processes that often include intimidating and stigmatizing certain groups (Kitzinger, 1987), setting and enforcing norms, creating culturally dominant language and imagery, and not least, creating and shaping individual desires and needs. As revolutionaries have repeatedly pointed out, *naming is power.*

In an era in which gender meanings and relations are being examined, destabilized, and renegotiated on every social and personal front, feminists must analyze any text on health, sexuality, bodies, children, domestic life, work life, emotion, laws, power—on *any* domain or metaphor of social life—as being at least in part *about gender,* and therefore as a location to be scrutinized. Eternal vigilance is the price of feminism.

The *DSM,* because of its powerful social location and its relations to most of the elements identified above, can be read as a work *about gender.* The task of feminist psychologists, as Michelle Fine and Susan Gordon (1989) suggested, is first to "interrupt the discipline," that is, to demystify ideology, to disrupt and problematize the seeming neutrality of theory and practice, to open ideological choices.

## *DSM* Listings of Sexual Dysfunctions

The sexual dysfunction nomenclature has changed dramatically over the different editions of the *DSM.* In the first edition (1952), there is no list of sexual dysfunctions, only the statement that "Sex impotence, psychogenic, [appeared in previous taxonomies, along with other specific conditions, but] since these are symptomatic diagnoses, they will be classified under any of several diagnoses dependent upon the clinician's opinion as to the basis" (APA, 1952, p. 107). That is, sexual difficulties (and note that only one is included) were considered *symptoms* of psychiatric disorders, not disorders themselves.

The second edition (1968) mentions sexual problems under "Psychophysiologic Disorders," in a subcategory of "Psychophysiologic Genitourinary Disorders." The text states: "This diagnosis applies to genito-urinary disorders such as disturbances in menstruation and micturition, dyspareunia [pain during intercourse] and impotence in which emotional factors play a causative role" (APA, 1968, p. 47). Here we have two sexual problems mentioned, and again both relate to the performance of intercourse, but now they are a type of psychophysiologic disorder, that is, psychiatric disorders that express themselves through physical dysfunction.

By the third and revised third editions (APA, 1980 and 1987), the list and description of sexual dysfunctions occupied six entire pages. This expansion indicates both the dramatic changes that had occurred in conceptualizations of psychiatric disorders and the importance of sexual function in the contemporary period. The list of dysfunctions in the *DSM-III and DSM-III-R* editions is similar:[1]

| *DSM-III* (APA, 1980) | *DSM-III-R* (APA, 1987) |
|---|---|
| *Sexual Disorders, subcategory Sexual Dysfunctions* | |
| Inhibited sexual desire | Hypoactive sexual desire disorder |
| | Sexual aversion disorder |
| Inhibited sexual excitement | Female sexual arousal disorder |
| | Male erectile disorder |
| Inhibited female orgasm | Inhibited female orgasm |
| Inhibited male orgasm | Inhibited male orgasm |
| Premature ejaculation | Premature ejaculation |
| Functional dyspareunia | Dyspareunia |
| Functional vaginismus | Vaginismus |

## Parameters of Sexuality in the *DSM*

In both editions, the description of each dysfunction is lengthy and technical, but the details disclose the subtext of sexuality as viewed by the psychiatric establishment. The definition of a dysfunction implies that sexuality is *universal and innate*. Since 1980 the definition of a sexual dysfunction has been as follows: "The essential feature of this subclass is inhibition in the appetitive or psychophysiologic changes that characterize the complete sexual response cycle" (APA, 1980, p. 290). Notice that it is "the" changes that characterize "the" complete cycle. Sexual abnormality is deviation from a fixed sequence (essentially desire, arousal, and orgasm). Although nothing is specifically mentioned about instinct, sections of the text clearly imply that sexuality is a sequence of universally encoded biological reactions of male or female body parts that are set into motion by "adequate" stimulation (e.g., "female arousal disorder" is defined as "failure to attain or maintain the lubrication-swelling response").

Second, sexuality consists of reactions of *body parts*. Despite the bodily emphasis throughout the terminology, the body as a whole has no meaning but instead has become a collection of disconnected physical parts. This compartmentalization lends itself to mechanistic images, to framing sexuality as the smooth operation of complex components, and to seeing sexual problems as calling for high-technology evaluation and repair. Much of the mystification of the *DSM* conceptualization of sexuality derives from this segmented physiologizing, and the implication is that only those who know a lot about tissues and organs can understand sexuality. In descriptions of the sexual dysfunctions, body parts and functions are either self-evidently gendered, as in "outer third of vagina," or the terms *male* and *female* are prominently included, as in the definition of dyspareunia as "genital pain in either a male or a female." Through this language the *DSM* affirms the centrality of gender even amidst the fragmented body parts.

Third, sexuality in the *DSM* is obsessively *genitally focused*. Every one of the dysfunction categories except for sexual desire mentions genital organs in one way or another. When the genitals perform correctly, there is no sexual problem; when they don't, there is always a sexual problem. Genitals, of course, remind us of generation, that is, procreation, and allusions to procreation inevitably connect sexuality to gender, reminding us of the necessary roles of biological male and female.

Fourth, the *DSM* validates *heterosexual intercourse* as the normative sexual activity, repeatedly describing dysfunctions as performance failures in coitus. *Sexuality, in the DSM, is heterosexual genital intercourse.* For example, *DSM-III-R* specifically points out that inhibited male orgasm "is restricted to an inability to reach orgasm in the [*sic*] vagina" (APA, 1987).

Gayle Rubin (1984) has argued that privileging heterosexual intercourse over other sexual activities establishes a scale in which "individuals whose behavior stands high in this hierarchy are rewarded with certified mental health" (p. 279). In addition, defining sexuality in terms of coitus associates sexuality with gender, since coitus is defined as an act occurring between a man and woman.

Thus, in at least four ways, the language of the *DSM* overtly and covertly speaks the language of gender and of the most biologically reductionist version. By using only the terms *males* and *females*, never *men* and *women*, the gender language fixes people in the world of animals and locates whatever governs sexuality in "the animal kingdom."

Although the changes are small, the 1987 revised version of the *DSM* is even more insistent than its 1980 predecessor in making sure the reader gets the gender message. There are five more mentions of *male* and *female* in 1987 than in 1980, for a total of fifteen rather than ten. No *women* appear in 1987 (there was one in 1980), but one additional *vagina*, and a new term, *penetration*.

*DSM* sexual dysfunction classification is laid out in a scrupulously gender-equal way. Men and women each have three dysfunctions. There is identical emphasis on difficulties with desire, arousal, orgasm, and pain. Yet, I would argue that the subtext of the *DSM* nomenclature rejects gender equality. The scrupulous insistence on males being males and females being females is of course the giveaway that we are not in the land of self-determination. But I am ahead of myself here.

## What's Omitted
## from the Classification?

By "reading back from the narrative to its excluded possibilities [in order to] comprehend its ideological operations" (Jeffords, 1989, p. 49), the *DSM* model of sexuality makes fundamental omissions that reveal it to be a deeply conservative document.

First, despite the scrupulous listing of women's sexual responses, which, by itself, could imply that women's sexuality is as important a concern to the *DSM* as is men's, *women's actual sexual voices are absent* from this conceptualization. The sexual concerns that women talk about, as we know these from popular surveys, questionnaire studies, political writings, and fiction, are absent here (Tiefer, 1988a).

There's nothing in the *DSM* about emotion or communication, whole-body experience, danger and taboo, commitment, attraction, sexual knowledge, safety, respect, feelings about bodies, breast cycles, pregnancy, contraception, or getting old. The only tiny reference to age is under "Inhibited *male* orgasm," where the clinician is reminded to take age into account. Pleasure is mentioned: A person has an arousal disorder if they don't have pleasure during sexual activity, but it's hardly highlighted. By making the choice to bypass the issues women have raised since anyone has been asking women to speak about sex, the *DSM* insults and dismisses women.

Second, the *DSM*, with its superficial gender equity based on sexual biology, denies women's social reality, that is, *gender inequality*. Women, lacking equal opportunity for sexual freedom, lacking equal encouragement to experiment, burdened with a poorer physical self-image and a weakened bargaining position in their intimate relationships, more often traumatized by past sexual exploitation, and far more often harassed by insecure reproductive rights and a limited window of sexual attractiveness, come to sexual opportunities severely disadvantaged compared to men. To speak of "a normal sexual excitement phase" as being determined by "activity that the clinician judges to be adequate in focus, intensity and duration" trivializes women's sociosexual reality and, by omission, perpetuates sexual patriarchy. The biological emphasis in the *DSM* that strips sexuality of its social context is a trick played on women, who need to understand social context as much as organs and tissues in order to steer a course for their sexual lives.

## Conclusion

On careful examination, we see that the *DSM-III* and even more the *DSM-III-R* are hardly neutral in the contemporary struggle over the construction of sexuality. Men's interests thrive in this discourse, and women's are secondary. John Gagnon has argued for the past twenty years that gender training and experiences during development result in fundamental gender differences in adult sexual scripts and responses (see Gagnon, 1979). Men's experiences in adolescence with genital arousal and orgasm, in conjunction with homosocial competitiveness and identification, create expectations and conditioning that bias men toward a goal-oriented, genital, self-focused sexual style. Masculinity depends on sexuality for its enactment (Jeffords, 1989). Put it all together and you get the heterosexualized and male-defined sexuality represented in "the" human sexual response cycle model of the *DSM*. Looking closely at this text reveals that nomenclature is a subtle agent of patriarchy.

This insight is not new. Some feminists have argued that throughout the twentieth century sexologists have played a consistent and significant role in indoctrinating women to adjust to men's sexuality. In "Sexology and the Universalization of Male Sexuality (from Ellis to Kinsey and Masters and Johnson)," Margaret Jackson (1984) argued that the role of sexology all along has been to normalize and universalize "the coital imperative" and the "primacy of penetration" in order to undermine women's resistance to compulsory heterosexuality. Similarly, Mariana Valverde (1987) argued that sexologists' role as marriage reformers in the twentieth century led them to insist that women, like men, have sexual needs and desires and that, conveniently, women's sexual needs and desires were just like men's, albeit a bit slower. Janice Irvine (1990), in her recent extended analysis of the history of sexology in the United States, likewise argued that sexologists' primary concern has been for their own professional status and legitimacy and that this emphasis has required strategies and alliances that have time and again co-opted any interests they may have had in women's self-determination.

So, it seems that the *DSM*'s choice to argue that anatomy is destiny once again limits women. Just because orgasm is in there doesn't mean this is a prowoman document. The construction of gender in the official psychiatric sexuality nomenclature is easily summarized: Men and women are the same, and they're all men.

# *11*

# Deconstructing
# Prefeminist Sexuality Research

## Why Deconstruct
## Prefeminist Sexuality Research?

*E*xamining prefeminist scholarship has both political and scholarly purposes. We can reinforce our commitment to feminism by showing how current scholarship is an improvement upon past work because it tells a richer and more complete story. By creating categories of prefeminist and feminist research, we can more easily identify important characteristics of contemporary feminist scholarship, which can in turn feed back to our political goals. For the purpose of this chapter, I will identify feminist sexuality research as *research on sexuality that is of, by, and for women's interests.*

Since *feminist* is a political term, introducing it as a modifier of *research* immediately draws attention to the claim that *scientific research is a social activity* undertaken in a *particular* sociocultural context and shaped by ideologies. Because the social construction of sexuality is always a crucial site for the negotiation of gender, analyzing sexuality will always illuminate processes of gender construction. As a feminist psychologist, I am drawn to this analysis because scientific research in the twentieth century plays a central role in the generation and enforcement of gender ideology. As Rachel Hare-Mustin and Jeanne Marecek (1990) have pointed out, constructing gender is a complex and multifaceted process requiring much imagination and hard work and employing untold numbers in every sector of society. Researchers and other intellectuals in the twentieth century are indispensable in creating the language and knowledge claims that maintain gender ideology.

Barbara Ehrenreich and Deidre English (1978) described scientists as the twentieth-century high priests entrusted with divining the laws of nature and showed all too well how scientists have interpreted nature's message to serve men's ends. To see clearly how science has worked for men is the first step in getting science to work for women.

# Conventional Reading
## of Prefeminist Sexuality Research

How would sex researchers describe their field and its history in the twentieth century? Most researchers, particularly younger ones, seem largely uninterested in history. Published papers indicate that they see scientific history as the gradual accumulation of facts amid shifting popularities of theories and areas of emphasis. Actually, most researchers seem to have very short memories and cite in their papers only a few recent publications that gave rise to their studies and that they critique for incompleteness or poor methodology.

In her 1973 presidential address to the American Psychological Association, Leona Tyler drew attention to this trend, pointing out that the choice of research projects had come to depend more on "such things as the availability of a new technique or instrument, the recognition of an unanswered question in a report of previous research, a suggestion from a friend or advisor, or just the fact that a federal program has made grant funds available" (p. 1025) than on commitment to a research issue because of any theoretical or humanitarian potential.

In sex research, the consequence of this nose-to-the-ground attitude has been the independent development of different subareas. A recent compilation of fifteen different theoretical approaches to sexuality edited by James Geer and William O'Donohue (1987) begins:

> The 20th century has witnessed the ascendancy of scholarly interest in human sexuality. This inquiry is by no means monolithic. Rather, a number of distinct, but as we will argue, largely compatible and logically independent scholarly approaches to human sexuality have developed within traditional academic disciplines. . . . Each discipline involved in the study of sex can be uniquely characterized by a particular set of questions about sex it is concerned with, and by particular methodologies it uses to investigate these questions. . . . For example, one can ask questions concerning how certain external stimuli modify an individual's sexual behavior, or how societal structures influence sexual functioning, or in what ways do cognitions influence sexual arousal, etc. . . . Strong cases can be made that these questions, and others, are all legitimate questions concerning sex. (Geer and O'Donohue, 1987, pp. vii, 3)

In other words, the conventional reading of prefeminist sexuality research is dominated by professionalism, a sort of parallel play wherein different disciplines carve out distinct methods and perspectives and each advances knowledge in its own ways.

One chapter in this collection, "A Feminist/Political Approach" by Catharine MacKinnon (1987), argues that a feminist approach views sexuality as "a construct of male power—defined by men, forced on women, and constitutive in the meaning of gender" (p. 67). That is, MacKinnon argues that the feminist approach begins with definition: "What is taken to be 'sexuality,' what sex means and what is meant by sex, when, how and by whom and with what consequences to whom, is the issue" (p. 69). The editors had no trouble with MacKinnon's challenge because sexuality research is long used to acknowledging and then ignoring definitional problems. The editor of one influential collection repeatedly drew attention to the "terminological confusion that characterizes the professional discourse on sexuality" (Katchadourian, 1979, p. 8) and noted, "One of the more serious handicaps facing the scientific study of sex is the lack of consensus among researchers in providing a clear and concise statement as to what, precisely, constitutes sexual behavior" (p. 35). Yet this problem had never seemed to pose insurmountable difficulties because each discipline defined sexuality for itself and ignored the others.

Perhaps this laissez-faire attitude resulted from sex researchers' bonding in the face of their many shared difficulties: ridicule and suspicion from the public and often even from professional colleagues, difficulty obtaining research money and subjects, limitations on research designs, and inability to easily observe the most interesting aspects of the subject matter. So, the conventional reading of prefeminist sex research portrays a potpourri of efforts from many different academic specialties loosely tied together by an undefinable but mutually assumed subject matter. Most researchers were largely ignorant of the field's history and were preoccupied with appropriate disciplinary methods and the shared experience of stigmatized status.

## Deconstructive Reading
## of Prefeminist Sexuality Research

How might a deconstructive reading of this same subject matter look? I remind the reader that deconstructing a text involves developing interpretive perspectives in addition to, or in opposition to, the prevailing one and that deconstruction often seeks to expose and destabilize covert (often dominant) ideologies.

Geer and O'Donohue (1987) allowed for the peaceful coexistence of many theories. They pointed out:

> There are several issues that appear with some regularity across chapters. This was not the result of planning on our part; but, rather, the cross-chapter commonalities reflect the fact that contemporary scholars view certain issues as central to understanding human sexuality. ... The two most obvious repeated themes are (a) the relative contribution of biological versus experiential variables, and (b) the nature and source of sex differences. (Geer and O'Donohue, 1987, p. 17)

This simple statement is like a bomb blast to a feminist. Each and every apparently separate little sex research compartment has been preoccupied with—what?—with sex differences. But have these studies been working toward women's liberation? Toward understanding how gender hierarchy is produced or maintained? Or, rather, have they been contributing to and justifying inequality by uncritically studying how women are different from men, especially when difference can be based on biology?

By focusing on this common theme, Geer and O'Donohue thus locate sex research as another of the many battlegrounds for the negotiation of gender relations in our time, and to the feminist it looks like this politically "unconscious" sex research has been used to develop beliefs and values that support male supremacy.

## Specific Themes in
## American Prefeminist Sexuality Research

### *Funding and Paradigms*

Let me illustrate these assertions with some digressions into sex research history. Historians Vern Bullough (1985) and Katherine Davis (1988) have examined the role of Rockefeller money in funding sex research in the United States. Following his experience on a New York City grand jury, and apparently also because of his son-in-law's experiences as a psychoanalytic patient, John D. Rockefeller, Jr., became interested in the sex reform issues of his day, venereal disease and prostitution. His first step, in 1913, was to facilitate the merger of a prominent public health organization with the nation's largest social purity organization. He then proceeded to support the new organization's many studies of prostitution. Research results were used to support progressive campaigns against red light districts, for prophylactics, and for limited sex education.

In 1921, Rockefeller underwrote a conference of noted medical researchers to discuss possibilities for human sexuality research. The conference had been rejected by several research groups unwilling to discuss sexuality even if money was available for it (how things have changed!). The 1921 conference advocated the formation of a Committee for Research in Problems of Sex, which Rockefeller continued to fund until the controversy surrounding Kinsey's second book in 1953 got too uncomfortable. That was about thirty years, 585 investigators, and $3 million later (Bullough, 1985). As Bullough put it, "One result of such funding was the establishment of a kind of dominant group in sex research, namely those with access to the funds supplied by the Committee for Sex Research, [a] 'sex establishment'" (p. 118).

But, and finally here's the point, until Kinsey began publishing in the late 1940s, this "establishment" supported, with these hundreds of researchers, almost exclusively biologically oriented studies on nonhuman species. The reason cited by Bullough is that human sex research was too controversial, but I would suggest that nonhuman sex research maintained its support because it was consistent with a particular naturalizing vision of sexuality.

The paradigm was sexuality as operationally defined by nonhuman animals' mating patterns: mounting, intromission, lordosis, ear-wiggling, and so on. My major professor in graduate school, the late noted comparative psychologist Frank Beach, repeatedly received these Rockefeller-funded committee grants to study the mating patterns and biology of small mammals from the late 1930s on. In the tradition of acknowledging but not worrying about definitions, which we can now see disguises gender politics, Beach began his second book in 1951 as follows:

> Although the phrase 'sexual behavior' is part of our common vocabulary, it is likely to mean different things to different people. As used in this book, the term refers exclusively to behavior involving stimulation and excitation of the sexual organs. Since heterosexual coitus, i.e., intercourse between a male and a female, is the means whereby the species is perpetuated, copulation between the sexes is taken as the core of our book. (Ford and Beach, 1951, p. 2)

The Rockefeller-funded group of sex researchers, which dominated the field, located sexuality as a product of human evolution, and their research elaborated concepts, methods, and metaphors with which to understand this sexuality. Need I point out that sexuality defined as evolutionarily driven, that is, as fundamentally organized for species reproduction, does not usually lead to women's sexual autonomy or self-determination? This particular meaning is most often related to systems of social regulation that enforce gender stratification and a sexual double standard (D'Emilio and Freedman, 1988). Thus we begin to see some of the ways that prefeminist sexuality research funding and paradigms maintained sexism and heterosexism.

### Paradigms and Methodolatry

Work based on the evolutionary paradigm of sexual behavior and the research that followed helped to legitimize a stigmatized business. Sexologists' preoccupation with the social peculiarities of their work was not an illusion—far from it. Public discourse about sexuality in our country seems to provide a permanent opportunity for conflict and intensity. The study of animal sexual patterns in the prefeminist era helped legitimize sex research and researchers because it seemed so objective and neutral and its methods and hypotheses seemed so removed from the political panics always attending human sexual issues. In fact, in her recent history of sexology in the United States, sociologist Janice Irvine (1990) saw biological sex research as providing *the* key to legitimacy for sexology.

I propose that an equally important strategy for legitimation has been the emphasis on methodological purity itself, regardless of topic area. With the same intense and magical identification with "hard science" as psychologists (Morawski, 1989), sexologists have persistently focused on proper methods as the royal road to success. In his 1981 presidential address to the Society for the Scientific Study of Sex, sociologist Ira Reiss drew the familiar line between "values" and "objectivity" as he repeatedly invoked a vague celebration of "science": "One reason it is crucial to have a sharp image of what is primary scientific research and theory is that such a conception can help in keeping out personal ideologies which may pose as scientific conclusions. . . . Values transform sexual science into an ideology and hinder those who wish to improve our scientific understanding" (Reiss, 1982). In the May 1990 issue of the same society's journal, the editor was still complaining about the neglect and stigmatization of sexology and still proposing the same solution:

> The academic community has generally regarded human sexuality and rigorous science as mutually exclusive endeavors. For example, how many tenured professors at major universities in the United States devote their research energies to human sexual behavior? . . . How many governmental agencies set aside funds to support basic research on human sexual behavior? How many sexual science programs exist? . . . Unfortunately, although sexuality is a vital part of human existence, it is an intrusive subject, usually relegated to poetry and fiction. . . . Furthermore, the study of human sexuality also raises emotional and ethical complications. . . . It is the purpose of the present paper to reaffirm the necessity of a rigorous sexual science. (Abramson, 1990, pp. 149–150)

Why this repeated call for rigor, which turns out to celebrate empirical data, explanation and prediction, measurement, reliability, and so on? Why the familiar call for "sexual data which can be measured or observed, with the added assumption that such data are capable of valid and reliable assessment" (Abramson, 1990, p. 153)?

I think it's no accident that this particular call for rigor is the first article in issue number 2 of the 1990 volume of *The Journal of Sex Research*. Issue number 1 of the 1990 volume was the first issue in the history of the journal devoted to feminist perspectives. It included a paper with quotations from focus groups of black women, a paper of excerpts from ten years of a lesbian magazine, a paper comparing information and imagery in biographies of two women artists authored by men and women, and a paper reproducing photographs of women's breasts from a collection owned by the Metropolitan Museum of Art. In the introduction to the issue, the editors wrote, "Feminist scholarship . . . can [no longer] afford to promote a concept of sexual science based on a narrow reading of science" (Vance and Pollis, 1990, p. 3). Can it be that methodolatry, that is, all that stuff about reliability and measurement, is mostly rhetoric to maintain the prefeminist status quo?

A recent example of this gatekeeping function is the role sexologists played in the furor over the publication of one of Shere Hite's (1987) books. From *Time* magazine's cover story of October 12, 1987, entitled "Are Women Fed Up? A Hotly Disputed Hite Report Says Yes—and that Men Are to Blame," to sober *New York Times* articles like "Hite's New Book is Under Rising Attack" (November 13, 1987, p. B4), "sexperts" were marshaled to attack the "inadequate," "badly flawed," and "appalling" methodology of Hite's research. The *Times* even got an Ann Arbor sociologist to condemn it as "the functional equivalent of malpractice for surveys."

What was all the fuss about? Why did anyone care *what* methods Shere Hite used? The litmus test of rigor was hauled out for Shere Hite because her book was *of, by, and for women's interests,* it challenged sexism and heterosexism, and it therefore mobilized the resistance of the sexological "establishment." In this case, the invocation of methodological purity was a brushfire to distract attention from content and usefulness.

Recall Leona Tyler's complaint about the irrelevance of most contemporary research despite its methodological success. Was Hite's book irrelevant? It got people thinking about the negotiation of gender in our time. Will all these wished-for research funds and sexual science programs and full professorships help women more? Where's the litmus test of beneficence to match the litmus test of rigor?

# Conclusion

Prefeminist sex research, despite its catholic claims to diversity and peaceful coexistence, can be deconstructed as a monolithic professional culture devoted to obtaining and maintaining academic respectability through methodological conformity. Sex differences and biological bases were the main topics of research, disguising persistent sexism and heterosexism. Fortunately, the women's revolution created a space and network of support for deviant sexology, and a critical mass of this work is beginning to influence the long-dominant "establishment." Recontextualizing sexuality, looking for new sets of voices, and making the results of our work usable, will be the tasks occupying feminist sexuality researchers for some time to come.

# 12

# The Feminist Revolution and Sexuality

## Recurrent Feminisms

When a new women's liberation movement began in the late 1960s, many participants thought something brand new was happening, that things were being seen and said that had never been seen or said before. The situation of women and the reasons for it seemed all silence and invisibility before. Suddenly, there was sound, the sound of women talking and marching and typing manifestos.

In retrospect, this sense of revelation seems not only naive but disrespectful toward our foremothers who supposedly swallowed all those lies about women's nature and meekly accepted their place in the world. It reflects a very grandiose idea that *we* were suddenly able to figure it all out for the first time. Well, our foremothers might not have had typewriters, but many times throughout history women have rediscovered themselves as an oppressed group, have recognized inequality and injustice based on gender, have named their oppression, and *voila*: women's uprisings. Myth, legend, and what written documentation exists show us that even when sex differences seemed ordained and irresistible, meek acceptance of women's lot has rarely been the order of the day in any culture.

As Robin Morgan (1984) wrote in *Sisterhood Is Global*, "An indigenous feminism has been present in every culture in the world and in every period of history since the suppression of women began. . . . It will be difficult for anyone to finish [*Sisterhood Is Global*] and ever again believe that feminism is a geographically narrow, imported, or even for that matter recent, phenomenon, anywhere" (p. 5).

Because of the unprecedented resources for research and communication available to women during this current uprising, perhaps this time we will finally understand *why* this is the world's longest revolution and be able to clarify the situation of women well enough that even if we don't achieve all our goals, at least history will not forget this phase of struggle.

## Tensions Within Feminism

Feminism means the fight on behalf of women as a class so that women will not be treated as a class. But *why* are women a class, and what is the best way to end the second-class status? Current scholarship identifies two incompatible but ever-present themes within feminism that lead to different answers to these questions. Various authors have identified the themes as the tendencies toward *maximizing* versus *minimizing* (Snitow, 1989).

The maximizing tendency within feminism seeks to deepen, empower, and maximize women's commonality by emphasizing women's culture (history, psychology) and women's unique experiences. It offers the *celebration* of what women have in common as opposed to patriarchal denigration, deprecation, or invisibility. It offers the rehabilitation and honoring of femininity. Its proponents argue that the (universalized) female body and bodily experience provide substantial input to consciousness and identity. Biology is valued as the source of women's power and women's bonds of motherhood are held to provide an enduring source of collective strength and insight. Above all, maximizers insist that women and men are different and always will be different and that the way for women to achieve political and social power is to celebrate women's unique contribution and voice.

Maximizers point to international women's peace activities—the power of women to mobilize around compassion as a way to settle group differences—as an example of this contribution. From the women who conducted antinuclear protests in Greenham Common in England to the Israeli women in black who resist the Israeli response to the Intifada with a weekly silent vigil proclaiming "End the Occupation" to the South and Central American mothers of the disappeared who demand human rights reform, examples abound to support the maximizers' claim that women bonding together as women can make change.

This maximizing emphasis on permanent differences should not be confused with the old gender stereotypes. This new celebration of women's commonality emphasizes that women's priorities can reverse the world's inexorable march toward military and environmental destruction. In some maximizers' writings, gender difference still equals hierarchy, but this time women's vision is praised and promoted as superior. In other writings, difference does not necessarily lead to hierarchy but eventually to mutual respect and coexistence.

The minimizing tendency within feminism is the more familiar women's liberation argument that the *dissolution* of gender stereotypes is a necessary condition for social liberation and peace. Minimizers take the position that observed differences between the genders are *not* inevitable but reflect persistent and internalized structural inequality. They argue that gender is a social construction with content quite different in different historical periods and cultural settings but always serving symbolically as a means for society to deal with human difference. Minimizer feminists believe that human differences based on biological or apparent biological groupings can wither away as a basis for social organization and be replaced by more individually oriented criteria for classification.

At one time, the minimization argument was ascendant in the women's movement, but I have gone into this division at some length because *both* views are now strong strands within feminism. The two themes will be apparent throughout my discussion about sexuality and will make it impossible to describe simply the feminist relation to any particular aspect of sexuality. For example, with regard to sexual violence against women, maximizers argue that male and female sexuality are fundamentally different because of both biology and early gender identity development and that objectification and aggression arise from male needs for psychological individuation and for sex as a fundamentally physical experience. Minimizers argue that sexual violence against women is a symptom, like other forms of sexism and misogyny, of a society where women are devalued and become targets for abuse.

It is well, however, to remember that the differences among feminists pale in comparison with the differences between those committed to the elimination of oppression against women and those committed to maintaining the traditional status quo in families, work settings, education, religion, and sexuality. Differences among feminists do not prevent coalitions on most important political issues, such as the need for more women in public office, the need for men to be more involved in childrearing, and the need for more acceptance of homosexuality.

## Sexuality

Sexuality is a complex modern construct that does not lend itself to a simple definition, and feminists have contributed to the current disputes over the various definitions of sexuality. Because feminists believe that *naming* is an expression of power, they see epistemology, or the study of the nature of knowledge, that is, how we know what things "really" are, as an important area of feminist scholarship. It's not "just semantics" to try to decide what sexuality is.

For example, do we want to construe sexuality as something *inside* a person, part of a person's identity? That is, does sexuality exist independently of a relationship, or is it something that emerges *in* a relationship embedded in a culture and a historical period? The two perspectives implied by these questions have very different consequences—in terms of clinical diagnosis and therapy, for example—and feminists attend to the ways in which different professions can promote or retard women's interests by their choice of language and emphasis.

The current professional diagnostic nomenclature for sexuality, for example, developed by the American Psychiatric Association (1987), lists as dysfunctions such matters as absence of sexual desire, inability to become aroused despite adequate stimulation, and difficulties with orgasm. This classification is based on the idea of an inborn and universal biological sexuality mechanism, the Masters and Johnson sexual response cycle, as the essence of sexuality. Proper functioning of this cycle is the definition of normal sexuality.

But this model is too narrow and does not promote women's interests in the real world, given what we know about women's relationships and status. "Health," if it is to have any meaning at all for sexuality, must include something about women's autonomy and knowledge, not just a collection of smoothly functioning anatomical parts. In discussing paraphilias—that is, habits of arousal to nonnormative objects or situations (voyeurism, exhibitionism, sadism, fetishism, transvestism)—again the psychiatric literature usually locates arousal as something *in the person*. Although it is claimed paraphilias interfere with reciprocal activity, there is no affirmative discussion of egalitarian relationships.

A feminist vision of sexuality, recognizing the importance of social context for facilitating or limiting women's experience, would focus on sexuality as it occurs within cultures and relationships. What women need is not more "official" rules for how to be "normal" but the recognition that women's sexuality in the past has been contained by patriarchal structures. To break from this past, women need professional support for diverse forms of expression (Tiefer, 1988a).

## Feminists and Women's Sexuality

Politically, contemporary feminists agree that sexuality is of the utmost importance, and indeed, sexual demands have been present since the beginning of the current uprising (Echols, 1989; Coote and Campbell, 1987). Even the best-known slogan of the movement, "The personal is political," is often thought to refer primarily to bringing sexuality, the most secret, hidden, and "personal" aspect of life, out into the open and exposing it as a major domain for the deployment and exercise of domination.

Sexuality is important, feminists argue, because *norms* regarding "proper" and "normal" sexual behavior function everywhere to socialize and control women's behavior. In traditional society, female fertility and thus sexuality are prime socioeconomic and political assets, and they are controlled by men through direct exercises of power and through extensions of men's familial control into every social institution, especially religion (Paige and Paige, 1981; Robinson, 1984). By contrast, in modern society there is *nominal* sexual equality because women are seen as sexual beings in their own right, not as sexual property.

Nevertheless, despite this nominal sexual equality the exercise of women's sexual choices continues to be constrained by many factors, including persistent socioeconomic inequality that makes women dependent on men and therefore sexually subordinate; unequal laws such as those regarding age of consent or rights in same-sex relationships; lack of secure reproductive rights; poor self-image or a narrow window of confidence because of ideals of female attractiveness; ignorance of woman-centered erotic technique; social norms about partner choice; and traumatic scars from sexual abuse.

One consequence of these restrictions is that we cannot say with any confidence what women's sexuality would be if it were not so restricted. This vacuum of knowledge has provided the opportunity for both minimizers and maximizers to rush in with their theories. So, for example, we have maximizer theorists (often called "cultural feminists," e.g., Echols, 1984) claiming that female sexuality, if free to develop and express itself without patriarchal constraint, would be nurturant, tender, egalitarian, sensual, and committed. Minimizer theorists usually claim agnosticism regarding female sexuality in a nonsexist world, although they suspect there would be much diversity, not only among women but even within one woman's life (Cartledge and Ryan, 1983; Valverde, 1987).

Women's sexual freedom and women's sexual victimization have both been more closely analyzed and more visible in recent years than ever before. In the first phase of the new wave of feminism, perhaps 1966–1974, feminists wrote at length about the need to transform erotic experience and relations. The emphasis on the clitoris as women's primary sexual organ was going to lead to massive sexual rechoreography and new status for the erotic potential of lesbianism. Masturbation for girls would become as expected and universal as for boys and lead to repertoires of sexual fantasy. Women would separate sexuality from reproduction as men did. Sexuality education would focus not just on plumbing but on the politics of pleasure and of relationships. Though "patriarchy" as a global and multifaceted process of repression was credited with brainwashing women to sexual subordination and ignorance, consciousness-raising, education, female-centered health care, and so on would all banish shame and passivity and women would discover or develop new sexual realities.

For a while there was a thrilling sense of new possibilities. But in the late 1970s and throughout the 1980s, the pendulum within feminist writings swung away from an emphasis on the power of self-definition to an emphasis on the immensity of sexual violence against women by rape, harassment, incest, and battery. Commercial pornography, once celebrated as a source of fantasy and female experimentation (not to mention employment) began to be seen by some feminists as the representation, and then even the cause, of sexual oppression against women. Despite the fact that many feminists continue to support explicit sexual imagery as offering more positive opportunity than harm for women (Ellis et al., 1988; Russ, 1985; Burstyn, 1985; Valverde, 1989), the public usually hears only the voices of feminists fighting pornography. The length of time female sexual freedom and pleasure were the main topic was brief as compared with the emphasis on victimization, danger, and repression. There has also been much attention to the international aspects of sexual victimization. Some feminists emphasize the need for greater prostitutes' rights and less stigmatization, whereas others militate for further action against "sex workers."

It is no surprise and far from a hopeless situation that there are disputes among feminists regarding the causes of sexual oppression and conflicts regarding strategy for overcoming oppression. When was there ever a revolution without factions? In the long run, the success of the revolution to change women's sexual lives probably depends less on whether feminists are unified in their analyses than on how well feminists can respond to larger sociocultural developments.

## Conclusion

There are many ways to be part of the feminist revolution; it is not monolithic. Whether the minimizers or the maximizers are ascendant at any particular time is important, but feminists must not lose sight of the practical fact that the movement is about ideas only insofar as they can improve women's material and social conditions. Movements for reform threaten to become movements of professionals who lecture to each other while real people's real lives are not improved. Those of us interested in feminism and sexuality must conscientiously monitor how our work improves the quality of life that women enjoy. As our world continues to shrink and societies become more pluralistic, the task will require broader levels of feminist analysis, but most of all the ability to take the time, sit down, and really listen to what women have to say.

# 13

# Feminisms and Pornographies

Since the early 1980s, there has been great and growing conflict within feminism about the importance of pornography as an issue, about strategy and tactics to deal with the issue, and even about the meaning of pornography—or pornographies, for there are many varieties.

Let me try to illuminate this conflict by first of all laying out some history and then by discussing some underlying conflicts within feminism that I think are responsible for this split over pornography. My belief, a suspicion before I began this chapter and a conviction by the time I finished it, is that this conflict is deep and important. Politically, I fear that alliances have been formed on the basis of simplistic and visceral reactions to what are complex issues. I think that both the antipornography feminists and the anticensorship feminists have made valuable contributions, and maybe my comments can go part of the way toward, if not a reconciliation, at least greater mutual appreciation and respect.

## Feminism Against Pornography

### Phase I: Theoretical Writings

Negative feminist interest in pornography arose in conjunction with the feminist analysis of rape in the 1970s. The initial blast may have been Robin Morgan's 1974 article, "Theory and Practice: Pornography and Rape." Morgan wrote: "The act of rape is merely the expression of the standard, 'healthy' even encouraged male fantasy in patriarchal culture, that of aggressive sex. And the articulation of that fantasy into a billion-dollar industry is pornography. . . . Pornography is sexist propaganda—no more, no less. Pornography is the theory: rape is the practice" (pp. 137, 139).

Morgan decided not to consider erotic art as pornography and explicitly rejected censorship as a tactic ("I'm aware that a phallocentric culture is more likely to begin its censorship purges with books on pelvic examination for women, or books containing lyrical paeans to lesbianism, than with 'See Him Tear and Kill Her'" [Morgan, 1974, p. 137]). Many feminists who agreed with her initial formulation of the connection between pornography and sexual violence against women, however, do not now support her in these details.

Major credit for providing the theoretical juice to this argument connecting rape and pornography must go to Susan Brownmiller's (1975) best-seller, *Against Our Will: Men, Women, and Rape*. This watershed book contains twelve chapters of unforgettable detail on the history and culture of rape, beginning with the conspicuous absence of "Thou shalt not rape" from the Ten Commandments and going through rape in the service of racism, war, manifest destiny, gang fights, cultural practices for obtaining or subduing a wife, and punishment for deviants.

In the final chapter, "Women Fight Back," Brownmiller discussed many of the goals raised by feminists in the struggle: eliminating testimony in rape trials about the victim's past sexual life, getting across the idea that it is rape unless women "consent" to sexual intercourse, getting rid of the red herring of false accusation, getting legislation passed to ban marital rape, gathering better statistics, mandating more expeditious and sensitive court proceedings, convincing police departments to hire more women police officers, and so on.

But Brownmiller argued that a new approach to the law and to law enforcement could take us only part of the way:

> The ideology of rape is aided by more than a system of lenient laws that serve to protect offenders. ... The theory of aggressive male domination over women as a natural right is so deeply imbedded in our cultural value system that all recent attempts to expose it—in movies, television commercials or even in children's textbooks—have barely managed to scratch the surface. As I see it, the problem is not that polarized role playing (man as doer; woman as bystander) and exaggerated portrayals of the female body as passive sex object are simply "demeaning" to women's dignity and self-conception, or that such portrayals fail to provide positive role models for young girls, but that cultural sexism is a conscious form of female degradation designed to boost the male ego by offering "proof" of his native superiority (and of female inferiority) everywhere he looks. ... The case against pornography [is] central to the fight against rape. ... Once we accept as basic truth that rape is not a crime of irrational, impulsive, uncontrollable lust, but is a deliberate, hostile, violent act of degradation and possession on the part of a would-be conqueror, designed to intimidate and inspire fear, we must look toward those elements in our culture that promote and propagandize these attitudes, which offer men, and in particular, impressionable, adolescent males, who form the potential raping population, the ideology and psychologic encouragement to commit their acts of aggression *without awareness, for the most part, that they have committed a*

*punishable crime,* let alone a moral wrong. (Brownmiller, 1975, pp. 389–391, emphasis in original)

Brownmiller argued that women's discomfort when viewing pornography comes from feeling degraded and humiliated, feelings that men need women to have to bolster their own masculine self-esteem. She went on to mourn that the same liberals who recognized the propagandistic power of Hitler's Nazi machines, or who saw through the antiblack messages of the shuffling servants in Hollywood productions, defended pornography as a valid extension of freedom of speech and denied that it was powerful antifemale propaganda.

Brownmiller's use of this analogy has been criticized by those who feel the importance thus accorded to pornography is vastly exaggerated and applauded by those who feel women's oppression has too often taken a back seat to the oppression of others. Brownmiller's (1975) book set the stage for a powerful feminist campaign against pornography as an, or perhaps *the,* essential symbol of misogynist culture and patriarchal philosophy.

## Phase II: Formation of Protest Groups, Rallies, and Marches

In the late 1970s, numerous grassroots feminist groups resisting violence against women emerged, building on the growth of antirape work earlier in the decade. These included Women Against Pornography (WAP), Women Against Violence Against Women, Feminists Fighting Pornography, and the Women's Alliance Against Pornography.

Large "Take Back the Night" marches, which were (and still are) held annually across the country to protest rape and promote women's safety, provided an opportunity for raising consciousness, arousing anger, and enlisting feminists who would be willing to leaflet, picket, develop slide shows and lectures, and even commit acts of violence against property. Beginning in the early 1980s, the focus of the marches shifted from being against sexual violence (rape, sexual abuse of children, and incest) to first including protests against pornography and prostitution and then to being almost entirely against pornography.

The National Organization for Women (NOW) got involved in the effort to raise consciousness about pornography and define the terms of the debate. In 1984, as a result of intensive lobbying by members of WAP, NOW passed a resolution stating, "Pornography is a factor in creating and maintaining sex as a basis for discrimination, and that pornography, as distinct from erotica, is a systematic practice of exploitation and subordination based on sex which differentially harms women and children through dehumanization, sexual exploitation, forced sex, forced prostitution, physical injury, and social and sexual terrorism presented as entertainment." In some ways, 1984 represented the highwater mark for the feminist antipornography movement. But I shall review one more development before looking at the change in the tide.

## Phase III: Shift from Public
## Demonstrations to Legal Activity

In the early 1980s the rhetoric about pornography began to expand and escalate. The prolific author Andrea Dworkin, longtime feminist activist, became the major feminist theorist in the antipornography camp. In the introduction to her first book, *Woman Hating* (1974), she discussed the need for "political action where revolution is the goal" (p. 17). She asserted that what was needed was not "academic horseshit" but "a planetary movement [committed] to ending male dominance as the fundamental psychological, political, and cultural reality of earth-lived life" (p. 17). The book contained a section on pornography that suggested that, like advertising and fairy tales, pornography teaches women to be subservient and defined by others. However, Dworkin was able to find some redeeming merit in the European pornographic newspaper *Suck*. She pointed out, "The emphasis on sucking cunt serves to demystify cunt in a spectacular way—cunt is not dirty, not terrifying, not smelly and foul. It is a source of pleasure, a beautiful part of female physiology to be seen, touched, tasted" (p. 79).

But by 1981, in *Pornography: Men Possessing Women,* Dworkin was unambiguously aggrieved: "Male power is the raison d'etre of porn; the degradation of the female is the means of achieving this power" (p. 25). By 1983, in *Right-Wing Women,* she was saying that pornography is "at the heart of the female condition. . . . One cannot be a feminist and support pornography. . . . [Any defense of it is] anti-feminist contempt for women" (pp. 223, 227).

Dworkin justified her attitude in lengthy discussions of the objectification and dehumanization of women in pornography and the functions for men and patriarchal society that are served. She especially emphasized the way pornography consolidates the male as an active seer and definer and the female as a passive object only important for parts of life and not for full human agency and autonomy. The female is defined by others, not self-defined.

The other major figure in this phase is a feminist lawyer, Catharine MacKinnon, author of an influential 1979 book, *Sexual Harassment of Working Women.* It defined sexual harassment as sex discrimination and described in detail its reality in the American workplace. By 1982, she, like Dworkin, was explicitly and theoretically focused on sexuality as the central issue for feminism. Not sexuality as discussed in the early 1970s, where a positive focus on getting equal pleasure in bed and equal rights in society was a central issue for feminism, but a new, critical focus locating women's oppression in the reality and the ideology of sexuality.

MacKinnon began an influential 1982 article, "Feminism, Marxism, Method, and the State: An Agenda for Theory," with a memorable analogy: "Sexuality is to feminism what work is to marxism: that which is most one's own, yet most taken away" (p. 515). Later in the article, she asserted that "feminism fundamentally identifies sexuality as the primary social sphere of male power" (p. 529) as shown by feminist work on abortion, birth control, sterilization abuse, domestic battery, rape, incest, lesbianism, sexual harassment, prostitution, female sexual slavery, and pornography. She wrote:

> The defining theme [in each of those issues] is male pursuit of control over women's sexuality. . . . Rape, incest, sexual harassment, pornography and prostitution are not primarily abuses of physical force, violence, authority or economics. They are abuses of sex. . . . Sexuality is the linchpin of gender equality. . . . Without a change in the very norms of sexuality, the liberation of women is a meaningless goal. . . . Sexual objectification is the primary process of the subjection of women. (MacKinnon, 1982, pp. 532–534, 541)

Here, MacKinnon reversed the familiar feminist formulation of the 1970s, "Rape is violence, not sex." Quite the opposite, she asserted, "Rape is sex, not violence." When discussing rape or incest, she argued, it makes no sense to determine whether the woman consented or not. How can women give consent to sex in a society constituted to oppress women?

This line of thinking is hard to understand for those not used to radical feminist thinking (Jaggar, 1983). Most of us are more familiar with liberal feminist thinking, where sexism results from stereotyped socialization and lack of equal rights. Or we might even be familiar with socialist feminist thinking, where sex discrimination is perpetuated because it serves important economic purposes. But radical feminist thinking starts from the premise that *patriarchy* is the problem; that having had men in control since time immemorial means that everything is designed to keep men in control. Radical feminism takes as its assumption that institutions, language, and customs are the way they are because they are better for men that way and posits that for things to improve, women need to challenge literally everything.

It's no surprise, then, that radical antipornography feminists advocate extreme legal solutions for problems such as violence against women. In 1983, MacKinnon invited Dworkin to participate in her course on pornography at the University of Minnesota Law School. The city council of Minneapolis hired the two of them to draft some antipornography legislation. There had been many antipornography efforts in the past, involving zoning or prohibiting ownership or manufacture, but Dworkin and MacKinnon tried a new approach.

They devised an antipornography ordinance to be part of the human rights ordinance already in force. It would define pornography and specific activities involving pornography. As with other provisions of the ordinance (e.g., equal opportunity in housing and employment), the legislation gave aggrieved citizens the right to sue ordinance violators in civil court for both punitive and compensatory damages. The important innovation about this approach to pornography legislation was that it did not make any of the acts penal code crimes but rather created a system of civil violations that gave women and others a right to sue for damages they could prove were caused by pornography.

In the draft legislation, pornography was defined as follows:

Pornography is the graphic sexually explicit subordination of women through pictures and/or words that also includes one or more of the following: (i) women are presented dehumanized as sexual objects, things or commodities; (ii) women are presented as sexual objects who enjoy pain or humiliation; (iii) women are presented as sexual objects who experience sexual pleasure in being raped; (iv) women are presented as sexual objects tied up or cut up or mutilated or physically bruised or physically hurt; (v) women are presented in postures of sexual submission, servility or display; (vi) women's body parts are exhibited such that women are reduced to those parts; (vii) women are presented as whores by nature; (viii) women are presented as being penetrated by objects or animals; (ix) women are presented in scenarios of degradation, injury, torture, shown as filthy or inferior, bleeding, bruised, or hurt in a context that makes these conditions sexual. (Dworkin and MacKinnon, 1988, p. 36)

The ordinance goes on to say that "it shall be sex discrimination" through pornography to:

1. "coerce, intimidate or fraudulently induce any person into performing for pornography" (Dworkin and MacKinnon, 1988, p. 41);
2. "produce, sell, exhibit, or distribute pornography, including through private clubs [trafficking]" (p. 44);
3. "force pornography on a person in any place of employment, education, home or public place" (p. 49);
4. "assault, attack or injure any person in a way that is directly caused by specific pornography" (p. 50).

This antipornography ordinance was defeated in Minneapolis, but it was passed in Indianapolis in 1984 and then defeated in Los Angeles; Suffolk County, New York; and Cambridge, Massachusetts. Its final legal test came in 1986, when a suit brought by the American Booksellers Association, the Association for American Publishers, an Indianapolis seller of videocassettes, and many others against the city of Indianapolis finally reached the U.S.

Supreme Court. *Mayor Hudnut v. the American Booksellers Association* had been held unconstitutional by the Seventh Circuit federal court. The Supreme Court affirmed this ruling in February 1986 without hearing any arguments on the basis that the ordinance violated the First Amendment right of free speech.

The language used by antipornography feminists in this ordinance may therefore no longer be legally viable (at least in the United States), but the language of "subordination, dehumanization and objectification" continue to thrive in much feminist writing.

## Feminists Against
## This Antipornography Approach

Barnard College in New York has had an annual "Scholar and the Feminist" conference with a different theme each year. The ninth conference, in 1982, was called "Towards a Politics of Sexuality." In the words of one organizer, "The conference attempted to explore the ambiguous and complex relationship between sexual pleasure and danger in women's lives and in feminist theory. The intent of conference planners was not to weaken the critique of danger. Rather, we wished to expand the analysis of pleasure" (Vance, 1984, p. 3).

The conference was designed to include feminists who were interested in including erotica in the feminist study of sexuality. In the days before the conference, a coalition of antipornography groups denounced the conference for inviting proponents of "antifeminist" sexuality to participate. The Barnard College administration was alerted and reacted by confiscating 1,500 copies of the conference program, which had many woman-made erotic images.

Following this conference, some feminists began meeting to organize an opposition to feminist antipornography, and, in 1984, the Feminist Anti-Censorship Task Force (FACT) was formed in New York during the time of the Suffolk County hearings on the Dworkin-MacKinnon ordinance. Eventually, there were several active FACT chapters around the country.

### Confusion of Pornography and Violence

Not all pornography is violent and degrading, and it is difficult to even agree on what fulfills those terms. Most pornography, as any cable TV or videocassette shop review will show, consists of sexual activities between consenting adults, emphasizing intercourse, oral sex, and lots of genital close-ups. Sadomasochistic (S&M) materials, which appear violent to those shocked or disgusted by the images, are actually a form of elaborate ritual to the participants rather than being literally violent or the cause of actual harm. Moreover, S&M materials are not as common as the slide shows prepared by Women Against Pornography groups allege.

If the target of the feminist campaign is violence against women, the question must be asked whether pornography is really the best place to try to make some headway against violence. Mainstream movies and TV are notorious for their violent imagery, and the claim that sexuality is the prime locus for violence against women ignores these genres entirely.

As feminists we might ask why sexuality and pornography need to be included at all. If what we are interested in eliminating is the subordination of women, why does it have to be sexually explicit material that we target? Servility, injury, enjoying pain—why do they get banned only if they involve sex? The honest political answer is that no one is about to ban violent images in this country—they are too mainstream. Only sexual images are sufficiently offensive to large diverse groups, and targeting seemingly violent sexual images would be the only way for feminists to get widespread public support. But the consequence of picking on sexual images is that sexuality itself becomes the target. This result is a major setback for those groups within the women's movement whose goal is to de-repress women's sexuality. Dworkin and MacKinnon's claim that sexuality is the prime and fundamental sphere for male power is not proven. Other feminists have claimed that the core location of female oppression is family structure and kinship systems, government and the rule of law, the division of labor, private property, or religion. The assertion that pornography is a cause rather than a symptom is a dangerous sleight of hand if it deflects attention from other causes.

### Images and Their Meaning:
### The Voices of Sex Workers

Assuming that one can know the meaning conveyed by an image merely from looking at it is simpleminded. In the Dworkin-MacKinnon ordinance, for example, the fifth element of the definition objects to women presented in postures of sexual display. How can we say that such images are inevitably degrading or humiliating? There can be many woman-made and prowoman images like this. Do all such images boost men's self-esteem by subjugating women? It seems dangerously simplistic to read universals of empowerment or subjugation from images. The relationship between personal, subjective fantasy and imagery is subtle and idiosyncratic, as we know from our own lives, from art, and from psychology. People interpret images from contexts of previous experience, and what each of us makes of images is certainly not generalizable.

Finally, women who are photographed or filmed in the making of pornography do not report that their work is inevitably harmful. Prostitute unions have repeatedly called for the decriminalization of prostitution so that working conditions and safety can be increased. They reject any approach that stigmatizes them further.

# The Popularity of Opposition to Pornography

There are many reasons why feminist opposition to pornography has been so popular. First, much pornography *is* sexist and conveys disrespect for women. Women's interests have not been considered, and accuracy about women's sexuality has not been a priority. As women become consumers and producers of pornography owing to the increased popularity of home video, however, it is likely that women will be able to influence the content through economic means.

Even without one iota of feminist support, pornography is already highly stigmatized in U.S. society. Most people are uncomfortable with the explicit and unfamiliar images. For most people it's a source of shame, not esteem, to say that they like or use pornography; it implies that one's sexuality is inadequate or abnormal. The stigma of pornography makes it easy for people to accept false statements about it. People cannot admit to more accurate knowledge of what is contained in pornography if they are not supposed to know at all. Even the words *obscene* and *pornographic* are often used to apply to things that are disliked or that disgust us, and people become used to the negative connotation.

## Phase IV: Attorney General Meese's Commission on Pornography

As the debate between feminists was heating up (competing tables at NOW conferences, counterattacking articles), pornography became an issue on the larger political stage and, incidentally, created another arena for the competing feminist positions. As part of his overall conservative agenda against sexual liberalism, President Reagan authorized the formation of an investigatory commission. Ever since the first Presidential Commission on Obscenity and Pornography had recommended the removal of barriers to pornography in 1970, political conservatives had been waiting for an opportunity to replace that report and its influence with one more to their liking.

Attorney General Edwin Meese announced an eleven-member investigatory commission in May 1985. Several commissioners had long histories as enforcers of antipornography legislation. The mandate of the commission was "to determine the nature, extent, and impact on society of pornography in the United States and to make specific recommendations to the Attorney General concerning more effective ways in which the spread of pornography could be contained" (Attorney General's Commission on Pornography, 1986, p. 1957). The commission held public hearings in Washington, Chicago, Houston, Los Angeles, Miami, and New York City. Hearings focused on the law, law enforcement, and First Amendment constraints; behavioral sciences; the production, distribution, and marketing industries; child pornography; and organized crime and its relation to trafficking.

Members of Women Against Pornography testified in Washington, Houston, New York, and Chicago, and their testimony is quoted at length in many sections of the commission's final report (Attorney General's Commission on Pornography, 1986). Andrea Dworkin's entire testimony in New York is reprinted (pp. 769–772). Two or three members of FACT testified, but other than an occasional phrase like "this point is disputed, but" with a footnote, there is no reference to a different feminist point of view in the report.

When the commission report, predictably critical of pornography and frequently using the feminist antipornography language, was released, Dworkin and MacKinnon held a press conference and released a statement which began, "For the first time in history, women have succeeded in convincing a national governmental body of a truth women have long known: pornography harms women and children." They went on to applaud the commission for endorsing the civil rights approach to legislation but then criticized it for recommending extension and escalated enforcement of obscenity laws.

In fact, the report recommended a repressive agenda for controlling sexual images and texts, vigorous enforcement of existing obscenity laws, and a variety of new measures that would surely lead to harassment of feminist bookstores, films, and art galleries more than they would target Times Square shops. They barely escaped recommending the outlawing of "any device designed or marketed primarily for the stimulation of human genital organs," that is, vibrators. The commission endorsed the types of citizen action groups that could well lead citizens to canvass local bookstores and newsstands with religious, parochial, or homophobic agendas in mind. Its conclusions may lead to a rash of local and state hearings and commissions where the language of *violent* and *degrading* will be used, in all probability still without accurate facts or a broad spectrum of feminist opinion.

## Conclusion

The 1985–1986 Meese Commission has passed, but violence against women goes on, along with the social and sexual oppression of women.

Feminist actions, strategies, and theories promoting women's sexual opportunities and well-being as they prevent women's endangerment are still much needed.

The feminist critics of the antiporn position emphasize that the focus on pornography trivializes real violence, distracts attention, drains activism from more fundamental legal, political, and economic issues, and fails to reduce violence against women. To win their battles, antipornography feminists ally with the antisexual conservatives and implicitly support agendas against women's sexual and reproductive rights. This alliance could result in poorer sex education opportunities for children and teenagers who need graphic information for their health and welfare. The antiabortion movement is gaining strength, and although the conservatives seem to be interested in feminist goals by using some of this "degrading" and "demeaning" rhetoric, there can be no confusion about the fundamental dissimilarity between conservatives and feminists.

The antipornography advocates have offered an analysis of sexual imagery that is simplistic but politically effective. Feminists who advocate greater sexual freedom for women need to develop their own analysis of sexual imagery that focuses on its power for freedom and for diverse growth. Such feminists need to understand, however, that women do face terrible danger in the world, much of it in conjunction with sexual activities, and until that danger is reduced by women's greater social and economic power, women seeking protection, and political groups capitalizing on women's fears, will find sexual freedom a convenient target.

# 14

# Some Harms to Women of Restrictions on Sexually Related Expression

*A*s a feminist and a psychologist specializing in research and clinical work on sexuality, I have concluded that *women are in more danger from the repression of sexually explicit materials than from their free expression.* If the vast range of items considered pornographic have anything in common, it is that they can be described as "sexually transgressive material." But because women's sexuality has been repressed, suppressed, and oppressed, what's needed is more transgressive opportunity, not less.

I want to justify this claim with five arguments and try to bring in some ideas about the current state of women's sexuality as I've learned about it through my experience in psychotherapy practice and work in several different medical centers. I have to begin with the usual disclaimers—that the people whose sexuality I know the best all come to me because they have complaints and dissatisfactions, and thus they probably do not reflect a cross-section of the culture. However, I have worked with a wide variety of patients, and although many of them have been Western, white, and middle class, I have also worked with many people of color, immigrants from Burma to Barbados, couples in their twenties and their seventies, and people raised in many different religions and ethnic groups.

The fundamental context of women's sexuality in our time is *ignorance and shame.* More than even fear, I would argue, women's experience is constructed and colored by ignorance and shame. And yet sexuality is given tremendous importance in terms of social norms. The societal message is that you *have* to be sexual, you have to *want* to be sexual, you have to be *good* at being sexual, and you have to be *normally* sexual. Yet there's no tradition of sexual coaching or intercourse training or masturbation training or honest feedback or places to go to get all your questions answered by a friendly expert. I and clinicians like me have become the friendly expert— which is ridiculous when you think about it in terms of cost, availability, and the medical model context of therapy.

I suspect that under managed care friendly sex therapy is not going to be included in the basic benefits package. That would be all right if there were better sex education or less social pressure to be sexual. So much of sex therapy is remedial sex education that should have occurred during childhood and adolescence. Too much of it is the untwisting of inhibitions that never should have gotten established in the first place.

In fact, a great deal of sex therapy focuses on expressing and undoing feelings of undesirableness, badness, and dirtiness. Many people are raised with the religious or cultural message that the feelings and pleasures of the body and mind are dangerous and dirty. Most women are ambivalent at best about their bodies throughout their lives. It's easy for politicians or the media to prey on the large variety of early negative feelings. And although anti-pornography arguments seem to rely on scientific research or moral principles, I often see just the projection of these internal feelings of shame and dirt that were taught at an early age.

## Women Need Power, Not Protection

Empowerment, not protection, is the route to women's sexual development. In May 1993 I read in the newspaper that on Mother's Day the Rev. Calvin Butts, pastor of the Abyssinian Baptist Church in New York, was going to show his respect for women by taking dozens of compact discs of rap songs that insult women into the street and running them over with a truck.

I think this is a silly and empty gesture, but unfortunately, it's a common gesture toward women. If Rev. Butts wants to increase the respect shown toward women, he needs to help increase the power held by women, not try to "protect" women from disrespect by riding in on a big truck (do I hear echoes of the knight in shining armor?) and whisking away the danger. He should preach that respecting women means giving women and men information and skill about safer sex practices to prevent HIV transmission. Better yet, he should go on a hunger strike to demand that the federal government research a female-controlled method of HIV virus-killing so women can protect themselves from AIDS. Women need to be able to protect themselves with information, power, and skill if they are to gain respect.

## Encourage Women's Tentative
## New Sexual Visions

If we accept that women's sexuality has been shaped by ignorance and shame and is just beginning to find new opportunities and voices for expression, then now is exactly the wrong time to even think about campaigns of suppression. Suppressing pornography will harm women struggling to develop their own sexualities: History teaches us that *any* crackdown on sexually explicit material always falls the hardest on experimental presses, alternative artists, small theaters, and the like. Little bookstores and individual galleries do not have the money for lawyers or the time to spend in endless legal disputes. Magazines will fold; performers will go hungry; sex educators, if any are left, will be too intimidated to teach more than the blandest facts of genital plumbing.

Criminalizing explicit sexual expressions will force erotic experimentation in art, video, books, and performances underground and deprive most women of access to unconventional inputs to their erotic imagination. Women will feel that old familiar shame when confronting anything but the most mainstream sexual concepts, and they will not be able to break out of their historic repression.

Now is the time for more sexual experimentation, not shame-soaked restraint. This experimentation should include freedom for new sexual science and art, new ideas about desire and pleasure, and new practices that will lead individuals, families, and couples away from the ruts worn by centuries of religious inhibition, fear of pregnancy and disease, and compulsory heterosexuality.

What is clear to the sex therapist and sex educator is that there will be no new options for sexual behavior or experience for women at all without open talk about sexual possibilities. And there will be no open sexual talk if every seedling effort is met by religious disapproval, talk-show or media ridicule, scientific neglect, or criticism from activist women.

Accusations that pornography harms women amount to a powerful form of backlash against new sexual forms. The consequence is a blanket of inhibition. I have often heard that inhibition in the form of defensive, reactionary voices almost whining, "Why do they need to do that? My husband and I have been getting along just fine for thirty-five years, and we would never do that!" This type of comment is a form of social control that prevents more experimental women from breaking out of historical limitations. Without freely available information, ideas, and images, women's sexual liberty is just a joke.

## Respect Sexual Imagination

A third harm to women from suppressing pornography is that it deprives people of learning more about the human imagination. The antiporn feminists argue that pornography is to be interpreted in a literal way—if it's a picture of a woman being fucked while lying across three tall stools in a coffee shop, it's a picture of an embarrassed, uncomfortable, and unhappy woman. But this isn't the way sexual fantasy actually works.

For example, I have a patient who came to me because she did not enjoy sex with her husband of six years. Every story is complicated, but to boil this down, some of the contributions to this state of affairs had to do with her strict religious upbringing of sexual shame and conflict, her compulsive and perfectionistic mental functioning learned from her immaculately clean hausfrau mother, her aversion toward her tyrannical father, and her obsession with her weight. Although she had chosen her husband for various good reasons, she did not find him sexually appealing. Most people who hear this description may think, "Good grief, this is truly hopeless," but in fact this combination of circumstances is not at all uncommon in women's lives given families, religion, and patterns of socialization for girls.

This woman had some sexual pleasure when she masturbated; however, this pleasure was diminished by her shame about the sexual fantasy she had developed. In the main part of this repetitious fantasy, she was the unhappy provider of sexual excitement to a group of seedy men in a seedy living room. She danced naked, encouraged them to undress, fondled them, and provided fellatio around the room. Although in the fantasy she was never excited, in real life she would get excited and masturbate to orgasm. This gave her a sense of pleasure and mastery but also feelings of shame and confusion.

This kind of story is more common than I can tell you and illustrates the paradoxes women often find themselves in today. Is it correct to interpret this woman's fantasy as the straightforward story of a degraded and humiliated and subjugated woman? No. Such a simplistic assessment does not accurately characterize the "meanings" of her fantasy. This woman felt aroused by the sexual power of her dancing and her power to arouse the seedy men. They were turned on; they wanted her. She felt desired and irresistible, and this feeling aroused her. Hers was a pretty sexually empowered fantasy, in its own way. The vicissitudes of her upbringing and this misogynist culture produced the more negative elements—the undesirable setting and partners and the lack of her own arousal in the fantasy. She couldn't feel entitled to openly enjoy sexual arousal, which was exactly what was going on with her husband.

Ellen Willis has pointed out that "women have learned, as a matter of survival, to be adept at shaping men's fantasies to their own purposes," and I think this patient's fantasy is a good example of this idea (Willis, 1988, p. 55). In another place and time, this woman and the vicissitudes of her life would have come up with a different way to deal with her sexual conflicts. Anyway, the point is that pornography is about fantasy and identification with characters in stories as symbols. It cannot really be understood just on a literal level. And if pornography is suppressed, women will not learn things about themselves and their imaginations that they can learn through experimenting with and reflecting upon their reactions to pornography.

## Don't Reject Women in Pornography

Opponents of pornography often argue that women in pornography are seriously harmed while doing the work and that eliminating pornography would help these women escape from abominable conditions. But the same argument has been made over and over again that eliminating prostitution would allow women to escape abominable conditions, when in fact prostitutes themselves repeatedly argue that what they want are safe and healthy working conditions, not further stigmatization.

Suppressing pornography and the production of sexual images will directly harm women who make their living in many sex industries, including models and sexual performers of various sorts. These women have appealed to feminists for support, not rejection. The more sex industry work is made antisocial and illegal, the more it goes underground and the more the women who work there are subject to abuse and oppression. Improved working conditions for these women will come from decriminalization, destigmatization, feminist support, and public pressure, not from being pushed underground and out of public sight. Sex industry workers, like all women, are striving for economic survival and a decent life, and if feminism means anything it means sisterhood and solidarity with these women who are also striving for self-determination.

## Masturbation, the Subtext of the Pornography Debate

Finally, and perhaps most important, suppressing explicit sexual materials will harm women by strengthening the power of the conservative religious lobbies. And since the goals of the religious right are incompatible with women's economic, spiritual, and reproductive freedoms, such influence must be resisted at all costs. Conservative religious groups have historically rejected pornography not because of "harm to women" but because of its connection to masturbation. In fact, the debate about pornography is in large part a debate about masturbation. I think the reason no one talks about *women's* use of pornography and *women's* interest in pornography has to do with discomfort with the idea of women masturbating. The "harm to women" argument arose from feminist theorizing and has been adopted as rhetoric by the religious right, but I do not believe that is where their real antipathy lies.

Another disclaimer is called for here. Whenever sexologists talk about sexual specifics it is assumed that we are talking in a normative way—this is good, this is bad, this is healthy, this is sick. So, in talking about masturbation, am I saying it is good or bad? Neither. Both. I really don't care! By talking about pornography and masturbation, I'm talking about sexual practices and what they are useful or not useful for.

Sexuality is an option in life, although one wouldn't think so to listen to many "experts" talk. If someone wants to have a long and lively sexual life— and believe me *I don't care* whether anyone does or does not want to, and I am making no recommendations—but a person who does want to needs to learn about sexuality and take time to practice. Masturbation is a form of learning and practice that is known in every culture. It's also a hobby, and like many hobbies it can be practiced frequently or rarely.

What always amazes me is people who want to have exciting and gratifying sex but who think it just comes "naturally" without practice or knowledge. I'm sorry, but no one can play Rachmaninoff without putting in a lot of piano practice! If someone just wants to have a little bit of sex in his or her life, or if the experience itself is not very important, then masturbation is of much less relevance or importance for that person. As a sexologist my goal is to discuss sexuality without choosing values, without endorsing particular acts or patterns.

For the religious right, however, sexuality is always a moral issue. Conservative religious organizations oppose women's autonomous sexuality and believe that sexuality is for procreation, for families, not for individual pleasure, identity, and exploration. Masturbation or individual sexuality is a threat to the vision of sexuality as the tie that binds a family. Ideally, the right wants to return to the years before the women's movement demanded and won the right to abortion, contraception, mandatory sex education, accessible day care, women's health centers, and so on. Picking on pornography to "protect" women attacks women's independence, and I propose that masturbation is an important subtext. Supporting women's sexuality requires supporting (though not mandating) women's masturbation and the availability of explicit sexual materials of all sorts.

## Conclusion

Shame and ignorance make cowards of us all, but now is no time for cowardice about women's sexual practices or imaginings. Censorship harms women because women need sexual empowerment, not sexual protection. Antiporn campaigns say that porn gives men power. But in fact, men already have power. Explicit sexual materials and performances can contribute to women's sexual power. People who do not like certain types of pornography can avoid them. Or better yet, they can create something completely new.

# PART FOUR

# Phallocentrism Redux

Working for the past ten years in hospital urology departments has given me a better window than I could have imagined into the social construction of sexuality. The medicalization of men's sexuality that I have witnessed may come to seem an obvious or inevitable development in the history of sexuality, but watching the piecemeal changes step by step, I have felt privileged and fascinated to see at close hand how such a development actually occurs. The changes did not appear at all inevitable at the time but rather resulted from steady pressure and effort exerted by various interest groups interacting with the public to create a particular set of sexual values, meanings, and practices.

There have been numerous times when I thought women and their interests might exert some influence, and it has repeatedly stunned me to see how little attention women are paid within this growing construction. That is why I've titled this section "Phallocentrism Redux." Although women's sexual "rights" were very much the topic of conversation in the 1970s and early 1980s, the penis seems now to have resumed its predominant role in sexual discourse. The medical management of men's sexuality has become a male preserve where masculinity is the name of the game and women are neither seen nor heard. Although satisfying women sexually is the alleged purpose of all the erectile research and repair, having an erection so men can feel equal to other men seems more what's "really" going on. I'll never forget the patient who, when asked why he wanted treatment for his erectile dysfunction, said, "So when I go into a bar I can feel as good as the other guys."

The human psychophysiological potential of sexuality can be adapted, as Foucault pointed out so well, to prevailing sociopolitical winds, and the job of the analyst is to identify and analyze those winds. In the case of the medicalization of male sexuality, the prevailing winds have to do with the economics and authority of contemporary medicine, the absence of competing discourses of sex as pleasure or hobby, and above all, gender politics as constituted and reflected in erotic relations.

# 15

# Sexism in Sex Therapy:
# Whose Idea Is "Sensate" Focus?

*A* feminist analysis of the patriarchal bias in sexology could do worse than begin with one of the fundamental elements of the new sex therapy: "sensate focus." In *Human Sexual Inadequacy*, Masters and Johnson (1970) introduced "sensate focus" as an important educational device:

> Sensate focus . . . was chosen to provide the sensory experience most easily and appropriately available to marital partners as a medium for physical exchange in reconstituting natural responsivity to sexual stimuli. . . . These 'exercises' are designed to free sexual dysfunctional individuals from inhibitions that deprive them of an opportunity to respond naturally to sensory experience. . . . Sensory awareness and its communication to another person can be extremely difficult for those who have not had the opportunity to develop sensate orientation gradually, under circumstances in which the experience was valued and encouraged, or at least not negated. . . . This educational process, as initiated in therapy by the sensate 'exercises,' permits gradual modification of negative reactions to sensory stimuli so that learning occurs. (Masters and Johnson, 1970, pp. 76, 77)

This argument for the importance of focusing on sensations during sexual relations sounds persuasive and even self-evident, and indeed "sensate focus" has continued to be a cardinal element of sex therapy while other aspects of Masters and Johnson's original design and rationale have been discarded.

But just *why* should *sensory* experience be the normative centerpiece of sexuality? Consider contrasting points of view expressed by participants in Shere Hite's research:

> Sex is important because during sex you can be as close as possible with another person.

> Sex is beautiful because such a complete contact with another person makes me feel my being is not solely confined to my own body.

137

Sex plays a very important part in my life because it is a symbol of the love I am sharing with my man. I know it is his way of showing that he loves me.

I become very emotionally involved in my sexual relations. I think I have sex almost always to consummate a bond, to develop and perpetuate closeness. (Hite, 1976, pp. 283–284)

These are quotes from people for whom emotional and not sensory focus is the centerpiece of sexual experience; it is no surprise that the quotes are from women. An emotional focus for sexual relations offers a dramatically contrasting point of view.

Ellen Frank, Carol Anderson, and Debra Rubinstein's (1978) study of 100 white couples with self-defined "successful marriages" found that 77 percent of the women reported sexual difficulties like "partner chooses inconvenient time, inability to relax, too little foreplay, too little tenderness." Their responses in this area correlated with overall ratings of sexual satisfaction. Hite's (1976) entire volume is dedicated to a "redefinition" of sexual relations wherein routine scripts of foreplay-to-intercourse-to-orgasm would be replaced or at least enhanced by more spontaneity, variety, verbal communication, fun, and tenderness. Such a redefinition requires appreciating the deep gender differences in sexual socialization in our society and rejecting the notion that sex-as-usual represents the interests of all men and women.

But the fact that *sex therapy* has remained sensate-focused shows that many women's interests are being bypassed. It would, it seems to me, take only a little imagination to design an alternate sex therapy stressing emotional homework assignments (heavy on loving communication, eye contact, expression of feelings, and the like). Alternate assessment instruments could be designed to evaluate a couple's emotional knowledge, comfort, and connectedness during sex instead of their satisfaction with the performance of various sexual acts.

Therapists' commitment to a sensate view of sexuality not only represents a choice about what sort of sexual experience is "real" or "best" but also assumes that all partners are already sensually adept or would be able to learn how to focus on sensation. This is part of the claim (I would say "myth") of universality and "naturalness" that is such a central element in the Masters and Johnson approach. Can such assumptions be made?

A minimum requirement for a sensate focus would seem to be a lack of competing or distracting thoughts. A person would have to feel comfortable, safe, and entitled in order to focus wholly on his or her tactile experience. Can we assume that most women can be thoroughly relaxed in sexual situations given the inequality of so many relationships, given women's concern with their appearance, given women's worries about safety and contraception? The fact that this question is ignored in *Human Sexual Inadequacy* and other sex therapy texts indicates how unimportant the social reality of women's lives is for most sex therapists. In the eyes of sex therapy, men's and women's interests are the same and they are focused "by nature" on sensory and physical experience and performance. This biological reductionism suggests that sex therapy is likely to be a patriarchal tool unless feminists intervene.

# *16*

# In Pursuit
# of the Perfect Penis:
# The Medicalization
# of Male Sexuality

$S$exual virility—the ability to fulfill the conjugal duty, the ability to procreate, sexual power, potency—is everywhere a requirement of the male role, and thus "impotence" is everywhere a matter of concern. Although the term has been used for centuries to refer specifically to partial or complete loss of erectile ability, the first definition in most dictionaries never mentions sex but refers to a general loss of vigor, strength, or power. Sex therapists, concerned about these demeaning connotations, have written about the stigmatizing impact of the label: "The word *impotent* is used to describe the man who does not get an erection, not just his penis. If a man is told by his doctor that he is impotent, and the man turns to his partner and says he is impotent, they are saying a lot more than that the penis cannot become erect" (Kelley, 1981, p. 126). Yet a recent survey of the psychological literature found that the frequency of articles with the term *impotence* in the title has increased dramatically since 1970. In contrast, *frigidity,* a term with equally pejorative connotations and comparable frequency of use from 1940 to 1970, has almost totally disappeared from the literature (Elliott, 1985).

In this chapter I would like to show how the persistence and increased use of the stigmatizing and stress-inducing label of *impotent* reflects a significant moment in the social construction of male sexuality. The factors that create this moment include the increasing importance of lifelong sexual activity in personal life, the insatiability of mass media for appropriate sexual topics, the expansionist needs of specialty medicine and new medical technology, and the highly demanding male sexual script. I will show how these factors interact to produce a medicalization of male sexuality and sexual impotence that limits many men even as it offers new options and hope to others. Let me begin with a discussion of men's sexuality and then discuss what medicine has recently had to offer it.

# Male Sexuality

Sexual competence is part—some would say the *central* part—of contemporary masculinity. This is true whether we are discussing the traditional man, the modern man, or even the "new" man:

> What so stokes male sexuality that clinicians are impressed by the force of it? Not libido, but rather the curious phenomenon by which sexuality consolidates and confirms gender. . . . An impotent man always feels that his masculinity, and not just his sexuality, is threatened. In men, gender appears to "lean" on sexuality . . . the need for sexual performance is so great. . . . In women, gender identity and self-worth can be consolidated by other means. (Person, 1980, pp. 619, 626)

John Gagnon and William Simon (1973) explained how, during adolescent masturbation, genital sexuality (i.e., erection and orgasm) acquires nonsexual motives—such as the desire for power, achievement, and peer approval—that have already become important during preadolescent gender role training. "The capacity for erection," they wrote, "is an important sign element of masculinity and control" (Gagnon and Simon, 1973, p. 62) without which a man is not a man. Allan Gross (1978) argued that by adulthood few men can accept other successful aspects of masculinity in lieu of adequate sexual performance.

Masculine sexuality assumes the ability for potent function, but the performances that earn acceptance and status often occur far from the bedroom. Observing behavior in a Yorkshire woolen mill, British sociologist Dennis Marsden described how working-class men engage in an endless performance of sexual stories, jokes, and routines: "As a topic on which most men could support a conversation and as a source of jokes, sexual talk and gesture were inexhaustible. In the machine noise a gesture suggestive of masturbation, intercourse, or homosexuality was enough to raise a conventional smile and re-establish a bond over distances too great for talking" (Marsden, quoted in Tolson, 1977, p. 60). Andrew Tolson argued that this type of ritualized sexual exchange validates working men's bond of masculinity in a situation that otherwise emasculates them and illustrates the enduring homosocial function of heterosexuality that develops from the adolescent experience (Gagnon and Simon, 1973).

Psychologically, then, male sexual performance may have as much or more to do with male gender role confirmation and homosocial status as with pleasure, intimacy, or tension release. This assessment may explain why men express so many rules concerning proper sexual performance: Their agenda relates not merely to personal or couple satisfaction but to acting "like a man" during intercourse in order to qualify for the title elsewhere, where it *really* counts.

I have drawn on the writings of several authorities to compile an outline of ten sexual beliefs to which many men subscribe (Doyle, 1983; Zilbergeld, 1978; LoPiccolo, 1978; LoPiccolo, 1985): (1) Men's sexual apparatus and needs are simple and straightforward, unlike women's; (2) most men are ready, willing, and eager for as much sex as they can get; (3) most men's sexual experiences approximate ecstatic explosiveness (the standard by which individual men compare their own experience, thus becoming disappointed over suspicions that they are not doing as well as others); (4) it is the responsibility of the man to teach and lead his partner to experience pleasure and orgasm(s); (5) sexual prowess is a serious, task-oriented business, no place for experimentation, unpredictability, or play; (6) women prefer intercourse, particularly "hard-driving" intercourse, to other sexual activities; (7) all really good and normal sex must end in intercourse; (8) any physical contact other than a light touch is meant as an invitation to foreplay and intercourse; (9) it is the responsibility of the man to satisfy both his partner and himself; (10) sexual prowess is never permanently earned; each time it must be reproven.

Many of these demands directly require—and all of them indirectly require—an erection. James Nelson (1985) pointed out that male sexuality is dominated by a genital focus in several ways: Sexuality is isolated from the rest of life as a unique experience with particular technical performance requirements; the subjective meaning for the man arises from genital sensations first practiced and familiar in adolescent masturbation and directly transferred without thought to the interpersonal situation; and the psychological meaning primarily depends on the confirmation of virility that comes from proper erection and ejaculation.

It is no surprise, then, that any difficulty in getting the penis to do what it "ought" can become a source of profound humiliation and despair, both in terms of the immediate blow to self-esteem and in terms of the eventual destruction of masculine reputation that is assumed will follow. Two contemporary observers expressed men's fears of impotence in these terms:

> Few sexual problems are as devastating to a man as his inability to achieve or sustain an erection long enough for successful sexual intercourse. For many men the idea of not being able to "get it up" is a fate worse than death. (Doyle, 1983, p. 205)

> What's the worst thing that can happen? I asked myself. The worst thing that can happen is that I take one of these hip, beautiful, liberated women to bed and I can't get it up. I can't get it up! You hear me? She tells a few of her friends. Soon around every corner there's someone laughing at my failure. (Parent, 1977, p. 15)

## Biomedical Approaches
## to Male Sexual Problems

Within the past decade, both professional and popular discussions about male sexuality have emphasized physical causes and treatments for sexual problems. There is greater awareness and acceptance within the medical profession of clinical and research work on sexuality, and sexually dissatisfied men are increasingly willing to discuss their problems with physicians (Bancroft, 1982). The professional literature on erection problems has focused on methods of differentiating between organic and nonorganic causes (LoPiccolo, 1985). Recent reviews survey endocrine, neurologic, medication-related, urologic, surgery-related, congenital, and vascular causes and contrast them with psychological and relationship causes (Krane, Siroky, and Goldstein, 1983).

Although the physiological contributions to adequate sexual functioning can be theoretically specified in some detail, there are as yet few diagnostic tests that enable specific identification of different types of pathophysiological contributions. Moreover, there are few medical treatments available for medically caused erectile disorders aside from changing medications (particularly in the case of hypertension) or correcting an underlying disease process. The most widely used medical approach is an extreme one: surgical implantation of a device into the penis to permit intromission. This is the penile prosthesis.[1]

The history of these devices is relatively short (Melman, 1978). Following unsuccessful attempts with bone and cartilage, the earliest synthetic implant (1948) consisted of a plastic tube placed in the middle of the penis of a patient who had had his urethra removed for other reasons. Today, several different manufacturers produce slightly different versions of two general types of implant.

One type is the "inflatable" prosthesis. Inflatable silicone cylinders are placed in the *corpora cavernosa* of the penis, the cylindrical bodies of erectile tissue that normally fill with blood during erection. The cylinders are connected to a pump placed in the scrotum that is connected to a small, saline-filled reservoir placed in the abdomen. Arnold Melman (1978) described how the prosthesis works: "When the patient desires a tumescent phallus, the bulb is squeezed five or six times and fluid is forced from the reservoir into the cylinder chambers. When a flaccid penis is wanted, a deflation valve is pressed and the fluid returns to the reservoir" (p. 278). The other type of prosthesis consists of a pair of semirigid rods, now made of silicone, with either bendable silver cores or hinges to allow concealment of the erection by bending the penis down or up against the body when the man is dressed.

Because these devices have been implanted primarily by private practitioners, the only way to estimate the number of implant operations conducted to date is from manufacturers' sales figures. However, many devices are sold that are not used. A French urologist estimated that 5,000 patients were given penile implants in 1977 alone (Subrini, 1980). It seems reasonable to guess that by the mid-1980s hundreds of thousands of men had received implants.

Needless to say, many articles have been written stressing the need to carefully evaluate men who might be candidates for the procedures. Surgeons are concerned to exclude

> patients at risk of becoming psychotic or suicidal, developing chronic psychogenic pain, or initiating inappropriate malpractice suits. . . . A second important concern has been to rule out patients whose erectile dysfunction is psychogenic and could be cured without surgery . . . although several urologists have reported high patient satisfaction when carefully selected patients with psychogenic dysfunction received penile prostheses. (Schover and von Eschenbach, 1985, p. 58)

Postimplant follow-up studies have typically been conducted by surgeons interested in operative complications and global measures of patient satisfaction (Sotile, 1979). Past reports have encouraged the belief that the devices function mechanically, that men and their partners are able to adjust to them without difficulty, and that the prostheses result in satisfactory sexual function and sensation. But recent papers challenge these simple conclusions. One review of the postoperative follow-up literature was so critical of methodological weaknesses (brief follow-up periods, rare interviews with patients' sexual partners, few objective data or even cross-validation of subjective questions about sexual functioning, among others) that the authors could not summarize the results in any meaningful way (Collins and Kinder, 1984). Another recent summary criticized the implants' effectiveness:

> First, recent reports indicate that the percentage of surgical and mechanical complications from such prosthetic implants is much higher than might be considered acceptable. Second, despite claims to the contrary by some surgeons, it appears likely that whatever degree of naturally occurring erection a man is capable of will be disrupted, and perhaps eliminated by the surgical procedures and scarring involved in prosthetic implants. Finally, it has been my experience that, although patients are typically rather eager to have a prosthesis implanted and report being very happy with it at short-term surgical follow-up, longer term behavioral assessment indicates poor sexual adjustment in some cases. (LoPiccolo, 1985, p. 222)

Three recent urological papers report high rates of postoperative infection and mechanical failure of the inflatable prosthesis, both of which necessitate removal of the device (Apte, Gregory, and Purcell, 1984; Joseph, Bruskewitz, and Benson, 1984; Fallon, Rosenberg, and Culp, 1984). The first paper reported that 43 percent of patients required at least one repeat surgery; the second found that 47 percent of 88 devices implanted since 1977 had malfunctioned; and the third reported that 48 percent of 95 patients had their prostheses malfunction in one way or another since 1977.

In perhaps the only paper reporting on the effectiveness of penile implants in gay men, a therapist who had worked with three such patients indicated that "the implants were less successful with homosexuals than with heterosexuals because there tends to be much more direct penile contact in gay sexuality than in heterosexual sexuality. The person with the implant is aware of the difference, not his partner" (Paff, 1985, p. 15). One of the patients had to have the implant removed because of a mechanical malfunction.

## Public Information
## About Penile Prostheses

Public sexual information is dominated by health and medical science in both language and substance. Newspapers present "new" discoveries. Magazines have "experts" with advanced health degrees outline "new" norms and ways to achieve them. Television and radio talk-show guests, also health-degreed "experts," promote their latest books or therapeutic approaches as "resources" are flashed on the screen or mentioned by the host. Sexuality is presented as a life problem—like buying a house, having a good relationship, dealing with career choices—and the "modern" approach is to be rational, orderly, careful, thorough, up-to-date, and in tune with the latest expert pronouncements.

The public accepts the assumption that scientific discoveries help enable people to manage and control their own lives and welcomes new biomedical developments in areas perceived to be matters of health and illness. Sexual physiology has a tangibility that "love" and "lust" lack and thus seems more suitable to people as a language for public discourse. When biomedicine, health, and physiology are considered the appropriate sexual discourse, scientists and health-care providers are the appropriate authorities.

The media have presented information about penile prostheses in the same straightforward, rational, scientific, informative way as they have presented other "news" about sexuality. An early article in the *New York Times* (Brody, 1979), for example, presented the findings of a urological paper that had appeared in the *Journal of the American Medical Association* the day before. But not only was the science discussed, the article also gave the address of the prosthesis manufacturer as well as typical financial cost, length of hospital stay, and insurance coverage. A *JAMA* editorial criticizing the study's inattention to the patients' sexual partners was mentioned in the final two paragraphs.

An article in the April 1985 issue of *Vogue* exclusively discussed the new medical and surgical approaches to impotence under a typically simple and optimistic title, "Curing Impotence: The Prognosis is Good." The article mentioned the financial cost of the devices as well as an in-development "electrostimulatory device to be inserted in the anus before intercourse and controlled by a ring or wristwatch-like switch so that patients can signal appropriate nerves to produce an erection" (Hixson, 1985, p. 406). The style of the writing was technical and mechanical and so simple and cheerful that it was hardly amazing to read: "While psychological impotence problems probably also require psychological treatment, the doctors feel that successful electronic intercourse may provide the confidence needed by some men" (p. 406).

Literature for patients has been developed by the major prosthesis manufacturers and is available at patient education centers, in doctors' waiting rooms, and through self-help groups such as Impotents Anonymous. A typical booklet is seven pages of high-quality glossy paper with photographs of healthy young couples sitting in a garden, watching a beautiful sunset, or sitting by the ocean (Brooks and Brooks, 1984). Entitled *Overcoming Impotence,* the text reads, "Impotence is a widespread problem that affects many millions of men. It can occur at any age and at any point in a man's sexual life. The myth of impotence as an 'old man's disease' has finally been shattered. Impotence is a problem of men but also affects couples and families. Now, as a result of recent medical advances, impotence need no longer cause frustration, embarrassment and tension. New solutions are now available for an age-old problem."

In the second section, on causes of impotence, the booklet reads as follows: "The causes can be either physical or psychological. For many years, it was believed that 90 percent of impotent men had a psychological cause for their problem; but as a result of recent medical research, it is now known that at least half of the men suffering from impotence can actually trace its origin to a physical problem." After a lengthy discussion of the methods used to distinguish between physical and psychological impotence, the booklet continues in its relentlessly upbeat way: "For the majority of men who are physically impotent and for those who are psychologically impotent and do not respond to counseling, a penile implant offers the only complete, reliable solution. It offers new hope for a return to satisfactory sexual activity and for the disappearance of the anxieties and frustrations of impotence."

This conclusion, of course, seems to provide a straightforward technological solution to a technical problem. No mention is made of individual differences in adjusting to the prosthesis or even the fact that adjustment will be necessary at all. The mechanical solution itself will solve the problem; the person becomes irrelevant.

Other patient information booklets are similar: informative about the device and reassuring about the outcome. In addition to lengthy and detailed discussion of specific physical causes of impotence, there is a brief mention of psychogenic impotence. One booklet says: "Another group of patients have some type of mental barrier [*sic*] or problem. This latter group may account for as high as 50% of the people with impotence, but only a small number of these people are candidates for a penile implant" (Medical Engineering Corporation, 1983). Is it any wonder that men who "fail" the physical tests and are diagnosed as having psychogenic impotence cannot understand why they should be deprived of the device?

Urologists have begun in recent years to specialize in the diagnosis and surgical treatment of impotence. A quarterly publication from a prosthesis manufacturer "for surgeons practicing prosthetic urology" devoted a front page to the subject "Impotence Clinics: Investments in the Future" (American Medical Systems, 1984). Newspaper advertisements appear from groups of urologists with names such as "Potency Plus" (a group in California). Another group (also in California), which calls itself "Potential," advertises, "Impotence. . . . There could be a medical reason and a medical solution." An ad in a New York newspaper is headlined "Potent Solution to Sexual Problem."

Another source of publicity about the physical causes and treatments for erectile difficulties has come from The Impotence Institute of America, an organization founded by a man who has described how his own search ended happily with an implanted penile prosthesis. Although the subhead on the not-for-profit institute's stationery is "Bringing a 'total-care' concept to overcoming impotence," the ten men on the board of directors are all urologists.

In 1982 the institute created two consumer-oriented groups, Impotents Anonymous (IA) and I-Anon, based on the Alcoholics Anonymous model (both the institute's founder and his wife had formerly been members of Al-Anon). Recent correspondence from the institute indicates there are now seventy chapters of IA operating and another twenty planned. A 1984 news article about IA, "Organization Helps Couples with Impotence as Problem" repeated the now familiar information that "until five years ago most physicians believed that up to 95% of all erectile impotence stemmed from psychological problems, [but that] medical experts now agree that about half of all impotence is caused by physical disorders." The IA brochure cites the same numbers.

Let us turn now to a critique of the biomedical approach to male sexuality, beginning with this question of organic and psychogenic etiology.

## Critique of the Biomedical Approach

The frequent claim that psychogenic impotence has been oversold and organic causes are far more common than previously realized has captivated the media and legitimated increased medical involvement in sexuality. An *International Journal of Andrology* editorial summarizes the shift:

> Medical fashions come and go and the treatment of erectile impotence is no exception. In the 20s and 30s, physicians and surgeons looked for physical causes and tried out methods of treatment, most of which now seem absurd. Since that time there has been a widely held view that 90–95% of cases of impotence are psychologically determined. Where this figure came from was never clear [some sources cite Havelock Ellis], but it has entered into medical folklore. In the past five years or so, the pendulum has been swinging back. Physical causes and methods of treatment are receiving increasing attention. (Bancroft, 1982, p. 353)

In the Center for Male Sexual Dysfunction in the Department of Urology at Beth Israel Medical Center, New York City, more than 800 men have been seen since 1981 for erectile problems (I began working there in 1983). Very few who, on the basis of a simple history and physical, could be unambiguously declared "psychogenic" were immediately referred for sex therapy; the remainder underwent a complete medical and psychological workup. Over 90 percent of these patients believed that their problems were completely or preponderantly physical in origin; yet we have found that only about 45 percent of patients have exclusively or predominantly medically caused erectile problems and 55 percent have exclusively or predominantly psychologically caused problems. This approximately fifty-fifty split is, in fact, what is often cited by the mass media. But most of our patients (more than 75 percent) are referred by their primary physicians because of their likely medical etiology and their need for a comprehensive workup.

A Chicago group found that 43 percent of the men coming to a urology clinic for impotence evaluation had at least partly an organic basis for their problems, whereas only 11 percent of the men coming to a psychiatry department sex clinic had organic contributing factors (Segraves et al., 1981). A review of all patients seen at the Johns Hopkins Sexual Behaviors Consultation Unit between 1972 and 1981 showed 105 men over fifty years old with a primary complaint of erectile dysfunction. Even in this age group, only 30 percent could be assigned an organic etiology (Wise, Rabins, and Gahnsley, 1984). After listing sixty-six possible physical causes of secondary impotence, Masters and Johnson (1970, pp. 184–185) reported that only seven of their 213 cases (3 percent) had an organic etiology.

Obviously, one cannot describe the actual rate of occurrence of any particular problem (e.g., "organic impotence") without describing the population from which the sample comes. The urology departments' findings that approximately half of the patients seen for erectile problems have a medical cause *cannot* be generalized to other groups (e.g., men in general practitioners' waiting rooms reading prosthesis manufacturers' literature, men watching a TV program about impotence) without further normative data collection. It is important to emphasize that even men with diabetes, a known cause of peripheral neural and vascular difficulties that could result in impotence, are as often potent as not (Schiavi, Fisher, Quadland, and Glover, 1984; Fairburn, McCulloch, and Wu, 1982), and impotence in a diabetic cannot be predicted from the duration of the diabetes or the presence of other physical complications.

An even more serious criticism of the biomedical trend is the common tendency to contrapose organic and psychogenic causes of impotence as mutually exclusive phenomena. Joseph LoPiccolo (1985) wrote, "Conceptually, most of the research suffers from the flaw of attempting to categorize the patients into discrete, nonoverlapping categories of organic or psychogenic erectile failure. Yet, many cases, and perhaps the majority of cases, involve both organic and psychogenic erectile factors in the genesis of erectile failure" (p. 221). Sally Schumacher and Charles Lloyd (1981), in a review of 102 cases seen at two different medical school centers, concluded, "All patients reported psychological distress associated with their impotence [including] inhibitions, shame, avoidance, insecurity, inadequacy, guilt, hostility, fear of intimacy" (p. 46). A urologic review of 388 cases concluded, "There are wholly organic bases and also totally psychological causes for impotency; yet the two generally coexist. It is most probable that in all cases of organic impotency a psychologic overlay develops" (Finkle and Finkle, 1984, p. 25).

The explanation, I believe, is not so much that all cases involve a mixture of factors but that all cases involve psychological factors in some degree. The director of a New York sexuality clinic summed up her impressions similarly: "We have found in our work . . . that, where organic determinants are diagnosed, inevitably there will also be psychological factors involved, either as co-determinants of the erectile dysfunction or as reactive to it. . . . A man's emotional reaction to his erectile failures may be such that it serves to maintain the erectile problem even when the initial physiological causes are resolved" (Schreiner-Engel, 1981, p. 116).

The consequences of this implication are particularly serious given that, as LoPiccolo (1985) noted, "many physicians currently will perform surgery to implant a penile prosthesis if any organic abnormality is found" (p. 221). The effect of psychological factors is to make the dysfunction look worse than the medical problem alone would warrant. Altering the man's devastated attitudes will improve the picture, whatever else is going on.

Michael Perelman (1984) referred to "the omnipresent psychogenic component existing in any potency problem regardless of the degree of organicity" (p. 181) to describe his successful use of cognitive-behavioral psychotherapy to treat men diagnosed with organic impotence. He reminded his readers that physical sexual function has a psychosomatic complexity that is not only poorly understood but may have the "ability to successfully compensate for its own deficits" (p. 181). Thus the search for *the* etiology that characterizes so much of the biomedical approach to male sexual problems seems to have less to do with the nature of sexuality than with the nature of the medical enterprise.

## The Allure of Medicalized Sexuality

Men are drawn to a technological solution such as the penile prosthesis for a variety of personal reasons that ultimately rest on the inflexible central place of sexual potency in the male sexual script. Those who assume that "normal" men must always be interested in sex and who believe that male sexuality is a simple system wherein interest leads easily and directly to erection (Zilbergeld, 1978) are baffled by any erectile difficulties. Their belief that "their penis is an instrument immune from everyday problems, anxieties and fears" (Doyle, 1983, p. 207) conditions them to deny the contribution of psychological or interpersonal factors to male sexual responsiveness. This denial, in turn, results from fundamental male gender role prescriptions for self-reliance and emotional control (Brannon, 1976).

Medicalized discourse offers an explanation of impotence that removes control over, and therefore responsibility and blame for, sexual failure from the man and places it on his physiology. Talcott Parsons (1951) originally argued that an organic diagnosis confers a particular social role, the "sick role," which has three aspects: (1) the individual is not held responsible for his or her condition; (2) illnesses are legitimate bases for exemption from normal social responsibilities; and (3) the exemptions are contingent on the sick person recognizing that sickness is undesirable and seeking appropriate (medical) help. A medical explanation for erectile difficulties relieves men of blame and thus permits them to maintain some masculine self-esteem even in the presence of impotence. According to Masters and Johnson,

> Understandably, for many years the pattern of the human male has been to blame sexual dysfunction on specific physical distresses. Every sexually inadequate male lunges toward any potential physical excuse for sexual malfunction. A cast for a leg or a sling for an arm provides socially acceptable evidence of physical dysfunction of these extremities. Unfortunately, the psychosocial causes of perpetual penile flaccidity cannot be explained or excused by devices for mechanical support. (Masters and Johnson, 1970, pp. 187–188)

Perhaps in 1970 "devices for mechanical support" of the penis were not widely available, but now, ironically, impotent men have precisely the type of medical vindication that Masters and Johnson suggested would provide the *most* effective deflection of the "blame" men feel for their inability to perform sexually.

Men's willingness to accept a self-protective, self-handicapping attribution (i.e., an illness label) for "failure" has been demonstrated in studies of excuse-making (Snyder, Ford, and Hunt, 1985). Reduced personal responsibility is most sought in those situations in which performance is related to self-esteem (Snyder and Smith, 1982). It may be that the frequent use of physical excuses for failure in athletic performance provides a model for men to use in sexuality. Medical treatments not only offer tangible evidence of nonblameworthiness but also allow men to avoid psychological treatments such as marital or sex therapy, which threaten embarrassing self-disclosure and admissions of weakness men find aversive (Peplau and Gordon, 1985).

The final allure of a technological solution such as the penile prosthesis is its promise of permanent freedom from worry. One of Masters and Johnson's (1970) major insights was their description of the self-conscious self-monitoring that men with erectile difficulties develop in sexual situations. "Performance anxiety" and "spectatoring," their two immediate causes of sexual impotence, generate a self-perpetuating cycle that undermines a man's confidence about the future even as he recovers from individual episodes. Technology seems to offer a simple and permanent solution to the problem of lost or threatened confidence, as doctors cited from *Vogue* to the *Journal of Urology* have noted.

## The Rising Importance of Sexuality in Personal Life

Even though we live in a time when the definition of masculinity is moving away from reliance on physical validation (Pleck, 1976), there seems to be no apparent reduction in the male sexual focus on physical performance. Part of the explanation for this lack of change must rest with the increasing importance of sexuality in contemporary relationships. Recent sociocultural analyses have suggested that sexual satisfaction grows in importance to the individual and couple as other sources of personal fulfillment and connection with others wither. Edmund White (1980) wrote,

> I would say that with the collapse of other social values (those of religion, patriotism, the family, and so on), sex has been forced to take up the slack, to become our sole mode of transcendence and our only touchstone of authenticity. . . . In our present isolation we have few ways besides sex to feel connected with each other. (p. 282)

German sexologist Gunter Schmidt concluded,

People are being deprived more and more of opportunities to feel they are worth something to others, to experience what they are doing as something of significance, and to know that they are indispensable to the lives of their families or at least a few friends. The experience of powerlessness, dependency, inner vacuum left behind sucks in any experiences which make one at least temporarily aware of one's own importance. . . . A particularly important mode of compensation for narcissistic deprivation is the couple relationship, or, more precisely, the emotions it can mobilize, such as falling in love and sexual desire and satisfaction. (Schmidt, 1983b, pp. 4–5)

The increasing pressure on intimate relationships to provide psychological support and gratification comes at the same time that traditional reasons for these relationships (i.e., economics and raising families) are declining. Both trends place pressure on compatibility and companionship to maintain relationships. Given that men have been raised "not to be emotionally sensitive to others or emotionally expressive or self-revealing" (Pleck, 1981, p. 140), much modern relationship success would seem to depend on sexual fulfillment. Although some contemporary research indicates that marriages and gay relationships can be rated successful despite the presence of sexual problems (Frank, Anderson, and Rubinstein, 1978; Bell and Weinberg, 1978), popular surveys suggest that the public believes sexual satisfaction to be essential to relationship success.

The importance of sexuality also increases because of its use by consumption-oriented capitalism (Altman, 1982). The promise of increased sexual attractiveness is used to sell products to people of all ages. Commercial sexual meeting places are popular in both gay and heterosexual culture, and a whole system of therapists, books, workshops, and magazines sells advice on improving sexual performance and enjoyment. Restraint and repression are inappropriate in a consumer culture in which the emphasis is on immediate gratification.

The expectation that sexuality will provide ever-increasing rewards and personal meaning has also been a theme of the contemporary women's movement, and women's changing attitudes have affected many men, particularly widowed and divorced men returning to the sexual "market." Within the past decade, sexual advice manuals have completely changed their tone regarding the roles of men and women in sexual relations (Weinberg, Swensson, and Hammersmith, 1983). Women are advised to take more responsibility for their own pleasure, to possess sexual knowledge and self-knowledge, and to expect that improved sexual functioning will pay off in other aspects of life. Removing responsibility from the man for being the sexual teacher and leader reduces the definition of sexual masculinity to having excellent technique and equipment to meet the "new woman" on her "new" level.

Finally, the new importance of sexual performance has no upper age limit.

> The sexual myth most rampant in our culture today is the concept that the aging process per se will in time discourage or deny erective security to the older age-group male. As has been described previously, the aging male may be slower to erect and may even reach the plateau phase without full erective return, but the facility and ability to attain erection, presuming general good health and no psychogenic blocking, continues unopposed as a natural sequence well into the 80-year age group. (Masters and Johnson, 1970, p. 326)

Sex is a natural act, Masters and Johnson said over and over again, and there is no "natural" reason for ability to decline or disappear as one ages. Erectile difficulties become "problems" that can be corrected with suitable treatment, and aging provides no escape from the male sexual role.

## The Medicalization of Impotence: Part of the Problem or Part of the Solution?

The increasing use of the term *impotence* that Mark Elliott (1985) reported can now be seen as part of a medicalization process of sexuality. Physicians view the medical system as a method for distributing technical expertise in the interest of improved health (Ehrenreich and Ehrenreich, 1978). Their economic interests, spurred by the profit orientation of medical technology manufacturers, lie in expanding the number and type of services they offer to more and more patients. Specialists in particular have dramatically increased their incomes and prestige during the postwar era by developing high-reimbursement relationships with hospitals and insurance companies (Starr, 1982). In the sexual sphere, all these goals are served by labeling impotence a biomedical disorder that is common in men of all ages and best served by thorough evaluation and appropriate medical treatment when any evidence of organic disorder is identified.

There are many apparent advantages for men in the medicalization of male sexuality. As discussed earlier, men view physical explanations for their problems as less stigmatizing and are better able to maintain their sense of masculinity and self-esteem when their problems are designated as physical. Accepting medicine as a source of authority and help reassures men who feel that they are under immense pressure from role expectations but who are unable to consult with or confide in either other men or women because of pride, competitiveness, or defensiveness. That "inhibited sexual excitement

... in males, partial or complete failure to attain or maintain erection until completion of the [*sic*] sexual act," is a genuine disorder (APA, 1980, p. 279) legitimates an important aspect of life that physicians previously dismissed or made jokes about. And, as I have said, permanent mechanical solutions to sexual performance worries are seen as a gift from heaven; one simple operation erases a source of anxiety dating from adolescence about failing as a man.

The disadvantages to medicalizing male sexuality, however, are numerous and subtle. (My discussion here is informed by Catherine Riessman's 1983 analysis of the medicalization of many female roles and conditions.) First, dependence on medical remedies for impotence has led to the escalating use of treatments that may have unpredictable long-term effects. Iatrogenic ("doctor-caused") consequences of new technology and pharmacology are not uncommon and seem most worrisome when medical treatments are offered to men with no demonstrable organic disease. Second, the use of medical language mystifies human experience, increasing the public's dependence on professionals and experts. If sexuality becomes fundamentally a matter of vasocongestion and myotonia (as in Masters and Johnson's famous claim, 1966, p. 7), personal experience requires expert interpretation and explanation. Third, medicalization spreads the moral neutrality of medicine and science over sexuality, and people no longer ask whether men "should" have erections. If the presence of erections is healthy and their absence (in whole or part) is pathological, then healthy behavior is correct behavior and vice versa. This view again increases the public's dependence on health authorities to define norms and standards for conduct.

The primary disadvantage of medicalization is that it denies, obscures, and ignores the social causes of whatever problem is under study. Impotence becomes the problem of an individual man. This effect seems particularly pertinent in the case of male sexuality, an area in which the social demands of the male sexual role are so related to the meaning of erectile function and dysfunction. Recall the list of men's beliefs about sexuality, the evaluative criteria of conduct and performance. Being a man depends on sexual adequacy, which depends on potency. A rigid, reliable erection is necessary for full compliance with the script. The medicalization of male sexuality helps a man conform to the script rather than analyzing where the script comes from or challenging it. In addition, "Medicine attracts public resources out of proportion to its capacity for health enhancement, because it often categorizes problems fundamentally social in origin as biological or personal deficits, and in so doing smothers the impulse for social change which could offer the only serious resolution" (Stark and Flitcraft, quoted in Riessman, 1983, p. 4). Research and technology are directed only toward better and better solutions. Yet the demands of the script are so formidable, and the pressures from the sociocultural changes I have outlined so likely to increase, that no technical solution will ever work—certainly not for everyone.


## Preventive Medicine:
## Changing the Male Sexual Script

Men will remain vulnerable to the expansion of the clinical domain so long as masculinity rests heavily on a particular type of physical function. As more research uncovers subtle physiological correlates of genital functioning, more men will be "at risk" for impotence. Fluctuations of physical and emotional state will become cues for impending impotence in any man with, for example, diabetes, hypertension, or a history of prescription medication usage.

One of the less well understood features of sex therapy is that it "treats" erectile dysfunction by changing the individual man's sexual script. Sex therapists have described the process as follows:

> This approach is primarily educational—you are not curing an illness but learning new and more satisfactory ways of getting on with each other. (Bancroft, 1989, p. 537)

> Our thesis is that the rules and concepts we learn [about male sexuality] are destructive and a very inadequate preparation for a satisfying and pleasurable sex life. . . . Having a better sex life is in large measure dependent upon your willingness to examine how the male sexual mythology has trapped you. (Zilbergeld, 1978, p. 9)

Sexuality can be transformed from a rigid standard for masculine adequacy to a way of being, a way of communicating, a hobby, a way of being in one's body—and *being* one's body—that does not impose control but rather affirms pleasure, movement, sensation, cooperation, playfulness, relating. Masculine confidence cannot be purchased because there can never be perfect potency. Chasing its illusion may line a few pockets, but for most men it will only exchange one set of anxieties and limitations for another.

# 17

# The Medicalization
of Impotence:
Normalizing Phallocentrism

*I*n our time, phallocentrism is perpetuated by a flourishing medical construction that focuses exclusively on penile erections as the essence of men's sexual function and satisfaction. In this chapter I shall describe how this medicalization is promoted by urologists, medical industries, mass media, and various entrepreneurs. Many men and women provide a ready audience for this construction because of masculine ideology and gender socialization. Women's sexual interests in anything other than phallocentric sexual scripting are denied. As one author has put it, "Taken by itself, the penis is a floppy appendage which rises and falls and is the source of a number of pleasures. The phallus is more than this. It is the physical organ represented as continuously erect; it is the inexhaustibility of male desire; it is a dominant element within our culture" (Bradbury, 1985, p. 134).

Much successful effort in the past two decades has been devoted to defining, describing, and analyzing the circumstances and forces affecting women's sexual socialization and the construction of female sexuality (Tiefer, 1991a). Among the contributing factors has been that of medicalization, including medical ideology and practice regarding menstruation, menopause, pregnancy, childbirth, premenstrual syndrome (PMS), physical appearance, and fertility. Riessman argued that these areas have become medicalized as "physicians seek to medicalize experience because of their specific beliefs and economic interests. . . . Women collaborate in the medicalization process because of their own needs and motives. . . . In addition, other groups bring economic interests to which both physicians and women are responsive" (1983, pp. 3–4).

Men and their bodies can also be objects of systems of surveillance and control, however. Medicalization perpetuates a phallocentric construction of men's sexuality that literally and symbolically perpetuates women's sexual subordination through silencing and invisibility and thus operates to preserve men's power (Bem, 1993).

# Method

This chapter is informed primarily by my impressions and observations working as a sexologist and psychologist in medical center urology departments for the past decade. My responsibilities have included conducting one-hour-long psychosocial interviews and preparing reports on men with sexual complaints who consult a well-known urologist (Melman, Tiefer, and Pedersen, 1988). At the time his appointment is made, each man is asked to bring his primary sexual partner to the interview, and I conduct a separate interview with any partner who comes (Tiefer and Melman, 1983).

To date (August 1993), I have interviewed and kept records on close to 1,600 men, approximately 60 percent of whom brought sexual partners. Only six of these patients said they were gay, and none of these brought a partner to the interview. Our patients are predominantly referrals from the biggest health maintenance organization in the New York metropolitan area. Their ages range from the twenties to the eighties, averaging late fifties; they are approximately two-thirds ethnic minorities; about half are high school graduates, with equal numbers having more or less education; and about half of them are blue-collar New York City government employees (transit, sanitation, corrections, etc.). In addition, my observations draw from sexology texts and conferences of the major U.S. and international sexology (and, occasionally, urology) organizations.

# A True Story

In June 1989, a conversation took place during the annual meeting of the International Academy of Sex Research in Princeton, New Jersey, in front of a poster titled "Healthy Aging and Sexual Function" (Schiavi et al., 1990). One of the figures displayed depicted nocturnal penile tumescence[1] measures for a group of healthy male volunteers aged sixty-five to seventy-four. Referring to a particular subgroup of the volunteers, a urologist studying the figure said to the poster's author, a psychiatrist, "So, these men did not have rigid nocturnal erections, [so] they may actually have had disease." "No," the psychiatrist replied, "they were healthy, and in fact they were having sex, their wives confirmed that there was no dysfunction." "But," continued the urologist, "their wives may be satisfied, even they may be satisfied, but since *some* men in that age group *can* have rigid erections, *these* men must have had some impairment."

The urologist was promoting a model championing the authority of "objective facts" as revealed by technologies and the evaluation of body parts. The psychiatrist was defending the authority of human subjectivity and personal experience. In the urologist's model, women were invisible and irrelevant; sexuality yielded to "the erection" as the subject of professional interest and intervention. In this chapter I examine the recent expansion in cultural authority of the urologist and the constructions he (almost all urologists are men) advocates, as well as their consequences. By *phallocentrism* is meant this preoccupying interest and focus on the penis or phallus in sexuality discourse.

## Medicalization

Medicalization is a major intellectual trend in the twentieth century, a gradual social transformation whereby medicine, with its distinctive modes of thought, its models, metaphors, and institutions, comes to exercise authority over areas of life not previously considered medical (Conrad and Schneider, 1980). For medicalization to work, the particular behavioral area must be divisible into good (i.e., "healthy") and bad (i.e., "sick") aspects and must somehow be relatable (albeit often distantly) to norms of biological functioning. It helps if medical technology can have some demonstrable impact on the behavior.

Two types of medicalization have been described. Type one occurs when a previously deviant behavior or event such as a sin, crime, or antisocial act comes to be redefined as a medical problem; type two occurs when a common life event (e.g., pregnancy, baldness, or memory problems) is redefined as a medical problem and often focuses on the physical changes associated with aging. Medicalization transforms unacceptable erectile performance into a subject for medical analysis and management. Surprisingly, definitions and norms for erections are absent from the medical literature. The assumption that everyone knows what a normal erection is forms a central part of the universalization and reification that supports both medicalization and phallocentrism.

Medicalization occurs over a period of time. In the case of male sexual function, there are four groups identifiably active on behalf of medicalization (urologists, medical industries, mass media, and entrepreneurs), and many men and their sexual partners form a receptive audience. In addition, institutions with a stake in sexual restrictiveness may indirectly support medicalization because of its potential for social control through specifying norms, eliminating deviance, and enforcing conformity.

## Advocates for the Medicalization of Male Sexuality

### Urologists

In the 1960s, in anticipation of an increased patient population to be generated by Medicare and Medicaid, the U.S. government stimulated the creation of additional medical schools and granted preferred immigration status to those holding an M.D. degree (Ansell, 1987). As a result, between 1970 and 1990 the number of physicians practicing in the United States jumped about 80 percent, from 325,000 to almost 600,000, and the number of surgeons increased from 58,000 to more than 110,000 (Rosenthal, 1989). This rapid expansion created competition within and between medical and surgical subspecialties, including urology.

Urologists began specializing in male sexual dysfunction in quest of new patients and research areas. Using the new nomenclature of sexual "dysfunctions" provided by clinical sexology and psychiatry (LoPiccolo, 1978), surveys began to show a significant prevalence of sexual complaints in the general population, in the medical population, and among patients taking prescription medications.

Urology-dominated treatments and technologies evolved in the 1970s. They currently consist of various penile surgeries, penile implants, injections of drugs into the penis to cause erection, and vacuum erection devices. Besides its economic potential, sexual dysfunction is an attractive subspecialty because patients are not chronically sick or likely to die from their "disease"; there are also opportunities for diverse outpatient and inpatient services.

It is probably in the realm of diagnostics, however, that urology has advanced medicalization the most (Nelkin and Tancredi, 1989). By promoting sophisticated technologies for "differentiating" among various erection problem etiologies and by ensuring publicity of the claim that physical causes of erection problems are paramount, over the past decade urologists have come to dominate the "proper" diagnostic evaluation of men's sexual complaints (Spark, White, and Connolly, 1983; Rosen and Leiblum, 1992a).

A recent issue of the monthly American Urological Association newspaper contained a bordered box that read: "AUA Policy Statement/Male Sexual Dysfunction/Sexual dysfunction in the male is a disease entity, the diagnoses and treatments of which deserve equal attention to that given other diseases" (Poll shows widespread use of three major impotence treatments, 1993, p. 6). This bold jurisdictional claim is an outgrowth of a decade's professional events. An informal 1978 meeting of urologists in New York had resulted in the 1982 formation of the International Society for Impotence Research (ISIR). The society began publishing its journal, *The International Journal of Impotence Research,* in 1989. The first "World Meeting on Impotence" was held in 1984, and a major overview of the new field of "impotence" was coauthored by three urologists a few years later (Krane, Goldstein, and deTejada, 1989).

Urologists have promoted their claims through consistent use of the words *impotence* and *impotent,* while sexologists' own language claims have been hesitant: "Although we strongly prefer the terms 'erectile disorder' or 'erectile dysfunction,' we have opted, after considerable discussion and debate, to grant each author editorial discretion and freedom of choice in this regard" (Rosen and Leiblum, 1992b, p. xviii).

In 1985, Mark Elliott reviewed the frequency of the terms *impotence* and *frigidity* (another term sexologists had rejected) in titles in the *Psychological Abstracts* from 1940–1981. Although initially, the terms were equally popular, the use of *frigidity* had almost disappeared in recent years while *impotence* was far more popular than ever before. In 1992, the National Institutes of Health (NIH) sponsored a Consensus Development Conference on Impotence.[2] I spoke on "Nomenclature" and suggested that the term *impotence* was pejorative and confusing (Tiefer, 1992a). The final conference statement begins:

> The term "impotence," as applied to the title of this conference, has traditionally been used to signify the inability of the male to attain and maintain erection of the penis sufficient to permit satisfactory sexual intercourse. However, this use has often led to confusing and uninterpretable results in both clinical and basic science investigations. This, together with its pejorative implications, suggests that the more precise term, "erectile dysfunction" be used instead. (NIH, 1992, p. 3)

Nevertheless, the final report (and all the media stories about it) was still titled "Impotence."

## Medical Industries

Manufacturers and suppliers of medical devices, products, and services have obvious economic interests in expanding a new medical specialty. Individual pieces of diagnostic and treatment equipment can easily cost tens of thousands of dollars, and the field is very competitive. Interest has grown rapidly among pharmaceutical companies since the first effective injections of drugs into the penis to cause erections were developed in the mid-1980s (Wagner and Kaplan, 1992); clinical trials in my department currently test drugs that can be applied to the penis in cream or pellet form.

Medical industries provide resources to create the cultural authority essential to medicalization. The Mentor Corporation, for example, one of the five major implant manufacturers in the United States (Petrou and Barrett, 1991), started an Impotence Foundation in 1986 as a "national information service" (Mentor Corporation, n.d.). It provides a toll-free information number, unlimited free patient education brochures and videos, and complete free information and materials for educational seminars (e.g., ad designs, slides, and script) for doctors.

Another contribution to medical hegemony comes from the U.S. health insurance industry's cutbacks in the area of multi-visit services, including mental health services (Kramon, 1989). For example, the majority of men with sexual problems whom I interview are New York City government employees with HMO-type insurance. The HMO will completely cover the cost of any surgical or pharmacological treatment for their sexual problems but will not pay one penny for psychological sex therapy treatment or education.

## Mass Media

The mass media play a fundamental role in conferring cultural authority and legitimacy in the modern world (Nelkin, 1987). My belief is that the mass media favor medicalized information about sex because focusing on "scientific developments" or "health advice" allows publication of sexual subject matter with no taint of obscenity or pornography. Medicalized writing about sex is "clean" and "safe." *New York Times* readers will not see articles on techniques of fellatio, but they will see dozens of stories on penile injections. By quoting medical "experts," using medical terminology, and swiftly and enthusiastically publicizing new devices and pharmaceuticals, the mass media legitimize, instruct, and model the proper construction and discourse (Parlee, 1987). People underline and save "sex health" articles, and I have had patients bring in such materials even years following publication.

A two-part health column article on impotence in the *New York Times* illustrates the medicalized media approach to men's sexuality. The first part begins by publicizing the claim about medical etiologies: "Less than a decade ago, more than 90% of impotence cases were attributed to emotional inhibitions . . . but . . . experts say that more than half, and perhaps as many as three-fourths of impotency cases have a physical basis" (Brody, 1988, p. B4).

The article uses the term *impotence* and credits unnamed "experts" with generating a major shift in knowledge about the etiology of sex problems, though no new epidemiological studies are mentioned. A climate of conviction is created, which is reinforced when the reader sees the same claim in the *Wall Street Journal* under the title: "Research on Impotence Upsets the Idea that It Is Usually Psychological" (Stipp, 1987, p. 1).

*Time* magazine repeated the assertion: "Medical researchers have determined that up to 75% of all cases of impotence stem from physical problems, most of which can be treated" (Toufexis, 1988). This article, brought to me by several patients, quotes a seventy-six-year-old man with a penile prosthesis implanted after prostate cancer who says, "You'd think we were 26 years old again," and describes a forty-year-old former policeman with a fractured back whose wife is represented as "signalling her mood with the question, 'Have you had your shot [penile injection] today?'"

The title of the *Time* article, "It's Not 'All in Your Head,'" reveals the stigma associated with "mental" causes of sexual malfunction. Popular articles on men's sexual problems often begin, as had the 1980 *JAMA* lead article "Impotence Is Not Always Psychogenic" (Spark, White, and Connolly, 1980), with the mantra, "Until recently, medical literature attributed [fill in a high number] per cent of impotence to psychological causes. But, now it is estimated that [fill in a high number] per cent can be traced to organic disorders" (e.g., Blaun, 1987; Blakeslee, 1993).

Science and health journalism seems so superficial and uncritical as to be little more than advertising (Burnham, 1987). Emphasis is placed on new technologies, often with the disclaimer, as in the current case of penile injections, "not yet FDA approved." There is rarely any follow-up of initial reports. The articles are sprinkled with individual accounts of satisfied customers provided to the print or electronic journalist by hospital or manufacturer publicists. The last time my name appeared in a popular magazine article (Sheehy, 1993), my hospital public relations director called to ask if I would like to prepare some materials and provide some patients for a possible news release and press conference. Television and radio talk shows also publicize and promote the new medical technologies for men's sexual problems, and I have met with many retirees whose perspectives on sexual problems were largely informed by such shows.

### Entrepreneurs

These advocates for medicalization include self-help group and newsletter promoters who have created a market by portraying themselves as something between consumers and professionals. The formation of Impotents Anonymous (IA), which is both a urologists' advocacy group and a self-help group, was announced in the *New York Times* in an article including cost and availability information on penile implants (Organization helps couples with impotence as problem, 1984). A story about the organization's founders, a married couple, was included. They had recently toured with their new book, *It's Not All in Your Head* (MacKenzie and MacKenzie, 1988; Naunton, 1989). Although the IA newsletter ("Impotence Worldwide") features their organizational slogan, "Bringing a total care concept to overcoming impotence," it has only urologists on the advisory board.

The advocates for medicalization portray sexuality in a rational, technical, mechanical, cheerful way. Sexuality as an area for the imagination, for political struggle, or for the expression of diverse human motives or as a sensual, intimate, or spiritual rather than performative experience is absent.

## Men as an Audience
## for the Medicalization of Sexuality

Men constitute a ready audience for the medicalization of sexuality because of male socialization and masculine ideology, both of which make erectile function central to masculine self-esteem (Pleck, Sonenstein, and Ku, 1993; Metcalf and Humphries, 1985). The chronic insecurity and intermittent desperation (Hall, 1991) that result from this situation render men vulnerable to offers of "magical" and permanent solutions such as those offered by the technological fixes of modern urology (Tiefer, 1986a).

In the past two decades, numerous texts have underscored the pressures experienced by heterosexual men as standards for masculine sexual performance escalate in response to the "sexual revolution" and women's "new" sexual expectations (Zilbergeld, 1992). Men themselves contribute to these insecurities by endorsing naturalizing belief systems about sexuality and women's sexual satisfaction. Patients I see often insist, despite my demurral, that women (a uniform class) cannot be sexually satisfied without intravaginal intercourse and claim that their motivation for the erectile dysfunction evaluation and treatment is to keep their wives from leaving them. Interviewed separately and asked if they thought their marriage could break up because of the erectile difficulties, the wives are often surprised and offended at the thought.

Phallocentric beliefs burden and pressure men, but at the same time they maintain sexual privilege for men. The "needs" of the naturalized erection dominate the sexual encounter script where phallocentric sexual activities generally ensure men's pleasure and satisfaction. Assumptions of universality free men from regarding themselves or their partners as sexual individuals.

In addition to maintaining the phallic focus, the medicalized construction of sexuality offers men an "objective" world of science and medicine to minimize anxieties provoked by public disclosures of sexual inadequacy. Although admitting any performance failure challenges masculinity as constructed within the ideology of "machismo" (Mosher, 1991), at least medicalized discourse keeps the sexuality focus on the physical and avoids inquiry into motives, values, wishes, feelings, or fantasies (Seidler, 1992). The mantra of sexual medicalization, "It's not all in your head," replaces the stigma of failed responsibility with the face-saving excuse of physical incapacity that men often learn in sports and the military.

Are all men equally attracted to a medicalized message? Schiavi et al. (1990) described a group of older men (not a clinical sample) who, because of inadequate erections, could not have vaginal intercourse with their wives on at least 50 percent of their attempts over a period of six months, yet who reported high levels of sexual and marital satisfaction. These men would seem to be have sexual activity scripts and masculinity constructions that do not require long-lasting, rigid erections. My urologist colleagues would say that these men (and their partners) are merely "adapting" to a second-best situation. They would say that such satisfaction is really "adjustment," and they would predict that offering such men the new penile technologies would get many of them to admit that more and better erections would really make them more satisfied.

# Women as an Audience
# for the Medicalization of Men's Sexuality

The literature produced by the medicalization advocates often depicts women as supporting the medicalization of men's sexuality. For example, women offer testimonial to their preimplant unhappiness and postimplant sexual and relationship satisfaction in patient education videos available from penile implant manufacturers.

What about women's actual voices and self-representations? My interviews with the women sexual partners of the urology patients suggest that some do subscribe to a medicalized and phallocentric construction of sexuality. Sometimes they derive physical pleasure primarily or exclusively from coitus and, like urologists, talk about sexuality as requiring and centering around erections. Women who wish to become pregnant often focus on their man's erectile function as the centerpiece of sexuality.

Another subgroup is unhappily resigned to male privilege. They say men and women are sexually different and that men's phallocentrism is limiting, but they go along with the status quo. When asked how they would conduct sexual relations, they say, "I'm not sure, but there's got to be something better."

Other women I've spoken with strongly diverge from the medicalized and phallocentric construction. They often "cannot understand why he is so upset" because both partners enjoy nonintercourse activities. Some worry that their own sexual enjoyment (often increased since their partners' erection difficulties began) is endangered by penile injections and implants. "He'll want to use it all the time, and what will that do for me?" one wife angrily asked. Many women have asked me or asked me to ask the urologist to "talk sense" to their partners and make them less obsessed and unhappy.

Feminists have problematized coitus as the prime form of sexual activity if women's erotic pleasure is as important as conception or men's pleasure, yet coitus remains the prime component of the script of heterosexual relations (Clement, 1990). The feminist critique, for the men and women I interview, has merely added the clitoris to the standard phallocentric script; intercourse is still the main event and anything else is considered foreplay, afterplay, or "special needs."

# Medicalization and Phallocentrism

I realized that medicalization was about phalluses rather than penises when I tried, at the NIH Consensus Development Conference on Impotence, to introduce the idea of multiple meanings of erections. Disputing the notion of the "standard normal erection," I argued that "different men and different couples expect and rely on different degrees and durations of penile rigidity to accomplish their sexual goals" (Tiefer, 1992a). Neither the audience nor the final report took any note of such an idea!

In the world of medicalization, erection is not a means to an end; there is a universal erection that is "normal," and deviations are abnormal and need treatment. The normal erection is implicitly defined as "hard enough for penetration" and lasting "until ejaculation"—informally that means a few minutes although I have never seen this in writing. Anything less is "impotence." Occasionally, men come in who have medically proper erections but who can't have two or three ejaculatory episodes. Like all our patients, they want their penis function to conform to their standards of masculinity. They request treatment, but nothing is available. Yet.

Medicalization reifies erections. Although no sexual encounter or relationship occurs in the examining room, within the medical context a man's sexuality is present when penile arteries or veins are technologically observed or when a history focusing on erections ("how hard?" "how often?") is taken. The message throughout the medical encounter is that the penis and the erection are what count—and are all that count. The patient takes home a machine to measure nocturnal erections (hardness and duration), but no instrument to assess his relationship, his knowledge of sexual techniques, his comfort with bodily expression, or anything about his partner.

Although the news reports make it sound like diagnosis and treatment of men's erectile problems follow well-established patterns, there is considerable disagreement within the field (NIH, 1992). The symbolic need for a universal phallus has prevented researchers from studying the range of real erections (not to mention variations in their subjectivity). Moreover, the available medical and surgical treatments for erectile problems can have worrisome psychological and interpersonal consequences, which are ignored by the media and the follow-up literature. John Kabalin and Robert Kessler (1989), for example, reported a 43 percent rate of malfunctioning and reoperation for 290 patients with penile prostheses operated on between 1975 and 1985. My own follow-up research documented that a variety of pervasive worries about health and safety may accompany the penile implant despite satisfactory function (Tiefer, Moss, and Melman, 1991).

An additional connection between medicalization and phallocentrism comes from classifications of mental disorders (APA, 1980; Tiefer, 1992b). The current edition of the *Diagnostic and Statistical Manual of Mental Disorders* lists nine "sexual dysfunctions"; heterosexual coitus, requiring proper erectile function, is the sole focus. This nomenclature legitimates medicalization by relating sexuality to the (supposed) universal, biological norms of "the human sexual response cycle" (Masters and Johnson, 1966; but see Tiefer, 1991b). There is no place in the medical model of sexuality for the idea that erection and orgasm are social constructions given meaning by personality, relationship, values, expectations, life experience, or culture (Tiefer, 1987).

# Conclusion

The new scholarship on men occasionally makes reference to the unbridgeable gap between the real and vulnerable penis and the mystical, all-powerful phallus (e.g., Metcalf and Humphries, 1985). Modern technology seems determined to bridge that gap or at least to keep hope alive that a perfectable biology is just around the corner. The complex ritual and devices attached to the penis in the examining room by white-coated technicians transform sexuality as they reduce it to neurology and blood flow. The spotlight directed on "the erection" within current medical practices isolates and diminishes the man even as it offers succor for his insecurity and loss of self-esteem.

Men may enter the system innocently looking to understand the cause of a change in their bodily and sexual experience; the options they are given for understanding and coping shape an ever more phallocentric experience. Their partners and any ideas or feelings these partners might have are usually irrelevant to the process (the protocol at the department where I work is unusual in this respect). Erections are presented as understandable and manipulable in and of themselves, unhooked from person or script or relationship. A discourse of vascular processes—blood flow, trapping mechanisms, venous outflow—takes over. Patient education literature teaches that organic factors account for erection problems, and patients may be led further and further into diagnostic tests to locate specific deficiencies. Since specific causes are usually not identifiable, some generalization ("your blood pressure medication," "some hardening of the arteries") is offered and a medical treatment recommended. Because the remedies do create rigid penile erections, the patient is understandably convinced that the biological rhetoric was correct.

Women occupy an essential place in the discourse (the need for vaginal "penetration" is the justification for the entire enterprise), but women are only present in terms of universalized vaginal needs; their actual desires and opinions are (conveniently) invisible, suppressed, neglected, denied.

It is not clear how one might slow or reverse this trend. Basic research continues to focus on the cellular and neurochemical operations of the penis, ensuring a future of more organic "defects." The new men's movement to the contrary notwithstanding, there is no end in sight to the medicalization of men's sexuality or to the phallocentrism it perpetuates.

# 18

# Might Premature Ejaculation Be a Physical Disorder? The Perfect Penis Takes a Giant Step Forward

*I*n the past, sexology has viewed premature ejaculation as a "man-made" disorder. Our literature suggests that ejaculation in response to physical and emotional stimulation is partly learned through practice and partly a result of differing constitutions. Just as men's anatomies and habits differ, their psychophysiological responses and abilities differ. In recent years, ejaculating "too rapidly"—that is, "too rapidly" for the partner's satisfaction—has come to be seen as a sexual "disorder" that can be treated by sex therapy.

Conceptualizing premature ejaculation as a physical disorder represents a new, but not unexpected, step in the medicalization of male sexuality and will contribute to further standardization, perfectionism, mechanization, and dehumanization of couple sexual relations.

The question is not whether medical and surgical treatments can be developed to modify aspects of human sexual response; of course they can. If we can put a man on the moon, we can certainly develop drugs and other interventions to speed up, slow down, intensify, stimulate, delay, or provoke orgasm (or erection, sexual desire, sexual fantasy, genital stimulation, or sexual memories). Sexual virtual reality is a reality, after all. How to get more technology into sexuality is not the problem. Rather, the question should be, What are the human goals of sexual relations, and how can we in the world of sexology best serve those human ends?

Where are we going with all this medicalization? The past few years have seen the development of many new devices, drugs, and surgical procedures to treat erectile dysfunction. Watching this explosion firsthand, I have often wondered whether our time and resources are really improving couples' sexual satisfaction. Medicalization certainly seems a one-sided development and is often grossly inattentive to the quality of couples' sexual interactions and experiences. Is sexology now going to go down the same road with premature ejaculation? I can see it already: scores of drug studies, dose level comparisons, side-effects comparisons, and checklists and objective measures of how many seconds and minutes erections are maintained. And what about intimacy and pleasure?

To tell you the truth, I'm getting a little sick of all this phallocentrism. At least sex therapy, whatever its limitations, stresses mutual pleasure, communication, and sexual skills. Women's concerns get equal time. By definition, partners' interests are not excluded or silenced. Even when quantitative measures of performance don't change, couples report enjoying sexual activities more.

Now, don't get me wrong. Lots of women are indeed benefited by harder and more prolonged erections. Lot of other women are benefited by their partners' increased self-esteem and improved mood as a result of their augmented performance measures. But it is also true that lots of women will be burdened by these erections and by the assumption of the professional community that harder and longer-lasting erections are automatically a boon to both man- and womankind.

I object to the neglect of women's interests by these medical developments. Medicine is becoming the phallus's best friend and is making sexual relations into even more of a competitive sport among men. I have interviewed too many women who merely "put up" with intercourse as a favor to their husbands or as part of marital bargaining. The thought of such women having to cope with rigid and long-lasting erections into their sixties, seventies, and eighties gives me a major panic attack.

For every dollar devoted to perfecting the phallus, I would like to insist that a dollar be devoted to assisting women with their complaints about partner impairments in kissing, tenderness, talk, hygiene, and general eroticism. Too many men still can't dance, write love poems, erotically massage the clitoris, or diaper the baby and let Mom get some rest. The fundamental problem is with the human sexual response cycle model of sexual relations. If we continue to work within this barren conceptualization, we will have nowhere to go but toward maximizing mechanical, compartmentalized sexual components.

I believe that discussing whether premature ejaculation is largely organic or psychogenic is yet another way to avoid dealing with women's sexuality and sexuality from women's point of view. It perpetuates sexology as concerned only with coital performance, perpetuates the erection as a be-all and end-all of sexual relations, and continues the tradition of heavy medical investment in perfecting the penis. From the feminist point of view, it's rearranging the deck chairs on the *Titanic*.

# PART FIVE

# Conclusion:
# The Politics of Sexology

*T*his book expresses a lot of worry about sexology: where it is headed, whose interests it serves, and what its impact may be. I have indeed spent no little time and effort in recent years trying to alert my colleagues in sexology to the dangers as well as the benefits of our various messages, omissions, and unconscious ideologies. Sometimes I think all this worry may be excessive. How much influence, after all, do sexologists have on real people's real sexual lives? Are not people's values and experiences determined more by factors such as family and religion than by the pontifications of medical and social science "experts"?

I don't know how to measure the impact of sexology or how to weigh it against the impact of other discourses. My professional and personal experience has been that sexological pontifications about sexual "normalcy" or about factors influencing sexuality are thoroughly disseminated throughout society, either by way of sex education, popular books, talk shows, or magazines and newspapers. Most people seem at least as familiar with Dr. Ruth as with Al Gore, and that, to me, suggests significant impact.

Although opinions on controversial issues such as homosexual civil rights, sex education, AIDS, teenage pregnancy, and pornography seem rarely informed by sex research, popular ideas about "normal" sexual relations do seem to have been affected by physiological sex research (e.g., the "human sexual response cycle," capacity for multiple orgasm, aging changes) and by research on rape and sexual abuse. Undergirding all the contemporary discourse is a quasi-Freudian impression that sex is a central part of personality and relationships and that events early in life have a serious impact on personal sexual interests and capacities. This message has had a big influence on how ordinary people think about sexuality. I think it's a self-fulfilling message, and I hope social constructionism can do much to destabilize it.

I got into sexology accidentally, and it has taken me many years to see it in its social context. Like many college graduates, I went from one subject major to another, and then one career focus to another, based on what seemed the most interesting of the available jobs. Becoming a feminist opened my eyes (and mouth!) first to the existence, and then to the limitations, of the paradigms within which I was working and helped me begin to understand that professions not only contribute services and expertise to society but also serve certain political and ideological interests.

It took me much of the past decade to see how the values and economics of science and medicine have combined with the values and operations of the mass media to medicalize the social construction of men's sexuality. Maybe a sociologist would have understood this in one day; my slower comprehension has had one virtue: I could credibly communicate to other sexologists that we needed to look beyond the psychological and the biological if we really wanted to understand the forces shaping people's sexual lives.

This section includes three chapters in which I describe why an understanding of the contexts, omissions, and uses of sexology is essential to understanding its role in the construction of sexuality discourse and popular ideas about sexuality. The concluding chapter summarizes how I have recently come to realize that the whole social constructionist project needs to be expanded (that's polite for "redone") in order to incorporate ideas about race and ethnicity.

# 19

# Three Crises
# Facing Sexology

$S$everal crises facing sexology today have placed sexology in grave danger of losing control of its subject matter and reputation, and as a result there is more than a small danger of our field fragmenting. Crises can sometimes be constructive, however, and in the case of sexology I actually think they are overdue and may lead to some very valuable transformations. But fragmentation would be an unwelcome turn of events, and I hope my warnings can result in timely reforms.

Each of the three issues I am going to describe has been brought home to me recently in a particularly forceful way. The urgency of the first issue, what is happening with *sexuality in the culture,* has been made apparent by a hobby, some might say an obsession, of mine. For many years, I have clipped articles on sexuality from the *New York Times* and various other magazines and newsletters. I file these in manila folders in file cabinets in my apartment. Occasionally, I amuse myself by going back to read what the pope said about sexual pleasure in 1978 or what the media were worrying about in terms of sex roles or children and sex in 1982. But *I can't keep up anymore!* What once was a nice, steady trickle turned into a big and growing wave and has now become a terrifying deluge. Newspapers and magazines continuously headline "lesbian chic," "the politics of date rape on campus," "new home roles for fathers," or "what the Navy is doing about sexual harassment." One week, for example, the two top U.S. news magazines had sex as their cover stories. The June 21, 1993, issue of *Newsweek* headlined "Lesbians: Coming Out Strong; What Are the Limits of Tolerance?" on its cover, and the *Time* cover issued on the same date warned "Sex for Sale: An Alarming Boom in Prostitution Debases the Women and Children of the World." The same week, the *New York Daily News* of June 18, 1993, had a photograph of St. Patrick's Cathedral on its front page; the headline was "Church Sex Crisis: Catholic Bishops Move to Restore Trust, Credibility." The tremendous avalanche of publicity about sex seems to be out of hand, and sexologists need to understand what this means.

The urgency of discussing the second issue, what is happening with *sexuality in academia,* was brought home to me at the ninth Berkshire Conference on the History of Women held at Vassar College, Poughkeepsie, New York, in June 1993. This large and exciting conference meets every three years, and 1993 was the third time I attended. Sexology was the subject of one session that focused on the work of several twentieth-century clinicians and researchers. The speakers argued that sexology's work has served to regulate and repress women's and gay people's sexuality. What upset me was not the content, a caricatured and stereotyped portrayal of some important biological and developmental work about homosexuality, but the disparaging tone in which the critique was delivered. What I learned was that it is permissible to ridicule sexology at a professional historical conference, and this seemed to me a serious problem that sexologists need to understand and address.

Finally, I feel an increasingly urgent need to respond to a third problematic area, the ongoing *medicalization of sexuality.* This is no brand new crisis, only a constantly escalating one. Each year more sexologists join medical and surgical departments and study sexuality only through the medical paradigm, and each year medical people make larger claims to legitimacy and authority as sex experts. The year 1992 saw the first National Institutes of Health Consensus Development Conference ever held on a sexual topic, impotence, and it was almost completely dominated by the medical perspective. This program gave a big boost to the imperialistic goals of urologists, who have dominated the medicalization of male sexuality. Moreover, women's sexuality is beginning to receive the same treatment. New York University Medical Center's new women's menopause, breast care, and assisted reproductive technologies center opened in May 1993 with rooms of gleaming machinery, a dozen technicians, billers, and schedulers, but a trivial psychosocial component. There are scores of such centers opening all over the country, and each one adds another building block to the medicalization of women's sexuality.

These three examples illustrate the crises facing sexology.

I think we are losing authority regarding our subject matter, sexuality, because social changes have made it impossible to study sexuality in the ways that we know how to study things. This doesn't mean that we can't learn new ways, but it does suggest that serious reform is in order or we are finished as the premiere researchers of anything remotely resembling what sexuality has become in real people's lived lives.

Moreover, I think we are in serious danger of losing control of our reputation, that is, our professional credibility, because of the verbal games being played by the medicalizers of sexuality, on the right hand, and the new historians and cultural theorists, on the left. This doesn't mean that we can't salvage our reputation, but we need to be proactive about our future. I want to suggest that it is only by standing on a securely defined, but intellectually complex, middle ground between biology and social context that sexology has any future at all.

Following a detailed examination of these three crises—sexuality in the culture, in academia, and in medicine—I will briefly turn to some responses, reforms, and predictions for the future.

## Sexuality in the Culture

### Relentless Publicity

The media barrage about sexuality over recent years results in part from media exploitation of a topic that has always attracted public interest. In addition to endless magazine and newspaper articles having to do with sexual and gender trends, there is an explosion of television and radio talk shows focusing on celebrity sex lives, uncommon and bizarre sexualities, and breakthroughs in medical science. Sex sells (indeed, tabloid journalism has exploited sexuality since its beginning) because it titillates, divulges secrets, provides moral lessons, and responds to the public yearning for sexual guidance. In the absence of widespread formal sex education, the public is attracted to the apparent objectivity of journalists. As electronic media continue to expand, there will be more and more competition for audiences and sex will continue to be a safe bet to lure business.

### Continuing Controversiality

Sexuality topics are also of interest to the media and the public because they're controversial, and therein lies an especially important historical point. As John Fout said in his introduction to the latest collection of articles from the *Journal of the History of Sexuality,* "Controversies about sexuality surely have evolved from the alterations in patterns of work, family organization, and gender relations that have been the driving force behind the continuing struggles over 'appropriate' sexual behavior for women and men" (Fout, 1993, p. 1).

That is, in the constantly reorganizing, heterogeneous, global culture of modern society, sexuality persists as a domain filled with controversy because of its connections to large social issues such as work, family organization, and gender relations. Sexual issues are political because of social changes. Diverse constituencies such as Catholic church authorities, art museum directors, educators, politicians, and self-help groups struggle to control cultural meanings, definitions, laws, and social policies surrounding sexuality. Sometimes the struggle is *directly* over sexual behavior, as when the U.S.

Supreme Court rules that abortion is constitutionally protected or sodomy is not protected, but often sexuality *symbols and proxies* are fought over—thus we have the "culture wars" over pornography and the funding of art exhibits, free speech and hate speech, books and curricula in schools, permissible questions in publicly funded surveys, and so on (Bolton, 1992).

Let's look for a moment at some of the issues grabbing the publicity and observe the larger contests over work, family, and gender. Replacing the focus on premarital and extramarital sexualities in the 1960s and 1970s, in the 1990s we have articles on domestic use of sex fantasies and erotic "toys," technological sex ("virtual reality sex"), and New Age sex (safe, spiritual, and sensual). Media preoccupation with the new and different (often based directly on a commercial interest) is largely driven by "commodification"—the tendency in a consumer culture to turn any life domain into something for sale. Nevertheless, the underlying focus is the culture's concern with shifting meanings of sexuality as indices of changing values of work, family, and gender.

Homosexuality is an endlessly popular topic that allows the media to obsess over definitions of femaleness and maleness: sexual orientation in the hypothalamus and in the high school, lesbian chic and lesbian genes, gays with children, gays in the military, and so on. Because the culture is so highly gender differentiated, almost any lifestyle topic taps into controversies over gender behavior. Sexual danger is a perennial favorite for media debate: AIDS and other sexually transmissible diseases, trafficking and prostitution, rape as a weapon of war, sexual harassment in the military and in the schools, sexual abuse of retarded girls, incest, child abuse, satanic rituals, and of course the perpetual evils of smut (aka pornography). "Sexual panics" have preoccupied journalists and "infotainers" as much as celebrity sex scandals, and for the same reasons—titillation, gossip, education, and moralizing. Each of these topics mobilizes public interest and controversy because of its link to the larger issues of identity and rights raised by the massive social changes in work, family, and gender relations.

### Sex as Substitution and Compensation

Gunter Schmidt (1983a) has often written about how interest in sexuality continues to grow in life importance as a source of solace, intimacy, pleasure, and identity in direct proportion to the absence of other sources. As long as public life, with its bureaucracy, mobility, and technology, deprives people of a sense of efficacy and self-worth, they will continue to turn to private life for emotional sustenance. Sex for pleasure, for intimacy, and for gender-affirmation matters when these needs are frustrated elsewhere. The importance of these needs, of course, is part of the changing social life fabric generated by the massive changes in work, family, and gender relations.

### Sexology Research

Now, in all honesty, how many of these complex sexual issues are we sexologists studying? Probably none of us in the International Academy of Sex Research is studying these matters at all, and as a result I believe we are losing control of our subject matter. The topics that are of interest to people about sexuality are of interest because of the struggle over norms and values taking place around the issues that sexuality symbolizes in our culture.

Scientific research on one of these topics—for example, the effects of pornography on attitudes toward sexual violence or the origins of sexual orientation—could be a very useful endeavor. But such science becomes a political football and we in sexology are horrified. It takes perseverance and a thick skin to conduct research on controversial subjects. Individual studies are always inconclusive, and when the political stakes are high, researchers are speedily vilified or lionized based on the position their (often preliminary) findings support. Unprepared to cope with this public dimension, sexologists avoid complex and controversial areas, sticking with simple designs and variables. The result is that whole areas of study are left to marginal and politically invested researchers. Qualified sexologists have less and less to say about sexuality in real people's lived lives. We cannot continue merely to burrow more and more deeply into "basic processes" while avoiding the hard work: How do these basic elements combine and connect in lived sexualities?

## Sexuality in Academia

The second crisis issue deals with sexuality in academia—in particular, two developments of great importance to our field: the growth of sexuality studies within the explosion of cultural studies and the attitude of these new theorists toward sexology.

### The "New" Sexuality Studies

The new *Journal of the History of Sexuality,* first published in 1990, is probably the best single entree into the new sexuality studies. Each issue contains not only substantive articles but also more than a dozen book reviews, an indication of the explosion of scholarship in this field. From ancient to modern history, from Europe and the Americas to Africa and Asia, every sort of document is used to examine every aspect of sex and gender. In the journal's first anthology, the editor makes some large claims about the new scholarship.

In the hundred-year period from the 1860s through the 1960s much of what was published on sexuality was authored by "medical authorities," who wrote from the perspective of a biological and gender imperative. . . . These medical authorities who theorized about sex increasingly came to be known as sexologists. . . . Over the past ten or fifteen years . . . scholars in history, other social sciences, literature and the humanistic disciplines have begun to study sex and gender from radically different viewpoints, and new theoretical perspectives have been developed by such individual theorists as Michel Foucault, by feminist thinkers, and by gay studies specialists; the study of sexuality will never be the same. (Fout, 1992, pp. 1–2)

One element of the new scholarship examines the body and bodily experience. Thomas Laqueur (1990), for example, has argued that the history of the body has not just been a series of more and more accurate understandings of anatomy and physiology; rather, the metaphors and models used to describe the sexual body have changed in response to changing popular social values about gender. Barbara Duden (1991) analyzed the interactions between patients and their doctors in eighteenth-century Germany to investigate how people experienced their bodies and thought about health in an era without drawings, models, X rays, photographs, or sonograms—that is, before the body became a machine of organs surrounded by a skin-boundary.

The new body studies in sociology are reviewed in "Bodies in a Social Landscape" (Morgan and Scott, 1993). Sociologists are looking at how body image and experience are constructed by factors such as nationalism, commercialism, individualism, and gender. The sexual body, expectations, and scripts for social experience are central to this new scholarship.

Literary studies form another element of the new sexual scholarship. Marjorie Garber's (1992) analysis of cross-dressing is a good example. Garber includes sexology's perspective on cross-dressing as just one among many points of view along with those of films, diaries, novels, and historical accounts. Sexology research is no longer "the" source of authority—sexologists provide just one of several competing perspectives. As Garber wrote in her introduction, "Academic studies have . . . shown a marked fascination with cross-dressing. Printed circulars announcing conferences on the topic [arrive] in my mail almost weekly. With the rise of new interdisciplinary studies under the general rubric of 'cultural criticism,' literary scholars, historians, anthropologists and others have found in such topics an ideal site for the study of cultural discourses about gender and sexuality" (p. 5).

The new discipline of cultural studies frequently focuses on the same issues as the "culture wars" being fought in the public sphere. The controversies within the field are intense, and they are debated with a sense that the answers will have important impacts on political processes. This sense of engagement in groundbreaking and important work is harder to sustain in sexology, a field chronically beleaguered by scientific insecurity and academic homelessness (Tiefer, 1988b, 1991b).

The new sexual scholarship is presented in many new journals. Consider *differences*, a "feminist cultural studies journal" published by Indiana University Press. A representative issue on sexuality from Summer 1991 was entitled "Queer Theory: Lesbian and Gay Sexualities." The large group of feminist and gay and lesbian scholars in cultural studies of gender and sexuality argue and advocate their topics as part of the broad movement for human rights within the aforementioned larger social changes in work, family, and gender relations. As Jennifer Terry (1991) wrote at the beginning of her essay in "Queer Theory," "The work of an historian of the present is today a form of political activism" (p. 55). To those of us raised in the good old days of positivist science, this sort of political claim is heretical, but science is not what it used to be, and the term "objective" has been out of favor for some time with philosophers of science (Guba, 1990).

In her introduction to the *differences* issue, Theresa deLauretis (1991) made further claims regarding the intentions of activist scholarship: "Homosexuality is no longer to be seen simply as marginal with regard to a dominant, stable form of sexuality (heterosexuality). . . . Instead, male and female homosexualities may be reconceptualized as social and cultural forms in their own right. . . . Same-sex desire may be potentially productive of new forms of self, community and social relations" (pp. iii, xi).

## *The Perspective on Sexology*

The second important aspect of what is happening with sexuality in academia has to do with what the new scholarship says about sexology. The December 1992 issue of *Discourse: Journal for Theoretical Studies in Media and Culture*, a University of Wisconsin cultural studies journal, offers a good example. The cover of this special issue on gay and lesbian studies includes photographs of two children accompanied by the text, "Is this child gay? How do we know? Why do we want to know? Who makes up these questions? Where do these questions get asked? Who gets to ask them?"

Obviously, one answer is that sexologists have been among the primary ones asking these questions. The new academics argue that sexologists have not only had certain privilege to ask questions and classify people by their answers but that sexology must not be seen only as a science but as a source of repressive social control over people's sexuality, especially nonmale and nonheterosexual people's sexuality. These academics deny that the concepts and methods common to sexology are neutral and objective and instead explore social interests that are supported by sexologists' work on gender and sexuality.

Let me illustrate this perspective with an example close to home—my own 1969 Berkeley dissertation. These new scholars wouldn't say, for example, that I did my dissertation on gonadal hormones and copulation patterns in the golden hamster to understand general mammalian processes of hormones and behavior. Rather, they would argue that I was privileging a tradition of biological determinism in sexology, perpetuating dichotomous gender language to describe behavior, using universalized terms to minimize differences between animals and humans, attending only to those aspects of sexuality that are linked to reproduction, and testing animals in circumstances that disguised species-specific behaviors in order to gain greater power for my universalizations. The new academics challenge us to examine the traditions and larger social meanings of our research techniques and theories.

There are now quite a significant number of books and articles examining sexology and sex research from this cultural, historical, political point of view. A few of the leading ones include Paul Robinson's *The Modernization of Sex* (1976), Jeffrey Weeks's *Sex, Politics and Society: The Regulation of Sexuality Since 1800* (1981), and Weeks's *Sexuality and Its Discontents* (1985).

Several feminist analyses have also appeared. Anthropologist Carole Vance published her examination of the sex and gender ideologies undergirding a two-week Kinsey Institute training workshop in *Feminist Studies* (Vance, 1980). British scholars Margaret Jackson, Sheila Jeffreys, and others published several papers in *Women's Studies International Forum* between 1982 and 1984 with titles such as "Sexology and the Universalization of Male Sexuality, from Ellis to Kinsey and Masters and Johnson." Janice Irvine (1990) published perhaps the most extensive analysis, *Disorders of Desire: Sex and Gender in Modern American Sexology.*

Last year, at the International Academy of Sex Research meeting in Prague, Marianne van den Wijngaard gave me a copy of her 1991 University of Amsterdam dissertation, *Reinventing the Sexes: Feminism and Biomedical Construction of Femininity and Masculinity, 1959–1985,* which deals extensively with the prenatal hormone sex research of that era. Most of the sexologists she discussed are or have been members of this Academy.

It has taken me about twenty years to thoroughly understand what it means that sexologists are historical actors and that because of the importance of sexuality in current social struggles over those changes, sexologists are inevitably *political* actors as well. Sexologists have a poor sense of history, or rather, our sense of history is simplistic and self-serving—it's of the "up the mountain" type. "We used to be blind and ignorant, but now we have greatly progressed, and our methods allow us to see clearly, blah, blah, etc. and so forth."

By contrast, historians and others in these new cultural studies argue that we sexologists *produce* knowledge rather than *discover* it. By defining through our research methods, for example, that sexuality occurs in acts that can be counted, and then by asking people on questionnaires how many of those acts they have participated in over the past week (a fairly common method), we don't just find out about sexual acts occurring during a week, *we create a certain way of thinking about sexuality that we then find out about.* When we then report our results, we influence, sometimes in important ways, sexuality in society by disseminating categories that people use to understand their own lives.

Some of the feminist articles I mentioned above criticize sexologists' methods, concepts, and theories and argue that the sexism and heterosexism of sexology has been *intentional,* part of a design to make heterosexuality better for women in order to bind them more tightly to marriage. When sex research counts sexual acts, what acts are being counted, they ask. Sexologists are actually classifying human interactions into sexual and nonsexual by the development of these concepts, and the new cultural analysts look at the larger social goals that are being served. This is what Foucault meant with his claim that *bodies of knowledge reflect, express, and especially generate relations of power.*

When the cultural theorists argue that sexologists are historical actors and that sexology is an instrument of power as well as a science, they are looking at this struggle over work, family, and gender relations—a struggle that has been taking place for hundreds of years—and asking, Where is sexology positioned? Whose interests has it been serving? Their answer, and I think their answer has some truth but is too narrow and regards sexology too monolithically, is that sexologic discourses are *normative discourses*—discourses of prescription and deviance management, discourses of social control and repression. Sexologists of gender, they say, want to reinforce gender; sex therapists want to reinforce marriage; biological researchers want to promote biological reductionism and a sense that sexual orientation as well as factors affecting sexual activities are fixed and unchangeable, inborn, and "natural." The intentionality can be questioned, the monolithicness of the field can be questioned, but the outcomes may be as they describe.

Thus, the new academic studies of sexuality see sexology not as the premiere source of valid sexuality scholarship but rather as a major player in the construction of sexuality, and, too often, of a conservative sexuality.

## Sexuality in Medicine

The final crisis is one that I have spoken and written of often in the ten years I have had the privilege of working in a urology department in a medical center and observing firsthand the increasing medicalization of male sexuality (Tiefer, 1986a, 1993). Briefly, I have argued that a sociological process of medicalization has been occurring in many behavioral domains of life, including sexuality (Conrad and Schneider, 1980). The current crisis for sexology comes via what one might call "the imperialism" of urology with regard to men's erectile problems. Sexology is being bypassed. For example, last month's newsletter of the American Urological Association (AUA) reported the results of a poll the association had commissioned asking U.S. urologists how they treat patients with erection problems (Poll shows widespread use of three major impotence treatments, 1993). The results were shown in a graph: Ninety-four percent use vacuum devices, 90 percent use surgical implants, and 84 percent use injection therapy.

There is just a little omission in this poll—the whole domain of behavioral and psychotherapeutic interventions is completely absent! Now, maybe the poll just covered the methods that urologists themselves employ and didn't inquire about referrals for psychotherapy. Even so, such an omission indicates that psychotherapy referrals must be rather minor for the AUA.

I would argue that there is a very real contest going on to define the nature of sexual problems and that urologists and other physicians are working hard to frame and define sexual problems in medical terms, to emphasize biological research on such problems, to publicize medical etiologies and treatments, and to institutionalize the primary care of sexuality within medicine. This is what is meant by medicalization. In the same issue of the AUA's newsletter appears this statement: "AUA Policy Statement: Sexual dysfunction in the male is a disease entity, the diagnoses and treatments of which deserve equal attention to that given other diseases. American Urological Association, Inc., Executive Committee, January, 1990." This statement is not the result of scientific investigation—it is a bold political claim with tremendous ramifications for sexology.

No one in our field can have failed to notice that a medical juggernaut is sweeping over the definition, diagnosis, and treatment of men's erection problems. There are scores of new technologies under development or in use to diagnose and create penile (and maybe soon clitoral) erections. There is obviously a snowball effect in progress; as new machines are being invented to detect new abnormalities, new treatments must be tested and used to correct these abnormalities. What's more, in the realm of basic research, teams of new scientists are hunting around the subcellular fractions of the penis identifying new constituents of the erectile process. This basic research, obviously a never-ending process, sets up a perpetual biological basis to maintain the medicalization of sexuality.

The academic sexuality scholars would say that a certain kind of sexuality is fostered by these developments—a sexuality of compartmentalized bodily functions, a sexuality dependent on mysterious technology, a sexuality where subjective experience is disregarded in favor of machine information, a sexuality defined as functions of universalized body parts of one person independent of any relationship or cultural context, a sexuality of lifelong youth-like performance, a penetration-centered sexuality, a sexuality dependent on experts.

They would also analyze the many economic interests that support medicalization, and it would not escape their notice that the medicalization of male sexuality is deeply neglectful of women's interests, that it essentially perpetuates a phallocentric sexuality. These are the ideological consequences of medical-technical trends that serve political purposes in the large, ongoing social struggles over family, work, and gender relations. Medicalization represents a crisis for sexology because it is a bold attempt to replace a multidimensional perspective with biological reductionism and medical privilege.

## Responding to These Crises

What can sexologists do about these crises? I have two suggestions, although each requires greater elaboration than I can offer here.

### Sexology and the New Cultural Scholars

First, we need to expand our definition of sexology to incorporate aspects of the new academic scholarship. Embracing the new cultural scholars, of course, could be merely a cynical political maneuver—by including them we defuse their ability to attack or undermine us. But I do not make this suggestion cynically. I think that our ahistorical and apolitical conferences and journals are missing a lot. For the reasons I discussed in the first section of this chapter, I am convinced that sexuality is a political topic. Understanding sexuality in our time requires that we understand more about how we fit into larger social and political schemes.

### Better Research Methods

The new academics are right to challenge traditional sexologists to examine how their research methods generate a particular construction of sexuality that seems to omit much of the complexity of sexuality in real people's lived lives. If we believe that sexuality is a holistic phenomenon, a psychobiosocial unity, and I think most sexologists do subscribe to this view, then our methods must follow from this assumption. We must abandon outdated experimental methods that oversimplify sexuality in the quest for a "rigorous" scientific design. We must pursue theories and concepts to explain how sexuality is constructed so differently in different historical and cultural milieux. As Richard Fox and T. J. Jackson Lears (1993) wrote in the introduction to their new collection in cultural studies, "We need to tell much more complicated and multilayered stories than most of us have been accustomed to telling" (p. 10).

I suggest that we make a major effort to develop in reality the psychobio-social model we all acknowledge but rarely use in actual research. We cannot afford to simply bide our time until someday the psycho- and the bio- and the socio- pieces of research finally all fit together. How do gender, culture, ethnicity, age, health, early life experience, and sexual history act simulta-neously? That is the challenge. The multifactorial paradigm is what sexology has had to offer, and we can make it the dominant vision if we seize the opportunity offered by these contemporary crises.

## Conclusion

I was talking with Danish historian Karin Lützen about these ideas at the Berkshire women's history conference. She was pessimistic about sexual-wissenchaft, pointing out that some things just don't go together, that some disciplines are too disparate and simply can't mesh.

Well, the challenge is to make them mesh. We are caught between the medical juggernaut and the new cultural studies, and we have a golden op-portunity to seize, define, and elaborate a complex middle ground. Sexol-ogy has existed in the past few decades with its members keeping one foot in their primary disciplines and one foot in the house of sexology. But this casual professional alliance may be too weak to resist the contemporary pres-sures. We need to advocate for more funding for multidisciplinary research and dialogue. We need to gain more visibility and credibility for our multi-disciplinary perspective. Those of us devoted to the study of sexuality must work out new research methods that respect the complexity and diversity of sexual experience. If we lose control of our subject matter, if it fragments under the economic and political pressures of the moment, then not only we but society will have lost an opportunity that may be a long time coming again.

# 20

# New Perspectives in Sexology: From Rigor (Mortis) to Richness

This is a chapter *about* rigor. Actually, it's a chapter *against* rigor! Here I propose that rigor-rhetoric is actually code language for the conservative position in a hot and important intellectual controversy in the politics of research. The politics of research is linked to larger cultural struggles, and I suggest that those struggles help explain the positions taken in debates over rigor in sex research. Rigor, once stripped of its superiority complex, may be able to take its place among a pantheon of approaches to the understanding of sexuality. In other words, my purpose is to argue for a more diverse and inclusive scientific vision that will take us *from rigor to richness.*

## The Current Emphasis on Rigor in Sex Research

A recent article in the *Journal of Sex Research* written by the journal's editor serves as a good example of the view I wish to criticize (Abramson, 1990). Although I'm going to focus on this article at some length, Paul Abramson is far from the only proponent of this point of view. Sexologists Ira Reiss (1982) and Donald Mosher (1989), among others, have also argued for this perspective.

Abramson's article, entitled "Sexual Science: Emerging Discipline or Oxymoron?" was an explicit defense of and plea for rigor in sexologic research. It was a paean, a fervent expression of approval, to rigor, as indicated at the beginning of the abstract: "The purpose of this paper is to argue for the necessity of a rigorous sexual science" (p. 147). What is a rigorous sexual science? Rigor, the dictionary has it, derives from the Latin for *stiff,* as in *rigor mortis* or *rigid,* and is usually taken to mean *strict* or *severe.* The latter definitions could signify severely high standards, but I feel the term *rigor,* as Abramson and others use it, is meant to signify severely narrow standards— the promotion of science of a *specific* type.

As the article unfolds, it appears that rigorous science is the application of those research methods that will produce "detailed quantitative information" (p. 148) on patterns of human sexual behavior, such as would be useful in current work on the transmission dynamics of HIV. Abramson is embarrassed by the reaction of prominent statisticians, epidemiologists, and population ecologists as they discover that sexology lacks detailed quantitative data on the prevalence of various sex acts, numbers of partners, frequencies of activities, and the like and become frustrated in their efforts to develop mathematical models for AIDS transmission.

His wish that sexology could play ball with these specialists, that sexology had the numbers to plug into the mathematical models, led Abramson to define a very traditional view of sexual science: "The intent of sexual science is to obtain careful observations or measurements of sexual phenomena which in turn, are expounded in a theoretical structure. Predictions . . . are deducted from these theories, which once again are measured against observations of sexual behavior. Progress in sexual science is facilitated by the inflating database and the continually reformulated theories" (Abramson, 1990, p. 149).

Abramson concludes his paean by threatening diminished public influence should the profession not heed his warning:

> There are profound consequences of the absence of a rigorous sexual science. . . . Most obvious are the limitations in predicting the spread of AIDS . . . [but there are other] key questions in the field of sexual science, e.g., what motivates human sexual behavior? what is the function of human sexual behavior throughout the lifespan? . . . Future generations will find it incomprehensible that so little effort was marshalled to obtain data on and establish a science of human sexual behavior. (Abramson, 1990, p. 162)

## Rigor-Rhetoric and the Quest for Professional Legitimacy

What's wrong with this plea for rigor? Isn't Abramson simply calling for *good quality* in sex research? In my opinion, the article is not about quality in research and not about the judgment of future generations but about a seat at the table of the current scientific establishment. If we demystify *rigor,* we find it really means professional legitimacy.

Sex researchers have a persistent inferiority complex. We're always afraid that people think there's something wrong with us for doing the work that we do, and we're always trying to compensate. This worry, of course, is not a delusion—many people *do* suspect the motives of sexologists, and we surely put up with far more snickering about our career motives than do fast-food entrepreneurs, police officers, or conservation advocates. The snickering comes when people repeatedly make the fundamental error of attribution—they know their own behavior is governed by situational factors but attribute *other* people's behavior to qualities of character and inner motivation (Ross, 1977; Harvey and Weary, 1985). Our motives for specializing in sex are always being scrutinized and snickered at.

Some scientists in the field of human sexuality have coped with this problem through emphasizing their methodological purity. Listen again to Abramson:

> The academic community has generally regarded human sexuality and rigorous science as mutually exclusive endeavors. For example, how many tenured professors at major universities in the United States devote their research energies to human sexual behavior? ... How many professors receive tenure at major universities in the United States as a consequence of their research on human sexual behavior? How many job advertisements, in the past 10 years, have sought professors with an expertise in human sexuality? How many governmental agencies set aside funds to support basic research on human sexual behavior? How many sexual science programs exist in the United States? How much grant money is allocated for basic research on human sexual behavior? The answers to all of these questions is very little or none. (Abramson, 1990, p. 149)

This is the plaint of a man who fears that because we are not perceived as rigorous, we are excluded from the party. He's not saying that more rigor would lead sexologists to a broader, deeper, richer, more enduring understanding of sexuality. Rather, his complaint is that no rigor means no respect.

## Legitimacy Through Rigor Is a False God

Suppose it turns out that rigor-rhetoric is not really about quality but about professional legitimacy. What's wrong with professional legitimacy? Isn't it all right to want tenure? promotions? grants? a seat at the table? a little respect? Won't these signs of legitimacy actually enable sexologists to make a more substantial contribution to the world than we could otherwise?

I think the argument is fundamentally flawed. The reason why sexology doesn't have the academic clout of some other disciplines is not because its methods are not rigorous. It is because our subject matter is inevitably and inexorably political.

Magnus Hirschfeld, the important turn-of-the-century sexologist, carved this hopeful commitment in his Berlin Institute: *"per scientiam ad justitiam"* (through science to justice) (Weeks, 1985, p. 71). And what happened to Hirschfeld? His institute was seized by the Nazis in 1933 and all its materials were destroyed. Did this happen because he wasn't rigorous enough? Would more quantitative methods have protected him?

Was it because of a concern over rigorous data that Attorney General Meese's Commission on Pornography preferred ex–film star Linda Lovelace's confessions to sexologist Gene Abel's extensive information, gathered over a period of many years, about rapists' use of pornography (U.S. Department of Justice, 1986)?

## Rigor-Rhetoric and the Politics of Research

Abramson's paper appeared in the May 1990 issue of the *Journal of Sex Research*, between two issues devoted to feminist perspectives on sexuality. The contrasts between the feminist issues and the May 1990 issue reveal strong differences of opinion regarding standards of quality in sex research.

Right off the bat, the introduction to the first feminist issue explicitly rejects "a concept of sexual science based on a narrow reading of science" and "a limited definition of strategies for increasing recognition and gaining respectability" (Vance and Pollis, 1990, p. 3). There is no paean to rigor here. Rather, the feminist editors argue that "the papers in this issue reflect *many* . . . new directions. . . . Employing *diverse* methods and sources of data, authors examine women's sexual experience and the cultural frame that constructs sexuality. . . . Examining the frameworks, methods and assumptions about women and gender which we employ in sexology is a vital part of this project" (pp. 4–5, emphasis added).

Why should examining the methods *used in sexology* be a vital part of understanding sexuality? Recall Abramson's (1990) assertion: "The intent of sexual science is to obtain careful observations or measurements of sexual phenomena which in turn, are expounded in a theoretical structure" (p. 149). Here, sexology is the means to understand sexuality. But in the feminist articles, sexology *itself* is part of the subject matter. How can sexology be both subject and method?

Michel Foucault ([1976] 1978) has had a profound impact on sexual studies with his argument that to understand "sexuality" we must understand *the texts* wherein it is defined. "The history of sexuality," he wrote, "must first be written from the viewpoint of *a history of discourses*" (p. 69, emphasis added). Foucault's position is that sexuality is constructed within particular sociohistorical contexts (Tiefer, 1987). Out of human potentials for consciousness and behavior, sociocultural forces of definition and regulation shape an experience that becomes "naturalized" and feels unlearned.

Foucault's argument helps to explain the feminist assertion that part of the project of understanding sexuality must be to examine sexology. Like it or not, sexology itself is one of the forces of definition and regulation constructing sexual experience.

The impact of these social constructionist ideas on sexology is tremendous, and one shattering implication has to do with scientific method and the notion of rigor. The social constructionists would argue that if sexologists follow the traditional model espoused by Abramson (1990), the only sexuality that will be studied will be that of the observer. Since scientists propose the definitions and meanings used in their research, they will actually be studying a projection of themselves, or at best, of the current state of the field. The observed person, whom we call the subject, but whose subjectivity is ignored, is not really consulted, is merely stuffed into the sexologist's categories (Danziger, 1988). The implications for sexology of the social constructionist project are that what purports to be the most neutral and objective perspective turns out to be highly and irrevocably subjective.

When I use the phrase "the politics of research," I am referring to this clash of definitions and models. The feminist issues of the *Journal of Sex Research* challenge sexology to face a significant contemporary intellectual debate over the definition and validity of traditional science, especially of social science. A challenge to the foundations of science has been building over the past few decades from a variety of perspectives that dispute the possibility of objectivity, operational definitions, or traditional quantitative methods, and claims for more rigor must now be seen in this larger context (Gergen, 1982).

The challenge to the status quo in science comes from the same team that is challenging the status quo elsewhere in culture—in art, in politics, in the law. This team consists of the coalition of women and ethnic and sexual minorities who no longer worry about getting a seat at the table through playing the game in the traditional way because they have been excluded no matter how well they have played the game. They have learned that legitimacy is conferred by matters other than quality, and they have turned to examine those other matters.

In the November 8, 1990, issue of the *New York Review of Books,* in an article entitled "A Lab of One's Own," anthropologist Clifford Geertz reviewed three books on feminism and science wherein feminists challenged the dominance of traditional models of science in the name of a more variegated vision. In acknowledging that there is a tide of revisionism in science, Geertz identified the 1962 publication of Thomas Kuhn's enormously influential book, *The Structure of Scientific Revolutions,* as the watershed event with ripples and repercussions extending into many academic fields. Geertz closed his not-very-favorable review with the prediction that the challenges raised by the new scholarship would "not soon disappear."

The editorial section of the October 28, 1990, *New York Times* joined the argument with a piece criticizing a "new orthodoxy" in academia (Bernstein, 1990). The author observed that "minorities, women and homosexuals," mostly radicals from the 1960s but now apparently tenured professors, were enforcing conformity to the view that Western civilization requires intellectual affirmative action. You know something is a political hotcake when the *New York Review of Books* and the *New York Times* publish opinion pieces on it in the same week, and you don't need a weatherman to know which way the wind is blowing when the opinions expressed in both publications are similar.

## Sexology and the Politics of Research

So poor beleaguered sexology, already suffering the slings and arrows of ridicule and delegitimation because of its risque subject matter, finds its discussions about scientific method located smack in the middle of a raging cultural struggle over diversity. Where will sexology position itself in the debate on methodology?

In an essay on the status of sex research, William Simon (1989) encouraged sexologists to become more familiar with the ideas of Foucault and postmodernism. He identified an "emergent consensus about the absence of consensus" (p. 18) as the central theme of postmodernism and suggested that plunging into this way of thinking results in "a sense of being forced to an unexpected and often discomforting pluralism" (p. 19).

Pluralism and diversity, of course, sound very appealing—very democratic, very tolerant. They also sweep under the table issues of power and domination—the construction of difference is, after all, about domination (Carby, 1990). Pluralism is confusing in academia, where evaluation and competition are so much a part of the playing field. What standards would be utilized in a pluralistic sexology? A single standard of rigor makes things a lot simpler.

## Richness and High-Quality Sexology

Surprisingly, a more inclusive vision may seem more appealing in light of one of Abramson's goals, a goal that I believe can only be accomplished with an attitude toward methodology that embraces difference. Recall Abramson's warning about the "profound consequences of the absence of a rigorous sexual science" and his warning that "most obvious are the limitations in predicting the spread of AIDS . . . [but there are other] key questions in the field of sexual science, e.g., what motivates human sexual behavior? what is the function of human sexual behavior throughout the lifespan?" (p. 162).

I agree that those are among the key questions, although as a social constructionist I would avoid language like *"the* function of human sexual behavior."* But another question is, How can we best get answers to these kinds of questions?

I propose that Simon's "unexpected and discomforting pluralism" is well demonstrated by the range of articles presented in the two feminist issues of *The Journal of Sex Research.* Sharon Thompson's (1990) interviews with teenage girls about their early sexual experiences is a study of narratives—open-ended interviews in which participants are asked to tell about their experience (Personal Narratives Group, 1989). Thompson divided her narratives into two groups: alienated narratives and pleasure narratives. But beyond that, there is no classification. There are no "careful measurements of sexual phenomena," though there is careful quoting and much theoretical discussion. We see the confusing terrain of coercion and choice and the role of expectation in experience. The author's values, pro-pleasure and pro-education, are clearly visible, but does that exclude the scholarship from science? The old definitions of science quoted by the rigor-defenders might say, "Yes, it's interesting, but it isn't science," but is the purpose of such exclusion merely rhetorical gatekeeping?

Ann Kaplan's (1990) paper on the images of motherhood and sexuality in contemporary film and fiction and Kathryn McMahon's (1990) analysis of sex and gender articles in twelve years of *Cosmopolitan* magazine follow Foucault's advice to understand texts wherein sexuality is constructed and defined. These papers, without any attempt at conceptual classification or quantitative measurement, expose themes and emphases in media sexual ideologies. Do they teach us about sexuality in our time? After reading these papers, do we understand anything more about "what motivates sexual behavior" or its "functions throughout the lifespan"? Assuming we've learned something, have we learned it through science? What about an article like Jan Clausen's (1990) lengthy monologue on her sexual and social experiences with partners of both sexes? Is that monologue science? Now, we're really talking lack of consensus; we're into pluralism for sure.

In an article introducing the ideas of social constructionism to psychology, Kenneth Gergen (1985) wrote that a constructionist analysis must "eschew the empiricist account of scientific knowledge . . . the traditional Western conception of objective, individualistic, ahistorical knowledge . . . [and embrace criteria such as] the analyst's capacity to invite, compel, stimulate or delight the audience. . . . Virtually any methodology can be employed so long as it enables the analyst to develop a more compelling case" (pp. 271, 272, 273).

I might put this notion a little differently. It's not that we have to eschew the empiricist account of knowledge, but rather that we have to demystify and desacralize that account as the most real or valid account (Sherif, 1979).

Instead of adhering, sheeplike, to a prestige hierarchy of methods with experimental, controlled, and quantitative methods at the top and correlational, descriptive, and qualitative methods at the bottom, we must accept that different approaches produce different insights, that all "facts" and other forms of understanding the world are limited by the circumstances of their production, and that methods are complementary, not competing, even when their premises conflict (Tiefer, 1978).

## Conclusion

At the beginning of this chapter, I called Abramson's article a paean but neglected to mention the Greek origins of the term. According to my dictionary, a paean was originally a war cry. And a paean to "rigorous science" now indeed turns out to be a war cry on behalf of one particular definition of what should count as knowledge about the world. I myself no longer hear that call to arms. I'm busy poking around in interview narratives, magazine analyses, and historical archives and—yes, *and*—looking at questionnaire and hormone studies. Do I sacrifice legitimacy? Will I get to sit at the table? History will judge where the rejection of rigor-rhetoric will get us. In the meantime, in the rich and complicated mixture of information of many colors, I find sexuality.

# 21

# Women's Sexuality:
# Not a Matter of Health

## The Power of Naming

*W*hat are the advantages and disadvantages of locating women's sexuality under the rubric of health? Designating sexuality a matter of "health" has important ramifications in terms of appropriate authorities, institutional control, language and imagery, methods for study, and, most important, people's views of its place in their own lives (Featherstone, Hepworth, and Turner, 1991; Conrad and Kern, 1981). In this context, it is important to note that "health" is not dictated by biology any more than "sexuality" is dictated by biology (Scott and Morgan, 1993); they are both matters of language and culture, sets of biological potentials expressed and constructed very differently in different sociohistorical situations. Diseases and illnesses are matters of classification, and they change as social values about "normal" aspects of age, fitness, and gender change. Yes, we all are born and die, and in that sense, biology dominates, but how we use and experience our bodily potentials in between those bookends is no more dictated by biology than is the style of our hats.

Thinking about the consequences of assigning categories, I am reminded that language does not name reality, it organizes reality (Potter and Wetherell, 1987). Topics within areas of health, mental health, and sexuality have been subject to repeated renaming and redefinition as social values have changed. Because sexuality is contested political terrain where various ideological forces struggle for legitimacy and cultural authority, all discourse about sexuality, including scientific and clinical discourses, represents some worldview and political agenda. The informed discussant accepts that there is no neutral ground, no apolitical ground of technical expertise where one can coolly and objectively discuss the facts and leave politics at the door.

## Appeals of the Health Model

Feminists are attracted to a health model for sexuality in large part because they want the "legitimacy" and "moral neutrality" for their claims about women's rights and needs offered by what purports to be reliance on the "objective" facts of biological "nature." Many feminists celebrated the publication of Masters and Johnson's (1966) physiological measures of people engaged in masturbation and coitus, for example, because the study seemed to provide objective proof that women's sexual capacities not only existed but equaled those of men (e.g., Ehrenreich, Hess, and Jacobs, 1986). Feminists felt they finally had ammunition against the tyranny of the Freudian vaginal orgasm, not to mention against the earlier claims of women's passionlessness and frigidity. As Masters and Johnson (1966) themselves boasted, "With orgasmic physiology established, the human female now has an undeniable opportunity to develop realistically her own sexual response levels" (p. 138).

The legitimacy offered by the medical/health model of sex extends beyond descriptions of women's sexual capacities to the implicit assumption that sexuality, at least of the medically approved "normal" sort, is actually a component of health, that is, that sexuality itself is healthy. Because *healthy* has become the premiere adjective meaning *goodness,* it can be used to endorse everything from behaviors to products and services (Barsky, 1988). The importance of such an imprimatur for sexuality cannot be overestimated in a culture where sexuality has long been located in the moral domain and where allegations about a woman's sexuality could easily destroy her social reputation and standing (Freedman and D'Emilio, 1988).

The legitimacy and entitlement offered women's sexuality by the medical model appear to derive directly from "nature" without the intervention of culture or cultural standards of right and wrong. I have elsewhere discussed how the discourse of "naturalism" and reliance on "laws of nature" are rhetorically tempting not only for the public but for sex researchers and activists (Tiefer, 1990b). Once having opted for biological justification, supporters of women's sexuality can even recruit evolutionary theory, that replacer of (or, sometimes, competitor of) divine law, as the ultimate and inarguable source of authority (Caporael and Brewer, 1991).

Locating women's sexuality under the rubric of health appeared to give it a strong, secure, and eminently respectable home that feminists could use as a base to press for improved sex education, protection against sexual violence, reproductive rights, elimination of the sexual double standard, and all the other components of the sexuality plank in the contemporary women's rights platform.

## Hidden Assumptions of the Health Model

But, alas, all is not so simple. There are hidden assumptions accompanying the health model that make it deeply worrisome when applied to women's sexuality: the four medical model assumptions of norms and deviance, universality, individualism, and biological reductionism (Mishler, 1981).

## Norms and Deviance

First and most important is the fundamentally normative structure of the health and medicine model—the assumption that there is such a thing as healthy sexuality that can be distinguished from nonhealthy (diseased, abnormal, sick, disordered, pathological) sexuality. The normative basis of the health model is absolutely inescapable—the only way we can talk about "signs and symptoms" or "treatments and cures" or "diagnosis and classification" is with regard to norms and deviations from norms. But where shall we get the norms for women's sexuality? What are the legitimate and compelling sources and what do they say?

In fact, sexuality norms are far better understood by sociologists than by health specialists. That is, sociologists have analyzed sexual category-making as part of the social discourse of sexuality with regard to such subjects as promiscuity, prostitution, masturbation, nymphomania, and frigidity (Schur, 1984; Sahli, 1984). Can health specialists demonstrate that their "sexual health" norms derive from scientific sources and not simply cultural values (Tiefer, 1986b)?

In my opinion there are no valid clinical norms for sexuality. There are diverse cultural and legal standards, and they have been selectively appropriated by the health and medicine domain. But just as playing canasta ten hours a day *may be* a sign of emotional malfunction, that doesn't mean there is a disease of "hypercanasta." That is, without being facetious, there's just too much lifestyle, historical, and cultural variability in sexual behavior standards for us to be able to establish *clinical* norms of sexual activity performance, choices, frequencies, partners, and subjectivities. One of my biggest worries about locating sexuality discourse within the domain of health is the potential abuse of norms. Sociologists point out that norms are the principal mode of social control over sexual behavior because the norms become internalized and even unconscious to the point where they can "police" people twenty-four hours a day (DeLamater, 1981). What we don't need in a society with a history of women's sexual disenfranchisement are additional sources of repression.

## Universality

The difference between clinical norms and cultural standards is, presumably, that health is based on pan-cultural standards of biological functioning and malfunctioning. The only such standards for sexual function currently derive from the physiological research of Masters and Johnson (1966), and I have written at length about how that research is based on a flawed and self-fulfilling design (Tiefer, 1991c). Masters and Johnson's finding of a universal "human sexual response cycle" of arousal and orgasm was not valid because they only took measurements on subjects who were able to exhibit masturbatory and coital arousal and orgasm in their laboratory. I do not doubt that many (most? all?) human bodies *can* produce genital vasocongestion and orgasm. But should those physical performance capacities constitute universal medical norms? In other words, is there any "health" consequence that merits the claim that absence of these features constitutes a disorder?

## *Individualism*

Although family medicine comes close sometimes, I know of no medical specialty that does not consider as the appropriate unit of analysis the individual person (or something smaller, such as the individual organ or organ-system) (Stein, 1987). Should we follow the medical model and situate sexuality in the individual person's physiology/psychology? Is sexuality better understood as an enduring or even essential quality of the self or as a phenomenon that emerges in a social context? Given the usefulness of systems perspectives in sexual therapy, sexuality as a concept may turn out to have much in common with friendship (Verhulst and Heiman, 1988). One can take a history of a person's lifetime experiences with friendship (or sexuality), but each experience will only be understood when contextual issues such as scripting, expectations, and negotiations are analyzed.

Moreover, women's sexual lives are embedded in, we might say "constructed by," sociohistorical frameworks that feminists have identified as patriarchal. Focusing on women's sexuality in terms of individual capacity and expression, as occurs within the biomedical framework, not only ignores the relationship context but also ignores the larger political framework, with the subsequent danger of mistaking something socially constructed and then internalized for some transhistorical essence (e.g., MacKinnon, 1987).

Finally, the individual focus of the health model "privatizes" sexual worries and difficulties, making them the result of some malfunctioning of a "natural" and "normal" capacity. The individual is often blamed for causing or contributing to the problem, which perpetuates shame and contributes to further ignorance about the way sexuality is socially constructed (Crawford, 1977). Any sense of entitlement to sexuality given by the health model is negated, it seems to me, when the same model misleadingly implies that sexuality is some individual and private birthright rather than a learned and deeply socialized phenomenon.

## *Biological Reductionism*

Finally, a health model of sexuality inevitably focuses on the biology of sexuality and on biological standards for normal and abnormal functioning.

When sexuality is seen primarily as a matter of health, research on biology predominates and is considered more central and definitive than research on sociocultural influences. An emphasis on biological research contrasts with what feminist historians have seen as the more progressive trend—an ever-widening awareness of the sociocultural factors that determine women's sexual opportunities and experiences (Duggan, 1990). "Social actors possess genitals rather than the other way around," as one feminist essay put it (Schneider and Gould, 1987, p. 123).

Biological reductionism is also antifeminist because it is far less likely to result in policies that limit or reverse negative social elements. Linnda Caporael and Marilynn Brewer (1991), for example, noted, "In the current Western milieu, people tend to feel a lesser responsibility to redress inequities attributed to biology than inequities that arise from defects in policy, law or social structure" (p. 2). Research showing the influence of hormones or neurotransmitters on women's sexual responsiveness will have a different impact on policy than research on the influences of rape prevalence, body image obsessions, gender socialization, or contraceptive availability.

## The Medicalization of Men's Sexuality: An Object Lesson

These hidden assumptions of the health model are not just abstract worries—they have had visible consequences in the medicalization of men's sexuality (see the chapters in Part 4). To make a long story short, sexual health for men has been reduced to the erectile functioning of the penis. Impotence research and treatment constitute a new and highly successful medical subspecialty for urologists, and diagnostic and treatment technologies are a growth industry. The field of men's sexuality focuses on a specific physical organ and dictates universalized standards of functioning and malfunctioning. There's no real interest in the sexuality of a person, not to mention that of a couple with a particular culture and relationship. There's just universalized biological organ norms—as for the heart or kidney.

This medical juggernaut has resulted from the collusion of men's interests in a face-saving explanation for poor "performance," the societal perpetuation of a phallocentric script for sexual relations, economic incentives for physicians and manufacturers, the media appeal of medicalized sexuality topics, and the absence of a strong alternative metaphor for sexuality that would affirm variability. These are powerful forces, and in the presence of continuing social pressure for sexual adequacy as defined by intercourse performance, they have created an explosive new medical development.

The clinical developments around "impotence" are supported by a tremendous quantity of basic cellular research on the penis, and the hunt for biological variables that might affect erectile functioning and become a source for new diagnostic or treatment interventions is assured a long life.

In 1992, the National Institutes of Health held its first Consensus Development Conference on a sexuality topic (there have been several Consensus Development Conferences annually since 1977). The topic of the conference, "Impotence," confirms these trends. The participants were overwhelmingly urologists. The outcome was a lengthy document essentially ignoring culture, partners, lifestyles, or lifetime differences; it was a document reifying "erection" as the essence of men's sexuality and asserting the medical model as the proper frame of reference for understanding and intervention.

I foresee the same outcome for women's sexuality, should some new physiological discovery about the genitalia emerge that could be developed into an industry and a clinical practice. For example, the *New York Times,* covering the 1993 American Urological Association, quoted one urologist as casually speculating that vascular abnormalities of the clitoris might play the same role in women's sexual problems as the extensively researched vascular penile abnormalities (Blakeslee, 1993). Discussing women's sexuality in terms of health leads directly, it seems to me, to a biologically reductionist, compartmentalized, economically driven system that ignores far more than it includes the real complexities of women's sexuality.

## A Man-Centered Sexology

It is not difficult to demonstrate that sexology is and has been man-centered (Tiefer, 1988b, 1991a). Despite the incorrect impression that sexology is friendly to women's interests (sex therapy seems to include a lot about communication and whole-body pleasure, lesbianism is considered a normal sexual orientation alternative, and so on), there is actually active resistance to feminist analysis within the field.

The most dramatic example of this resistance comes from a careful examination of the nomenclature for sexual dysfunction (Tiefer, 1988a, 1990a, 1992b; Boyle, 1993). Although there appears to be scrupulous gender equality in the numbers of sexual dysfunctions, and remarkable similarity in the types of dysfunctions listed, women's complaints as they are reported in their own voices are absent (Hite, 1976; Frank, Anderson, and Rubinstein, 1978). Women's official dysfunctions are directly related to performing coitus—proper vaginal lubrication, orgasm, absence of vaginal constriction, desire, and absence of genital aversions. There's nothing about love, gentleness, kissing, passion, body freedom, freedom from fear, lack of coercion, communication, emotional involvement, manual skills, cooperative contraception, infection avoidance, and the like. Although I have sent numerous letters to the authors of the 1994 edition of the nomenclature, there will be no changes.

Thus, sexology, in its current phase of tunnel vision, continues to neglect many variables important to women. Popular authors and feminist activists fill bookstores addressing women's issues and presenting diverse women's voices, but these voices are not represented in the professional texts, training programs, and licensing requirements or in insurance-reimbursible complaints, sex education curricula, or government conferences. Until the schism between the feminist literature and sexology is closed, the male-centered paradigm of sexology is dangerous for women.

## Women-Centered Sex Research

My experiences with men's medicalized sexuality and with the unyielding male-centered sexology paradigm frighten me about the future of women's "sexual health." Ordinary people are especially vulnerable to mystification and exploitation. As feminists, our efforts on behalf of women's sexuality should be in terms of providing and financially supporting education and consciousness raising rather than health care at the present time. Sex research should raise up women's diverse voices, not impose a preexisting paradigm through questionnaires or measurements. And, of course, the most beneficial effects of all will come from efforts to promote women's political and economic power.

# 22

# Sex Is Not a Natural Act:
# The Next Phase

The astute reader will have noticed that issues of race and ethnicity have rarely been mentioned in these essays. I should say that the nonwhite reader will have noticed—white readers do not often seem to notice such omissions, and therein lies both the problem and its solution (Spelman, 1988). Nor have I dwelt on real-world differences other than gender—nationality, age, able-bodiedness, sexual orientation, and so on. These omissions will doubtlessly have been noticed mostly by nonheterosexuals, people with disabilities, and others who are aware of "difference" from their own experiences.

As a white, heterosexual, able-bodied, American-born feminist, I, not surprisingly, have focused in my writing on correcting the errors of omission and commission in sexology that pertained to "women." I have argued that these errors could not be corrected by a few deft changes here and there but would require transformation of the concepts and categories sexologists use to understand what kind of thing sexuality is (Tiefer, 1991a). Such a transformation would take into account the experiences and perspectives of "women."

Of course, at some level I knew that "women" were not all of a kind and did not necessarily have the same sexual interests. Yet it did not occur to me that differences among women were so important as to undermine gender generalizations. Both my work in urology departments and feminist reading supported my impression that there were important issues stressed by many women that were not represented anywhere in sexology, and I took it on myself to expose some of the resistances to recognizing women's perspectives. Rereading all these chapters as I prepared this book has left me feeling that this effort was worthwhile but grievously incomplete. An understanding of sexuality and of sexology must not only address "women's" issues but must also address other issues of social difference, such as race and class, and must show how one's specific cultural background—the fact that one is a white woman or an African-American woman, for example—will have an important influence on one's outlook and experience with regard to sexuality.

Social constructionist thinking actually leads quite easily to this expansion; one might say it even demands it. If the key element in the critique of the biological and psychological reductionism of sexology today is that it strips sexuality of important elements of social context, then the context of gender is extremely important. But no one has only a gender! There is no man or woman anywhere whose sexual life has not been influenced by race and class. The very experience of gender itself is shaped within the crucible of a race and class location.

Although I have grasped this point intellectually for a long time, it is ironic that it was emotionally brought home to me by men. In my urological work, as I mentioned in the chapters in Part 4, in the past few years I have largely treated and evaluated men who belong to a particular health insurance plan in the greater New York area. They came from diverse backgrounds in terms of nationality, religion, race, and occupation, but they were largely middle and lower-middle class and employed in New York City government departments such as transit, sanitation, corrections, housing, parks, police, social services, and education. Their insurance plan covered any of the medical or surgical treatments for erectile problems but paid not one penny toward any psychotherapeutic or psychoeducational treatments.

This bias in the coverage annoyed me for years (I felt psychology was disregarded and discredited), and early on I saw it as sexist, as depriving these men's partners of opportunities to improve communication, intimacy, and sensuality in their relationships. But I only gradually came to see this insurance condition as a link in understanding how men's sexuality is shaped within a class context. White-collar (and almost always white color) men came to us with insurance coverage that could be applied to *any* recommended form of treatment from couple sex therapy to penile implant surgery. We took more time with these men to describe the psychological treatment options and in the process perhaps taught these men a few connections between sexual function and emotions or thinking.

The restrictions imposed on the health plan users contributed to an assumption that they would not be interested in talk-therapies, that their sexuality was "only" mechanical and genital, and that all their sexual problems could be fixed with mechanical means. Since they would have to pay out of pocket for nonapproved services such as sex therapy, we rarely dwelt on its virtues, and they rarely asked for more information. The men's partners, too, dismissed an "option" that would involve an added financial burden.

This financial situation is a reality shaping real people's sexual lives; I could name hundreds of names. In a similar fashion, I have recently been thinking about the sexual lives of my black patients and couples in light of the demographics of heterosexual relationships within the black community.

Ronald Braithwaite (1981) reported that there was only one acceptable black man available for every five black women when one excludes married, imprisoned, drug-addicted, and homosexual men and takes into account the high death rates of young black men from accidents and homicides. How does this scarcity affect the negotiating powers of black women within relationships? How does it affect single women's projections about their sexual lives, and how do they behave in response to their projections? How does the scarcity affect the attitudes and behaviors of black men toward their sexual partners? And so on.

A terrible consequence of the racism that affects all intellectual work is that white researchers (and clinicians and teachers) cannot ask very good questions because they have so little understanding of the lives of nonwhite people. Moreover, patients and other people of color whom the white sex researcher meets are often skeptical and mistrustful of the researcher's motives for inquiring deeply into sexual values and practices in their lives and communities. Yet, there are few nonwhite sex researchers as yet, and only a small amount of work has been done in this area.

Fortunately, there is a growing body of feminist scholarship by women of color and growing acceptance and enthusiasm about scholarship with a multicultural focus. Fortunate, too, is the availability of new methods of research that allow researchers to explore qualitative aspects of experience and avoid the intellectual barrenness and suffocation of sexuality questionnaires and checklists. Using more open-ended methods helps immeasurably when you are heading off into uncharted but politically sensitive waters.

My hope is to take advantage of these new opportunities over the next few years to better understand the social construction of sexuality with regard to race and class as well as gender. I hope that the almost-all-white sexological community will rapidly see that as scholars we must situate our research participants and patients in their full social context before we can claim to understand their sexualities. This new trajectory of research and thinking should show, even more definitively, how sex is not, and never has been, a "natural" phenomenon.

# Notes

## Chapter 1

1. These letters were written years before the risk of HIV transmission had inspired "safer sex" practices.

2. With technology and commercialization moving as fast as they are, I wonder if this assertion is still true for North Americans and Europeans in the 1990s.

3. At least the language shifted. It may be that the public has never surrendered the attitude that sexual transgressions really do represent moral violations, as witnessed by the return to a public discourse dominated by moralistic language in the 1970s and 1980s.

## Chapter 2

1. This discussion is based on an unpublished manuscript by Carol Tavris and Leonore Tiefer, 1983, "The 'G' Spot, the Media and Science."

## Chapter 4

1. Robinson suggests that Masters and Johnson's "scheme of four phases" is "irrelevant" and "merely creates the impression of scientific precision where none exists" (Robinson, 1976, p. 130). The reader is referred to his dissection of the model's stages.

2. The same introduction persists in the just-released *DSM-IV* (APA, 1994). See Chapter 10, note 1, for further information about *DSM-IV*.

3. Again, it must be emphasized that subject selection plays a large role, as acknowledged by Masters and Johnson: "Study subjects were selected because they were specifically facile in sexual response. . . . The carefully selected homosexual and heterosexual study subjects employed in the Institute's research programs must not be considered representative of a cross-section of sexually adult men and women in our culture" (Masters and Johnson, 1979, pp. 61–62).

## Chapter 9

1. This speech was given to the Midcontinent Region of the Society for the Scientific Study of Sex, May 28, 1993, in response to being awarded the 1993 Alfred C. Kinsey Award for Distinguished Contribution to Sexology.

## Chapter 10

1. In the just-released *DSM-IV* (APA, 1994), sexual dysfunctions are listed under Sexual and Gender Identity Disorders (pp. 493–519). The same nine dysfunctions are listed as in 1987, although Inhibited Female Orgasm has been renamed Female Orgasmic Disorder and Inhibited Male Orgasm has been renamed Male Orgasmic Disorder. A most interesting and potentially significant addition has been made to the criteria listed for each of the nine dysfunctions: "The disturbance causes marked distress or interpersonal difficulty." This statement adds a substantial psychological qualification to the definition of each disorder. There are two new categories, "Sexual dysfunction due to a general medical condition" and "Substance induced sexual dysfunction."

## Chapter 16

1. It should be noted that this chapter was written a year or two before a dramatic change occurred in the treatment of erectile problems. By 1994, the penile prosthesis, although still in widespread use, was a less popular treatment than the technique of self-injection of medication into the penis (discussed in Chapter 17).

## Chapter 17

1. "Nocturnal penile tumescence" refers to the fact that men have erections (penile tumescence) periodically throughout sleep. Measurement of these erections is a diagnostic test conducted with portable take-home measurement instruments worn during sleep. Men complaining of erectile dysfunction who display normal nocturnal erections are assumed not to have physical impairment.

2. The purpose of a Consensus Development Conference is to assess competing conceptualizations, assessments, and treatments in some medical domain and to arrive at a consensus of the current knowledge to serve as a guideline for practitioners.

# References

Abramson, P. R. (1990). Sexual science: Emerging discipline or oxymoron? *Journal of Sex Research* 27, 147–165.

Altman, D. (1982). *The Homosexualization of America: The Americanization of the homosexual.* New York: St. Martin's Press.

American Medical Systems (1984). Impotence clinics: Investments in the future. *Colleagues in Urology Newsletter,* Fourth Quarter, p. 1. Minnetonka, Minn.: American Medical Systems.

American Psychiatric Association (APA) (1952). *Diagnostic and Statistical Manual of Mental Disorders.* Washington, D.C.: APA.

———. (1968). *Diagnostic and Statistical Manual of Mental Disorders,* 2nd ed. Washington, D.C.: APA.

———. (1980). *Diagnostic and Statistical Manual of Mental Disorders,* 3rd ed. Washington, D.C.: APA.

———. (1987). *Diagnostic and Statistical Manual of Mental Disorders,* 3rd rev. ed. Washington, D.C.: APA.

———. (1994). *Diagnostic and Statistical Manual of Mental Disorders,* 4th ed. Washington, D.C.: APA.

Ansell, J. S. (1987). Trends in urological manpower in the United States in 1986. *Journal of Urology* 138, 473–476.

Apte, S. M., Gregory, J. G., and Purcell, M. H. (1984). The inflatable penile prosthesis, reoperation and patient satisfaction: A comparison of statistics obtained from patient record review with statistics obtained from intensive followup search. *Journal of Urology* 131, 894–895.

Attorney General's Commission on Pornography (1986). *Final Report.* Washington, D.C.: U.S. Department of Justice.

Bancroft, J. (1982). Erectile impotence: Psyche or soma? *International Journal of Andrology* 5, 353–355.

———. (1989). *Human Sexuality and Its Problems,* 2nd ed. Edinburgh: Churchill-Livingstone. (1st ed. published in 1983.)

Barsky, A. J. (1988). *Worried Sick: Our troubled quest for wellness.* Boston: Little, Brown.

Bayer, R. (1981). *Homosexuality and American Psychiatry.* New York: Basic Books.

Beach, F. A. (1956). Characteristics of masculine "sex drive." In M. R. Jones, ed., *Nebraska Symposium on Motivation.* Lincoln: University of Nebraska Press.

———. (1965). Retrospect and prospect. In F. A. Beach, ed., *Sex and Behavior.* New York: Wiley and Sons.

———. (1976). Sexual attractivity, proceptivity, and receptivity in female mammals. *Hormones and Behavior* 7, 105–138.

Bell, A. P., and Weinberg, M. S. (1978). *Homosexualities: A study of diversity among men and women.* New York: Simon and Schuster.

Bem, S. L. (1981). Gender schema theory: A cognitive account of sex typing. *Psychological Review* 88, 354–364.

———. (1993). *The Lenses of Gender: Transforming the debate on sexual inequality.* New Haven: Yale University Press.

Bernstein, R. (1990). The rising hegemony of the politically correct. *New York Times,* October 28, section 4, pp. 1, 4.

Birke, L. (1986). *Women, Feminism and Biology: The feminist challenge.* New York: Methuen.

Blakeslee, S. (1993). New therapies are helping men to overcome impotence. *New York Times,* June 2, section C, p. 12.

Blaun, R. (1987). Dealing with impotence. *New York,* March 30, pp. 50–58.

Bleier, R. (1986). Sex differences research: Science or belief? In R. Bleier, ed., *Feminist Approaches to Science.* New York: Pergamon.

Bloch, M., and Bloch, J. H. (1980). Women and the dialectics of nature in 18th century French thought. In C. P. MacCormack and M. Strathern, eds., *Nature, Culture and Gender.* Cambridge: Cambridge University Press.

Bolton, R., ed. (1992). *Culture Wars: Documents from the recent controversies in the arts.* New York: New Press.

Boswell, J. (1990). Concepts, experience and sexuality. *differences* 2, 67–87.

Boyle, M. (1993). Sexual dysfunction or heterosexual dysfunction? *Feminism and Psychology* 3, 73–88.

Bradbury, P. (1985). Desire and pregnancy. In A. Metcalf and M. Humphries, eds., *The Sexuality of Men.* London: Pluto Press.

Braithwaite, R. L. (1981). Interpersonal relations between black males and black females. In L. E. Gary, ed., *Black Men.* Beverly Hills, Calif.: Sage Publications.

Brannon, R. (1976). The male sex role: Our culture's blueprint of manhood, and what it's done for us lately. In D. David and R. Brannon, eds., *The Forty-Nine Percent Majority: The male sex role.* Reading, Mass.: Addison-Wesley.

Brecher, R., and Brecher, E., eds. (1966). *An Analysis of Human Sexual Response.* New York: Signet.

Bridenthal, R., Grossmann, A., and Kaplan, M., eds. (1984). *When Biology Became Destiny: Women in Weimar and Nazi Germany.* New York: Monthly Review Press.

Brody, J. (1979). Surgical implants correct impotence. *New York Times,* June 12, section C, p. 3.

———. (1988). Personal health. *New York Times,* August 12, section B, p. 4.

Brooks, M. B., and Brooks, S. W. (1984). *Overcoming Impotence.* Minneapolis: Mentor Corporation.

Brownmiller, S. (1975). *Against Our Will: Men, women and rape.* New York: Simon and Schuster.

Bullough, V. (1976). *Sexual Variance in Society and History.* New York: Wiley and Sons.

———. (1985). The Rockefellers and sex research. *Journal of Sex Research* 21, 113–125.

Burnham, J. C. (1987). *How Superstition Won and Science Lost: Popularizing science and health in the United States*. New Brunswick: Rutgers University Press.

Burris, A. S., Banks, S. M., and Sherins, R. J. (1989). Quantitative assessment of nocturnal penile tumescence and rigidity in normal men using a home monitor. *Journal of Andrology* 10, 492–497.

Burstyn, V., ed. (1985). *Women Against Censorship*. Toronto: Douglas and McIntyre, Ltd.

Caporael, L. R., and Brewer, M. B. (1991). The quest for human nature: Social and scientific issues in evolutionary psychology. *Journal of Social Issues* 47, 1–9.

Carby, H. (March 1990). Racism in the academy. Keynote address at the 17th annual Scholar and Feminist Conference, Barnard College, New York.

Carlson, R. (1971). Where is the person in personality research? *Psychological Bulletin* 75, 203–219.

Cartledge, S., and Ryan, J., eds. (1983). *Sex and Love: New thoughts on old contradictions*. London: The Woman's Press.

Churcher, S. (1980). The anguish of the transsexuals. *New York*, June 16, pp. 40–49.

Clausen, J. (1990). My interesting condition. *Journal of Sex Research* 27, 445–459.

Clement, U. (1990). Surveys of heterosexual behavior. *Annual Review of Sex Research* 1, 45–74.

Collins, G. F., and Kinder, B. N. (1984). Adjustment following surgical implantation of a penile prosthesis: A critical overview. *Journal of Sex and Marital Therapy* 10, 255–271.

Conrad, P., and Kern, R., eds. (1981). *The Sociology of Health and Illness: Critical perspectives*. New York: St. Martin's Press.

Conrad, P., and Schneider, J. W. (1980). *Deviance and Medicalization: From badness to sickness*. St. Louis: C. V. Mosby.

Coote, A., and Campbell, B. (1987). *Sweet Freedom: The struggle for women's liberation*. Oxford: Basil Blackwell.

Corner, G. W. (1961). Foreword. In W. C. Young, ed., *Sex and Internal Secretions*, Vol. 1, 3rd ed. Baltimore: Williams and Wilkins.

Crawford, R. (1977). You are dangerous to your health: The ideology and politics of victim blaming. *International Journal of Health Services* 7, 663–680.

Danziger, K. (1988). A question of identity: Who participated in psychological experiments? In J. Morawski, ed., *The Rise of Experimentation in American Psychology*. New Haven: Yale University Press.

Davis, K. B. (1988). Sex research and the Rockefeller Foundation. *Bulletin of the History of Medicine* 62, 74–89.

DeLamater, J. (1981). The social control of sexuality. *Annual Review of Sociology* 7, 263–290.

deLauretis, T. (1991). Queer theory: Lesbian and gay sexualities, an introduction. *differences* 3, iii–xviii.

D'Emilio, J., and Freedman, E. B. (1988). *Intimate Matters: A history of sexuality in America*. New York: Harper and Row.

Doyle, J. A. (1983). *The Male Sexual Experience*. Dubuque, Iowa: William C. Brown.

DuBois, E. C., Kelly, G. P., Kennedy, E. L., Korsmeyer, C. W., and Robinson, L. S. (1987). *Feminist Scholarship: Kindling in the groves of academe.* Urbana: University of Illinois Press.

Duden, B. (1991). *The Woman Beneath the Skin.* Cambridge: Harvard University Press.

Duggan, L. (1990). Review essay: From instincts to politics: Writing the history of sexuality in the US. *Journal of Sex Research* 27, 95–109.

Dworkin, A. (1974). *Woman Hating.* New York: E. P. Dutton.

———. (1981). *Pornography: Men possessing women.* New York: E. P. Dutton.

———. (1983). *Right-Wing Women.* New York: E. P. Dutton.

Dworkin, A., and MacKinnon, C. A. (1988). *Pornography and Civil Rights: A new day for women's equality.* Minneapolis: Organizing Against Pornography.

Echols, A. (1984). The taming of the id: Feminist sexual politics: 1968–1983. In C. S. Vance, ed., *Pleasure and Danger: Exploring female sexuality.* Boston: Routledge and Kegan Paul.

———. (1989). *Daring to Be Bad: Radical feminism in America: 1967—1975.* Minneapolis: University of Minnesota Press.

Edwardes, A. (1959). *The Jewel in the Lotus: A historical survey of the sexual culture of the East.* New York: Julian Press.

Ehrenreich, B., and Ehrenreich, J. (1978). Medicine and social control. In J. Ehrenreich, ed., *The Cultural Crisis of Modern Medicine.* New York: Monthly Review Press.

Ehrenreich, B., and English, D. (1978). *For Her Own Good: 150 years of the experts' advice to women.* Garden City, N.Y.: Anchor Press/Doubleday.

Ehrenreich, B., Hess, E., and Jacobs, G. (1986). *Re-making Love: The feminization of sex.* Garden City, N.Y.: Anchor Press, Doubleday.

Elliott, M. (1985). The use of "impotence" and "frigidity": Why has "impotence" survived? *Journal of Sex and Marital Therapy* 11, 51–56.

Ellis, K., Jaker, B., Hunter, N. D., O'Dair, B., and Tallmer, A. (1988). *Caught Looking: Feminism, pornography and censorship.* Seattle: Real Comet Press.

Fairburn, C. G., McCulloch, D. K., and Wu, F. C. (1982). The effects of diabetes on male sexual function. *Clinics in Endocrinology and Metabolism* 11, 749–767.

Fallon, B., Rosenberg, S., and Culp, D. A. (1984). Long-term follow-up in patients with an inflatable penile prosthesis. *Journal of Urology* 132, 270–271.

Featherstone, M., Hepworth, M., and Turner, B. S., eds. (1991). *The Body: Social process and cultural theory.* Newbury Park, Calif.: Sage Publications.

Festinger, L. (1954). A theory of social comparison processes. *Human Relations* 7, 117–140.

Fine, M., and Gordon, S. M. (1989). Feminist transformations of/despite psychology. In M. Crawford and M. Gentry, eds., *Gender and Thought: Psychological perpectives.* New York: Springer-Verlag.

Finkle, A. L., and Finkle, C. E. (1984). Sexual impotency: Counseling of 388 private patients by urologists from 1954–1982. *Urology* 23, 25–30.

Flax, J. (1987). Postmodernism and gender relations in feminist theory. *Signs* 12, 621–644.

Ford, C. S., and Beach, F. A. (1951). *Patterns of Sexual Behavior.* New York: Harper and Row.

Foucault, M. (1978). *The History of Sexuality,* Vol. 1, *An introduction.* New York: Pantheon. (Originally published in 1976.)

———. (1982/1983). An interview with Michel Foucault. *Salmagundi,* no. 58–59, 10–24.

Foucault, M., and Sennett, R. (1982). Sexuality and solitude. *Humanities in Review* 1, 3–21.

Fout, J. C. (1992). Introduction. In J. C. Fout, ed., *Forbidden History: The state, society, and the regulation of sexuality in modern Europe.* Chicago: University of Chicago Press.

———. (1993). Introduction. In J. C. Fout and M. S. Tantillo, eds., *American Sexual Politics: Sex, gender and race since the Civil War.* Chicago: University of Chicago Press.

Fox, R. W., and Lears, T.J.J., eds. (1993). *The Power of Culture: Critical essays in American history.* Chicago: University of Chicago Press.

Frank, E., Anderson, C., and Rubinstein, D. (1978). Frequency of sexual dysfunction in "normal" couples. *New England Journal of Medicine* 299, 111–115.

Freedman, E. B., and D'Emilio, J. (1988). *Intimate Matters: A history of sex in America.* New York: Harper and Row.

Gagnon, J. H. (1973). Scripts and the coordination of sexual conduct. *Nebraska Symposium on Motivation* 21, 27–60.

———. (1977). *Human Sexualities.* Glenview, Ill.: Scott, Foresman.

———. (1979). The interaction of gender roles and sexual conduct. In H. A. Katchadourian, ed., *Human Sexuality: A developmental perspective.* Berkeley: University of California Press.

———. (1985). Attitudes and responses of parents to pre-adolescent masturbation. *Archives of Sexual Behavior* 14, 451–466.

Gagnon, J. H., and Simon, W. (1969). Sex education and human development. In P. J. Fink and V. O. Hammet, eds., *Sexual Function and Dysfunction.* Philadelphia: F. A. Davis.

———. (1973). *Sexual Conduct: The social sources of human sexuality.* Chicago: Aldine.

Garber, M. (1992). *Vested Interests: Cross-dressing and cultural anxiety.* New York: Routledge.

Geer, J. H., and O'Donohue, W. T., eds. (1987). *Theories of Human Sexuality.* New York: Plenum Press.

Geertz, C. (1980). Sociosexology. *New York Review of Books,* January 24, pp. 3–4.

———. (1990). A lab of one's own. *New York Review of Books,* November 8, pp. 19–23.

Gergen, K. J. (1982). *Toward Transformation in Social Knowledge.* New York: Springer-Verlag.

———. (1985). The social constructionist movement in modern psychology. *American Psychologist* 40, 266–275.

Gilligan, C. (1982). *In a Different Voice.* Cambridge: Harvard University Press.

Green, R., and Wiener, J. (1980). *Methodology in Sex Research.* Report No. 80-1502. Washington, D.C.: Department of Health and Human Services.

Greer, G. (1971). *The Female Eunuch.* New York: McGraw-Hill.

Gross, A. E. (1978). The male role and heterosexual behavior. *Journal of Social Issues* 34, 87–107.

Grossman, A. (1983). The new woman and the rationalization of sexuality in Weimar Germany. In A. Snitow, C. Stansell, and S. Thompson, eds., *Powers of Desire: The politics of sexuality*. New York: Monthly Review Press.

Guba, E. G. (1990). *The Paradigm Dialog*. Newbury Park, Calif.: Sage Publications.

Hall, D. L. (1974). Biology, sex hormones and sexism in the 1920s. *Philosophical Forum* 5, 81–96.

Hall, L. A. (1991). *Hidden Anxieties: Male sexuality, 1900–1950*. Cambridge, U.K.: Polity Press.

Haraway, D. (1986). Primatology is politics by other means. In R. Bleier, ed., *Feminist Approaches to Science*. New York: Pergamon.

———. (1991). *Simians, Cyborgs and Women: The reinvention of nature*. New York: Routledge.

Hare-Mustin, R. T., and Marecek, J. (1990). *Making a Difference: Psychology and the construction of gender*. New Haven: Yale University Press.

Harvey, J. H., and Weary, G., eds. (1985). *Attribution: Basic issues and applications*. New York: Academic Press.

Haug, F., ed. (1987). *Female Sexualization: A collective work of memory*. London: Verso Books.

Hawton, K. E. (1985). *Sex Therapy*. Oxford: Oxford University Press.

Hite, S. (1976). *The Hite Report*. New York: Macmillan.

———. (1987). *Women and Love: A cultural revolution in progress*. New York: A. Knopf.

Hixson, J. R. (1985). Curing impotence: The prognosis is good. *Vogue,* April, p. 406.

Hoch, Z., Safir, M., Peres, Y., and Shepher, J. (1981). An evaluation of sexual performance: Comparison between sexually dysfunctional and functional couples. *Journal of Sex and Marital Therapy* 7, 195–206.

hooks, b. (1984). *Feminist Theory, from Margin to Center*. Boston: South End Press.

———. (1989). *Talking Back: Thinking feminist, thinking black*. Boston: South End Press.

Hornstein, G. (1989). Quantifying psychological phenomena: Debates, dilemmas and implications. In J. G. Morawski, ed., *The Rise of Experimentation in American Psychology*. New Haven: Yale University Press.

Hrdy, S. B. (1979). The evolution of human sexuality: The latest word and the last. *Quarterly Review of Biology* 54, 309–314.

Hubbard, R. (1990). *The Politics of Women's Biology*. New Brunswick: Rutgers University Press.

Irvine, J. M. (1990). *Disorders of Desire: Sex and gender in modern American sexology*. Philadelphia: Temple University Press.

Jackson, M. (1984). Sexology and the universalization of male sexuality (from Ellis to Kinsey and Masters and Johnson). In L. Coveney, M. Jackson, S. Jeffreys, L. Kaye, and P. Mahony, eds., *The Sexuality Papers*. London: Hutchinson.

Jaggar, A. M. (1983). *Feminist Politics and Human Nature*. Totowa, N.J.: Rowman and Allanheld.

Jeffords, S. (1989). *The Remasculinization of America: Gender and the Vietnam War*. Bloomington: Indiana University Press.

Jordanova, L. (1989). *Sexual Visions: Images of gender in science and medicine between the 18th and 20th centuries*. Madison: University of Wisconsin Press.

Joseph, D. B., Bruskewitz, R. C., and Benson, R. C. (1984). Long-term evaluation of the inflatable penile prosthesis. *Journal of Urology* 131, 670–673.

Kabalin, J. N., and Kessler, R. (1989). Penile prosthesis surgery: Review of ten year experience and examination of reoperations. *Urology* 33, 17–19.

Kaplan, E. A. (1990). Sex, work and motherhood: The impossible triangle. *Journal of Sex Research* 27, 409–425.

Kaplan, H. S. (1979). *Disorders of Sexual Desire*. New York: Brunner/Mazel.

Katchadourian, H. A. (1979). The terminology of sex and gender. In H. A. Katchadourian, ed., *Human Sexuality: A comparative and developmental perspective*. Berkeley: University of California Press.

Katcher, A. (1955). The discrimination of sex differences by young children. *Journal of Genetic Psychology* 87, 131–143.

Kelley, S. (1981). Some social and psychological aspects of organic sexual dysfunction in men. *Sexuality and Disability* 4, 123–128.

Kent, R. (1979). *Aunt Agony Advises: Problem pages through the ages*. London: W. H. Allen.

Kessler, S. J., and McKenna, W. (1985). *Gender: An ethnomethodological approach*. Chicago: University of Chicago Press. (Originally published in 1978.)

Kilmann, P. R., Boland, J. P., Norton, S. P., Davidson, E., and Caid, C. (1986). Perspectives of sex therapy outcome: A survey of AASECT providers. *Journal of Sex and Marital Therapy* 12, 116–138.

Kinsey, A. C., Pomeroy, W. B., and Martin, C. E. (1948). *Sexual Behavior in the Human Male*. Philadelphia: W. B. Saunders Co.

Kinsey, A. C., Pomeroy, W. B., Martin, C. E., and Gebhard, P. H. (1953). *Sexual Behavior in the Human Female*. Philadelphia: W. B. Saunders Co.

Kirkeby, H. J., Andersen, A. J., and Poulsen, E. U. (1989). Nocturnal penile tumescence and rigidity: Translation of data obtained from normal males. *International Journal of Impotence Research* 1, 115–125.

Kitzinger, C. (1987). *The Social Construction of Lesbianism*. Newbury Park, Calif.: Sage Publications.

Kramon, G. (1989). Psychiatric care: Orphan of insurance coverage. *New York Times*, November 7, section B, p. 16.

Krane, R. J., Goldstein, I., and DeTejada, I. S. (1989). Impotence. *New England Journal of Medicine* 321, 1648–1659.

Krane, R. J., Siroky, M. B., and Goldstein, I. (1983). *Male Sexual Dysfunction*. Boston: Little, Brown.

Kuhn, T. (1962). *The Structure of Scientific Revolutions*. Chicago: University of Chicago Press.

Ladas, A. K., Whipple, B., and Perry, J. D. (1982). *The G Spot and Other Recent Discoveries About Human Sexuality*. New York: Holt, Rinehart and Winston.

Laqueur, T. (1990). *Making Sex*. Cambridge: Harvard University Press.

Larson, M. S. (1977). *The Rise of Professionalism: A sociological analysis*. Berkeley: University of California Press.

Laws, S. (1990). *Issues of Blood: The politics of menstruation.* New York: Columbia University Press.

Lehrman, N. (1970). *Masters and Johnson Explained.* Chicago: Playboy Press.

Lewinsohn, R. (1958). *A History of Sexual Customs.* New York: Harper and Row.

Lloyd, G. (1984). *The Man of Reason: "Male" and "female" in Western philosophy.* Minneapolis: University of Minnesota Press.

LoPiccolo, J. (1977). The professionalization of sex therapy: Issues and problems. *Society* 14, 60–68.

———. (1978). Direct treatment of sexual dysfunction. In J. LoPiccolo and L. LoPiccolo, eds., *Handbook of Sex Therapy.* New York: Plenum Press.

———. (1985). Diagnosis and treatment of male sexual dysfunction. *Journal of Sex and Marital Therapy* 11, 215–232.

Lowe, M., and Hubbard, R., eds. (1983). *Woman's Nature: Rationalizations of inequality.* New York: Pergamon Press.

MacCormack, C. P., and Draper, A. (1987). Social and cognitive aspects of female sexuality in Jamaica. In P. Caplan, ed., *The Cultural Construction of Sexuality.* New York: Tavistock Publications.

MacKenzie, B., and MacKenzie, E. (1988). *It's Not All in Your Head.* New York: E. P. Dutton.

MacKinnon, C. A. (1979). *Sexual Harassment of Working Women.* New Haven: Yale University Press.

———. (1982). Feminism, marxism, method, and the state: An agenda for theory. *Signs* 7, 519–544.

———. (1987). A feminist/political approach. In J. H. Geer and W. T. O'Donohue, eds., *Theories of Human Sexuality.* New York: Plenum Press.

McMahon, K. (1990). The *Cosmopolitan* ideology and the management of desire. *Journal of Sex Research* 27, 381–396.

Martin, B. (1993). The critique of science becomes academic. *Science, Technology and Human Values* 18, 247–259.

Maslow, A. H. (1966). *The Psychology of Science.* New York: Harper and Row.

Masters, W. H., and Johnson, V. E. (1966). *Human Sexual Response.* Boston: Little, Brown.

———. (1970). *Human Sexual Inadequacy.* Boston: Little, Brown.

———. (1975). *The Pleasure Bond.* Boston: Little, Brown.

———. (1979). *Homosexuality in Perspective.* Boston: Little, Brown.

Mead, M. (1955). *Male and Female: A study of the sexes in a changing world.* New York: Mentor.

Medical Engineering Corporation (1983). *Patient information booklet discussing the surgical correction of impotency.* Racine, Wis.: Medical Engineering Corporation.

Melman, A. (1978). Development of contemporary surgical management for erectile impotence. *Sexuality and Disability* 1, 272–281.

Melman, A., Tiefer, L., and Pedersen, R. (1988). Evaluation of first 406 patients in urology department based center for male sexual dysfunction. *Urology* 32, 6–10.

Mentor Corporation. (n.d.). *A Guide for Setting Up Educational Seminars.* Goleta, Calif.: Mentor Corporation.

Metcalf, A., and Humphries, M., eds. (1985). *The Sexuality of Men.* London: Pluto Press.

Miller, P. Y., and Fowlkes, M. R. (1980). Social and behavioral construction of female sexuality. *Signs* 5, 783–800.

Millman, M., and Kanter, R. M., eds. (1975). *Another Voice: Feminist perspectives on social life and social science.* Garden City, N.Y.: Doubleday.

Mishler, E. G. (1981). Viewpoint: Critical perspectives on the biomedical model. In E. G. Mishler, L. R. AmaraSingham, S. T. Hauser, R. Liem, S. D. Osherson, and N. E. Waxler, *Social Contexts of Health, Illness and Patient Care.* Cambridge: Cambridge University Press.

Morawski, J. G., ed. (1989). *The Rise of Experimentation in American Psychology.* New Haven: Yale University Press.

Morgan, D., and Scott, S. (1993). Bodies in a social landscape. In S. Scott and D. Morgan, eds., *Body Matters: Essays on the sociology of the body.* London: Falmer Press.

Morgan, R. (1980). Theory and practice: Pornography and rape. In L. Lederer, ed., *Take Back the Night: Women on pornography.* New York: William Morrow and Co. (Originally published in 1974.)

———. (1984). *Sisterhood Is Global: The International women's movement anthology.* Garden City, N.Y.: Anchor Press.

Mosher, D. (1989). Advancing sexual science: Strategic analysis and planning. *Journal of Sex Research* 26, 1–14.

———. (1991). Macho men, machismo and sexuality. *Annual Review of Sex Research* 2, 199–243.

National Institutes of Health (NIH) (1992). Consensus Development Conference Statement on Impotence. Office of Medical Applications of Research. Bethesda, Md.: NIH.

Naunton, E. (1989). Answers to impotence: Support groups IA and I-Anon offer hope to the millions. *Sunday New York Daily News,* April 9.

Nelkin, D. (1987). *Selling Science: How the press covers science and psychology.* New York: W. H. Freeman.

Nelkin, D., and Tancredi, L. (1989). *Dangerous Diagnostics: The social power of biological information.* New York: Basic Books.

Nelson, J. (1985). Male sexuality and masculine spirituality. *Siecus Report* 13, 1–4.

Nelson, M. K. (1983). Working-class women, middle-class women, and models of childbirth. *Social Problems* 30, 284–297.

New psychiatric syndromes spur protest. (1985). *New York Times,* November 19, section C, p. 16.

Nyrop, C. (1901). *The Kiss and Its History,* trans. by W. F. Harvey. London: Sands and Co.

Organization helps couples with impotence as problem. (1984). *New York Times,* June 24, section 1, pt. 2, p. 42.

Ortner, S. B., and Whitehead, H., eds. (1981). *Sexual Meanings: The cultural construction of gender and sexuality.* Cambridge: Cambridge University Press.

Osherson, S. D., and AmaraSingham, L. (1981). The machine metaphor in medicine. In E. G. Mishler, L. AmaraSingham, S. T. Hauser, R. Liem, S. D. Osherson, and N. E. Waxler, eds., *Social Contexts of Health, Illness and Patient Care.* Cambridge: Cambridge University Press.

Padgug, R. A. (1979). On conceptualizing sexuality in history. *Radical History Review,* no. 20, 3–23.

Paff, B. (1985). Sexual dysfunction in gay men requesting treatment. *Journal of Sex and Marital Therapy* 11, 3–18.

Paige, K. E., and Paige, J. M. (1981). *The Politics of Reproductive Ritual.* Berkeley: University of California Press.

Parent, G. (1977). *David Meyer Is a Mother.* New York: Bantam.

Parlee, M. B. (1987). Media treatment of premenstrual syndrome. In B. E. Ginsburg and B. F. Carter, eds., *Premenstrual Syndrome: Ethical and legal implications in a biomedical perspective.* New York: Plenum.

Parsons, T. (1951). *The Social System.* New York: Free Press.

Pastore, N. (1949). *The Nature-Nurture Controversy.* New York: Kings Crown Press (Columbia University).

Peplau, L. A., and Gordon, S. L. (1985). Women and men in love: Gender differences in close heterosexual relationships. In V. E. O'Leary, R. K. Unger, and B. S. Wallston, eds., *Women, Gender and Social Psychology.* Hillsdale, N.J.: Lawrence Erlbaum Associates.

Perelman, M. (1984). Rehabilitative sex therapy for organic impotence. In R. T. Segraves and E. J. Haeberle, eds., *Emerging Dimensions of Sexology.* New York: Praeger.

Person, E. S. (1980). Sexuality as the mainstay of identity: Psychoanalytic perspectives. *Signs* 5, 605–630.

Personal Narratives Group, ed. (1989). *Interpreting Women's Lives: Feminist theory and personal narratives.* Bloomington: Indiana University Press.

Petras, J. W. (1973). *Sexuality in Society.* Boston: Allyn and Bacon.

Petrou, S. P., and Barrett, D. M. (1991). Current penile prostheses available for the treatment of erectile dysfunction. *Problems in Urology* 5, 594–607.

Pleck, J. H. (1976). The male sex role: Definitions, problems and sources of change. *Journal of Social Issues* 32, 155–164.

———. (1981). *The Myth of Masculinity.* Cambridge: MIT Press.

Pleck, J. H., Sonenstein, F. L., and Ku, L. C. (1993). Masculine ideology and its correlates. In S. Oskamp and M. Costanzo, eds., *Gender Issues in Contemporary Society.* Newbury Park, Calif.: Sage Publications.

Plummer, K., ed. (1981). *The Making of the Modern Homosexual.* London: Hutchinson.

———. (1982). Symbolic interactionism and sexual conduct: An emergent perspective. In M. Brake, ed., *Human Sexual Relations: Towards a redefinition of sexual politics.* New York: Pantheon.

Poll shows widespread use of three major impotence treatments. (1993). *AUA Today,* May, p. 6.

Potter, J., and Wetherell, M. (1987). *Discourse and Social Psychology: Beyond attitudes and behavior.* London: Sage.

Rado, S. (1949). An adaptational view of sexual behavior. In P. Hoch and J. Zubin, eds., *Psychosexual Development in Health and Disease.* New York: Grune and Stratton.

Read, D. (1989). Deconstructing pornography. In K. Peiss and C. Simmons, eds., *Passion and Power: Sexuality in history.* Philadelphia: Temple University Press.

Reiss, I. (1982). Trouble in paradise: The current state of sexual science. *Journal of Sex Research* 18, 97–113.

Rhode, D. L., ed. (1990). *Theoretical Perspectives on Sexual Difference.* New Haven: Yale University Press.

Riessman, C. K. (1983). Women and medicalization: A new perspective. *Social Policy* 14, 3–18.

Robinson, P. (1976). *The Modernization of Sex.* New York: Harper and Row.

———. (1984). The historical repression of women's sexuality. In C. S. Vance, ed., *Pleasure and Danger: Exploring female sexuality.* Boston: Routledge and Kegan Paul.

Rosen, R. C., and Leiblum, S. R. (1992a). Erectile disorders: An overview of historical trends and clinical perspectives, In R. C. Rosen and S. R. Leiblum, eds., *Erectile Disorders: Assessment and treatment.* New York: Guilford.

———, eds. (1992b). *Erectile Disorders: Assessment and treatment.* New York: Guilford.

Rosenthal, E. (1989). Innovations intensify glut of surgeons. *New York Times,* February 9, section C, p. 1.

Rosenthal, R. (1966). *Experimenter Effects in Behavioral Research.* New York: Appleton-Century-Crofts, 1966.

Rosenthal, R., and Rosnow, R. L. (1969). The volunteer subject. In R. Rosenthal and R. L. Rosnow, eds., *Artifact in Behavioral Research.* New York: Academic Press.

Ross, L. (1977). The intuitive psychologist and his shortcomings. *Advances in Experimental Social Psychology* 10, 174–220.

Rossi, A. S. (1973). Maternalism, sexuality and the new feminism. In J. Zubin and J. Money, eds., *Contemporary Sexual Behavior: Critical issues in the 1970s.* Baltimore: Johns Hopkins University Press.

Rubin, G. (1984). Thinking sex: Notes for a radical theory of the politics of sexuality. In C. S. Vance, ed., *Pleasure and Danger: Exploring female sexuality.* Boston: Routledge and Kegan Paul.

Russ, J. (1985). *Magic Mommas, Trembling Sisters, Puritans and Perverts.* Trumansburg, N.Y.: The Crossing Press.

Sahli, N. (1984). *Women and Sexuality in America: A bibliography.* Boston: G. K. Hall and Co.

Sandfort, T. (1983). Pedophile relationships in the Netherlands: Alternative lifestyles for children. *Alternative Lifestyles* 5, 164–183.

Sarrel, L., and Sarrel, P. (1983). How to have great new sex with your same old spouse. *Redbook,* March, pp. 75–77, 172.

Schiavi, R. C. (1988). Nocturnal penile tumescence in the evaluation of erectile disorders: A critical review. *Journal of Sex and Marital Therapy* 14, 83–97.

Schiavi, R. C., Fisher, C., Quadland, M., and Glover, A. (1984). Erectile function in nonimpotent diabetics. In R. T. Segraves and E. J. Haeberle, eds., *Emerging Dimensions of Sexology.* New York: Praeger.

Schiavi, R. C., Schreiner-Engel, P., Madeli, J., Schanzer, H., and Cohen, E. (1990). Healthy aging and male sexual function. *American Journal of Psychiatry* 147, 766–771.

Schiebinger, L. (1986). Skeletons in the closet: The first illustrations of the female skeleton in 18th century anatomy. *Representations* 14, 42–82.

Schmidt, G. S. (1983a). Foreword. In J. Bancroft, *Human Sexuality and Its Problems.* Edinburgh: Churchill-Livingstone.

———. (1983b). Introduction: Sexuality and relationships. In G. Arentewicz and G. S. Schmidt, *The Treatment of Sexual Disorders*. New York: Basic Books.

Schneider, B. E., and Gould, M. (1987). Female sexuality: Looking back into the future. In B. B. Hess and M. M. Ferree, eds., *Analyzing Gender: A handbook of social science research*. Newbury Park, Calif.: Sage Publications.

Schover, L. R., and von Eschenbach, A. C. (1985). Sex therapy and the penile prosthesis: A synthesis. *Journal of Sex and Marital Therapy* 11, 57–66.

Schreiner-Engel, P. (1981). Therapy of psychogenic erectile disorders. *Sexuality and Disability* 4, 115–122.

Schumacher, S., and Lloyd, C. W. (1981). Physiological and psychological factors in impotence. *Journal of Sex Research* 17, 40–53.

Schur, E. M. (1984). *Labeling Women Deviant: Gender, stigma, and social control*. New York: Random House.

Scott, S., and Morgan, D., eds. (1993). *Body Matters: Essays on the sociology of the body*. London: Falmer Press.

Segal, L. (1983). Sensual uncertainty, or why the clitoris is not enough. In S. Cartledge and J. Ryan, eds., *Sex and Love: New thoughts on old contradictions*. London: The Women's Press.

Segraves, R. T., Schoenberg, H. W., Zarins, C., Camic, P., and Knopf, J. (1981). Characteristics of erectile dysfunction as a function of medical care system entry point. *Psychosomatic Medicine* 43, 227–234.

Seidler, V., ed. (1992). *Men, Sex and Relationships: Writings from Achilles Heel*. New York: Routledge.

Shapiro, J. (1980). The battle of the sexes. *Science* 207, 1193–1194.

Sharlip, I. (1989). Editorial. *International Journal of Impotence Research* 1, 67–69.

Sheehy, G. (1993). The unspeakable passage: Is there a male menopause? *Vanity Fair*, April, pp. 164–167, 218–227.

Sherif, C. (1979). Bias in psychology. In J. A. Sherman and E. T. Beck, eds., *The Prism of Sex: Essays in the sociology of knowledge*. Madison: University of Wisconsin Press.

Simon, W. (1973). The social, the erotic, and the sensual: The complexities of sexual scripts. *Nebraska Symposium on Motivation* 21, 61–82.

———. (1989). Commentary on the status of sex research: The postmodernization of sex. *Journal of Psychology and Human Sexuality* 2, 9–37.

Simon, W., and Gagnon, J. H. (1986). Sexual scripts: Permanence and change. *Archives of Sexual Behavior* 15, 97–120.

Snitow, A. (1989). A gender diary. In A. Harris and Y. King, eds., *Rocking the Ship of State: Toward a feminist peace politics*. Boulder and London: Westview Press.

Snitow, A., Stansell, C., and Thompson, S. (1983). *Powers of Desire: The politics of sexuality*. New York: Monthly Review Press.

Snyder, C. R., Ford, C. E., and Hunt, H. A. (1985). *Excuse-making: A look at sex differences*. Paper presented at American Psychological Association annual meeting, August, Los Angeles.

Snyder, C. R., and Smith, T. W. (1982). Symptoms as self-handicapping strategies: The virtues of old wine in a new bottle. In G. Weary and H. L. Mirels, eds., *Integration of Clinical and Social Psychology*. New York: Oxford University Press.

Soble, A. (1987). Philosophy, medicine and healthy sexuality. In E. E. Shelp, ed., *Sexuality and Medicine*, Vol. 1, *Conceptual roots*. Dordrecht, Holland: D. Reidel Publishing Co.

Sotile, W. M. (1979). The penile prosthesis: A review. *Journal of Sex and Marital Therapy* 5, 90–102.

Spark, R. F., White, R. A., and Connolly, P. B. (1980). Impotence is not always psychogenic: Newer insights into hypothalamic-pituitary-gonadal dysfunction. *Journal of the American Medical Association* 243, 750–755.

Spelman, E. V. (1988). *Inessential Woman: Problems of exclusion in feminist thought.* Boston: Beacon Press.

Spitzer, R. L., Williams, J.B.W., and Skodol, A. E. (1980). DSM-III: The major achievements and an overview. *American Journal of Psychiatry* 137, 151–164.

Starr, P. (1982). *The Transformation of American Medicine*. New York: Basic Books.

Stein, H. F. (1987). Polarities in the identity of family medicine: A psychocultural analysis. In W. J. Doherty, C. E. Christianson, and M. B. Sussman, eds., *Family Medicine: The maturing of a discipline*. New York: The Haworth Press.

Stipp, D. (1987). Research on impotence upsets idea that it is usually psychological. *Wall Street Journal,* April 14, pp. 1, 25.

Stock, W. (1984). Sex roles and sexual dysfunction. In C. S. Widom, ed., *Sex Roles and Psychopathology*. New York: Plenum Press.

Subrini, L. P. (1980). Treatment of impotence using penile implants: Surgical, sexual, and psychological follow-up. In R. Forleo and W. Pasini, eds., *Medical Sexology*. Littleton, Mass.: PSG Publishing.

Sulloway, F. J. (1979). *Freud: Biologist of the mind*. New York: Basic Books.

Surgical implants correct impotence. (1979). *New York Times,* June 12, section C, p. 3.

Symons, D. (1979). *The Evolution of Human Sexuality*. New York: Oxford University Press.

Tavris, C., and Sadd, S. (1977). *The Redbook Report on Female Sexuality*. New York: Delacorte Press.

Terry, J. (1991). Theorizing deviant historiography. *differences* 3, 55–75.

Thompson, S. (1990). Putting a big thing into a little hole: Teenage girls' accounts of sexual initiation. *Journal of Sex Research* 27, 341–361.

Tiefer, L. (1970). Gonadal hormones and mating behavior in the adult golden hamster. *Hormones and Behavior* 1, 189–202.

———. (1978). The context and consequences of contemporary sex research: A feminist perspective. In W. McGill, D. Dewsbury, and B. Sachs, eds., *Sex and Behavior: Status and prospectus*. New York: Plenum Press.

———. (1986a). In pursuit of the perfect penis: The medicalization of male sexuality. *American Behavioral Scientist* 29, 579–599. (Reprinted in this volume as Chapter 16.)

———. (1986b). "Am I Normal?": The question of sex. In C. Tavris, ed., *Everywoman's Emotional Well-Being*. Garden City, N.Y.: Doubleday. (Reprinted in this volume as Chapter 1.)

———. (1987). Social constructionism and the study of human sexuality. In P.

Shaver and C. Hendrick, eds., *Sex and Gender*. Newbury Park, Calif.: Sage Publications. (Reprinted in this volume as Chapter 2.)

————. (1988a). A feminist critique of the sexual dysfunction nomenclature. *Women and Therapy* 7, 5–21.

————. (1988b). A feminist perspective on sexology and sexuality. In M. M. Gergen, ed., *Feminist Thought and the Structure of Knowledge*. New York: New York University Press.

————. (1990a). Gender and meaning in the DSM-III and DSM-III-R sexual dysfunctions. Paper delivered at American Psychological Association, Boston, August. (Reprinted in this volume as Chapter 10.)

————. (1990b). Sexual biology and the symbolism of the natural. Paper presented at the International Academy of Sex Research, Sigtuna, Sweden, and subsequently published (in German translation) in *Zeitschrift für Sexualforschung* 4 (1991), 97–108. (Reprinted in this volume as Chapter 3.)

————. (1991a). Commentary on the status of sex research: Feminism, sexuality and sexology. *Journal of Psychology and Human Sexuality* 4, 5–42.

————. (1991b). New perspectives in sexology: From rigor (mortis) to richness. Plenary address given to the Society for the Scientific Study of Sex, New York, 1990, and subsequently published in *Journal of Sex Research* 28 (1991), 593–602. (Reprinted in this volume as Chapter 20.)

————. (1991c). Historical, scientific, clinical and feminist criticisms of "the human sexual response cycle" model. *Annual Review of Sex Research* 2, 1–23. (Reprinted in this volume as Chapter 4.)

————. (1992a). Nomenclature and partner issues. Paper presented at National Institutes of Health Consensus Development Conference on Impotence, Bethesda.

————. (1992b). Critique of the DSM-IIIR nosology of sexual dysfunctions. *Psychiatric Medicine* 10, 227–245.

————. (1992c). Feminism and sex research: Ten years' reminiscences and appraisal. In J. C. Chrisler and D. Howard, eds., *New Directions in Feminist Psychology*. New York: Springer Publishing Co.

————. (1993). Über die Medikalisierung männlicher Sexualität. *Zeitschrift für Sexualforchung* 6, 119–131.

Tiefer, L., and Melman, A. (1983). Interview of wives: A necessary adjunct in the evaluation of impotence. *Sexuality and Disability* 6, 167–175.

Tiefer, L., Moss, S., and Melman, A. (1991). Follow-up of patients and partners experiencing penile prosthesis malfunction and corrective surgery. *Journal of Sex and Marital Therapy* 17, 113–128.

Tiefer, L., Pedersen, B., and Melman, A. (1988). Psychosocial follow-up of penile prosthesis implant patients and partners. *Journal of Sex and Marital Therapy* 14, 184–201.

Tolson, A. (1977). *The Limits of Masculinity*. New York: Harper and Row.

Toufexis, A. 1988. It's not "all in your head." *Time*, December 5, p. 94.

Trilling, L. (1950). The Kinsey Report. In L. Trilling, ed., *The Liberal Imagination: Essays on literature and society*. Garden City, N.Y.: Doubleday Anchor.

Tyler, L. (1973). Design for a hopeful psychology. *American Psychologist* 28, 1021–1029.

Unger, R. K. (1983). Through the looking-glass: No wonderland yet! (The reciprocal relationship between methodology and models of reality). *Psychology of Women Quarterly* 8, 9–32.

U.S. Department of Justice (1986). *Attorney General's Commission on Pornography: Final Report,* Vols. 1 and 2. Washington, D.C.: U.S. Government Printing Office.

Valverde, M. (1987). *Sex, Power, and Pleasure.* Philadelphia: New Society Publishers.

———. (1989). Beyond gender dangers and private pleasures: Theory and ethics in the sex debates. *Feminist Studies* 15, 237–254.

Vance, C. S. (1980). Gender systems, ideology and sex research: An anthropological analysis. *Feminist Studies* 6, 129–143.

———, ed. (1984). *Pleasure and Danger: Exploring female sexuality.* Boston: Routledge and Kegan Paul.

Vance, C. S., and Pollis, C. A. (1990). Introduction: A special issue on feminist perspectives on sexuality. *Journal of Sex Research* 27, 1–5.

van den Wijngaard, M. (1991). Reinventing the sexes: Feminism and the biomedical construction of femininity and masculinity, 1959–1985. Unpublished doctoral dissertation, University of Amsterdam.

Verhulst, J., and Heiman, J. R. (1988). A systems perspective on sexual desire. In S. R. Leiblum and R. C. Rosen, eds., *Sexual Desire Disorders.* New York: Guilford Press.

Vicunus, M. (1982). Sexuality and power: A review of current work in the history of sexuality. *Feminist Studies* 8, 133–156.

Wagner, G., and Kaplan, H. S. (1992). *The New Injection Treatment for Impotence.* New York: Brunner Mazel.

Weeks, J. (1981). *Sex, Politics, and Society: The regulation of sexuality since 1800.* London: Longman.

———. (1982). The development of sexual theory and sexual politics. In M. Brake, ed., *Human Sexual Relations: Towards a redefinition of sexual politics.* New York: Pantheon.

———. (1985). *Sexuality and Its Discontents.* London: Routledge and Kegan Paul.

Weinberg, M. S., Swensson, R. G., and Hammersmith, S. K. (1983). Sexual autonomy and the status of women: Models of female sexuality in U.S. sex manuals from 1950 to 1980. *Social Problems* 30, 312–324.

White, E. (1980). *States of Desire.* New York: E. P. Dutton.

Williams, R. (1976). *Keywords: A vocabulary of culture and society.* New York: Oxford University Press. (Rev. ed. published in 1983.)

Willis, E. (1988). Feminism, moralism, and pornography. In K. Ellis, B. Jaker, N. D. Hunter, B. O'Dair, and A. Tallmer, eds., *Caught Looking: Feminism, pornography, and censorship.* Seattle: The Real Comet Press.

Wilson, E. O. (1975). *Sociobiology: The new synthesis.* Cambridge: Harvard University Press.

Wise, T. N., Rabins, P. V., and Gahnsley, J. (1984). The older patient with a sexual dysfunction. *Journal of Sex and Marital Therapy* 10, 117–121.

Zilbergeld, B. (1978). *Male Sexuality.* Boston: Little, Brown.

———. (1992). The man behind the broken penis: Social and psychological determinants of erectile failure. In R. C. Rosen and S. R. Leiblum, eds., *Erectile Disorders: Assessment and treatment.* New York: Guilford.

# About the Book
# and Author

This collection of sexologist Leonore Tiefer's essays includes popular as well as professional writings and lectures on the social construction of sexuality. Tiefer's background as a sexologist is unusually broad, including rodent copulation research, sex therapy, classification of dysfunctions, and feminist analysis. Her wit and passion are evident in such essays as "The Kiss," "Advice to the Lovelorn," "Sexual Biology and the Symbolism of the Natural," "In Pursuit of the Perfect Penis: The Medicalization of Male Sexuality," and "New Perspectives in Sexology: From Rigor (Mortis) to Richness," and they all add up to a lively, controversial presentation of the forces shaping sex in our culture.

As Tiefer provocatively states toward the end of her introduction to Part 1, "A kiss is not a kiss; . . . your orgasm is not the same as George Washington's, premarital sex in Peru is not premarital sex in Peoria, abortion in Rome at the time of Caesar is not abortion in Rome at the time of John Paul II, and rape is neither an act of sex nor an act of violence—all of these actions remain to be defined by individual experience within one's period and culture." This book explores sex and its "experts" in colorful, original, and perceptive ways.

Leonore Tiefer is associate professor of urology and psychiatry at the Albert Einstein College of Medicine in the Bronx and a psychologist at the Montefiore Medical Center, Bronx, New York.

# Index